WORLD BANK STUDY

Challenges to Enterprise Performance in the Face of the Financial Crisis

Eastern Europe and Central Asia

AF769687

THE WORLD BANK
Washington, D.C.

Copyright © 2011
The International Bank for Reconstruction and Development/The World Bank
1818 H Street, NW
Washington, DC 20433
Telephone: 202-473-1000
Internet: www.worldbank.org

1 2 3 4 14 13 12 11

World Bank Studies are published to communicate the results of the Bank's work to the development community with the least possible delay. The manuscript of this paper therefore has not been prepared in accordance with the procedures appropriate to formally-edited texts. This volume is a product of the staff of the International Bank for Reconstruction and Development / The World Bank. The findings, interpretations, and conclusions expressed in this volume do not necessarily reflect the views of the Executive Directors of The World Bank or the governments they represent.

The World Bank does not guarantee the accuracy of the data included in this work. The boundaries, colors, denominations, and other information shown on any map in this work do not imply any judgement on the part of The World Bank concerning the legal status of any territory or the endorsement or acceptance of such boundaries.

Rights and Permissions

The material in this publication is copyrighted. Copying and/or transmitting portions or all of this work without permission may be a violation of applicable law. The International Bank for Reconstruction and Development/The World Bank encourages dissemination of its work and will normally grant permission to reproduce portions of the work promptly.

For permission to photocopy or reprint any part of this work, please send a request with complete information to the Copyright Clearance Center Inc., 222 Rosewood Drive, Danvers, MA 01923, USA; telephone: 978-750-8400; fax: 978-750-4470; Internet: www.copyright.com.

All other queries on rights and licenses, including subsidiary rights, should be addressed to the Office of the Publisher, The World Bank, 1818 H Street NW, Washington, DC 20433, USA; fax: 202-522-2422; e-mail: pubrights@worldbank.org.

ISBN: 978-0-8213-8800-6
eISBN: 978-0-8213-8801-3
DOI: 10.1596/978-0-8213-8800-6

Library of Congress Cataloging-in-Publication Data

Challenges to enterprise performance in the face of the financial crisis : Eastern Europe and Central Asia.
p. cm.
Includes bibliographical references.
ISBN 978-0-8213-8800-6 -- ISBN 978-0-8213-8801-3
1. Industries--Europe, Eastern. 2. Industries--Asia, Central. 3. Business enterprises--Europe, Eastern. 4. Business enterprises--Asia, Central. 5. Global Financial Crisis, 2008-2009. 6. Europe, Eastern--Economic conditions--21st century. 7. Asia, Central--Economic conditions--21st century. I. World Bank.
HC244.C42 2011
338.50947--dc23

2011018824

Contents

Acknowledgments ix

Acronyms and Abbreviations xi

Executive Summary xiii

1. Overview 1

Introduction 1

Main Issues Reflected in the Report 2

Data and Methodology 5

The Structure of This Report 5

2. Access to Finance 7

Financial Sector Developments in the Eastern Europe and Central Asia Region 8

Data and Methodology 14

Financial Constraints 15

Firm Survival 22

Understanding Foreign Bank Presence 24

Conclusions 25

3. Infrastructure Bottlenecks 29

Infrastructure in the Eastern Europe and Central Asia Region 30

Data and Methodology 31

Electricity: A Growing Concern 32

Telecommunications Usage on the Rise, but Access and Reliability Remain Issues 39

The Role of Regulation and Governance 42

Conclusion 47

4. Labor: Challenges Ahead of the Crisis 50

Recent Labor Market Developments in the Eastern Europe and Central Asia Region 51

Data and Methodology 52

Labor Constraints in ECA 53

Responding to the Rising Skills Constraints 65

Effects of the Crisis on Labor 69

Conclusion 69

References 73

Appendixes ... 81
Appendix 1. Technical Notes and Data Tables ... 83
Appendix 2. Notes on Sampling and the Survey Methodology ... 120
Appendix 3. Summary of Obstacles Doing Business ... 123

Boxes
Box 2.1. Effects of Easy Money ... 12
Box 2.2. Fixed vs. Floating—Example of Bulgaria and Poland ... 22
Box 3.1. Cost of Power Outages in Kosovo ... 37
Box 3.2. Progress in Armenia's Telecom Sector ... 41
Box 3.3. Weak Governance and Infrastructure Services: Getting Electricity in Ukraine ... 43
Box 3.4. Transport Constraints Tighten Across ECA ... 46
Box 4.1. Strides in Labor Regulations ... 54
Box 4.2. Are the Trends Emerging from the BEEPS Data Consistent with Other Sources? ... 57
Box 4.3. Wages and Productivity Increases: Do They Reflect Rising Skills and Labor Shortages? ... 60
Box 4.4. Emigration and Brain Drain in ECA ... 61
Box 4.5. Information Technology Use and Skills ... 65
Box 4.6. Early Effects of the Financial Crisis ... 68

Figures
Figure 2.1. Liquid Liabilities as a Share of GDP ... 9
Figure 2.2. Foreign Controlled Banking Sector Assets ... 10
Figure 2.3. Access to Credit ... 11
Figure 2.4. Foreign Claims as a Share of GDP ... 12
Figure B2.1.1. Private Credit/GDP Change (2004–2007) vs. 2009 GDP Growth ... 12
Figure B2.1.2. Change in Foreign Bank Claims to GDP Ratio (2004-2007) vs. 2009 GDP Growth ... 13
Figure 2.5. Firm Perceptions of Access to Finance ... 16
Figure 2.6. Demand for External Funding ... 17
Figure 2.7. Predicted Probability of Access to Finance Being No Obstacle ... 18
Figure 2.8. Predicted Probability of Applying for a Loan ... 18
Figure 2.9. Predicted Probability of Access to Finance Not Being an Obstacle, by Current Account Deficit (Fixed Exchange Rate Regime) ... 20
Figure 2.10. Predicted Probability of Access to Finance Not Being an Obstacle, by Current Account Deficit (Crawling Exchange Rate Regime) ... 20
Figure 2.11. Predicted Probability of Applying for a Loan by Current Account Deficit and Exchange Rate Regime ... 21
Figure 2.12. Predicted Probability of Firm Exit Based on Firm Size ... 23

Figure 2.13. Predicted Probability of Firm Exit Based on Firm Age 23
Figure 3.1. Electricity as No Obstacle, 2005 and 2008 32
Figure 3.2. Electricity as No Obstacle by Region 33
Figure 3.3. Power Outages vs. GDP Per Capita 34
Figure 3.4. Breadth of Power Outages 35
Figure 3.5. Losses Due to Power Outages 35
Figure 3.6. Losses Due to Power Outages by Income Classification 36
Figure 3.7. Generator Use 38
Figure 3.8. Telecommunications as No Obstacle, 2005 and 2008 39
Figure 3.9. Email Use vs. GDP Per Capita 40
Figure 3.10. Email Use vs. Labor Productivity 41
Figure B3.3.1. Duration of Procedures for Getting an Electricity Connection in Ukraine 43
Figure 3.11. Outage Costs and Government Effectiveness 44
Figure 3.12. Outage Costs and Control of Corruption 44
Figure 3.13. Internet Access and Government Effectiveness 45
Figure 3.14. Internet Access and Control of Corruption 45
Figure B3.4.1. Transport as No Obstacle, 2005 and 2008 46
Figure B4.1.1. Labor Regulations vs. GDP Per Capita 55
Figure B4.1.2. EPL Rigidity vs. Innovation 55
Figure 4.1. Skills and Education of Labor as No Obstacle, 2005 and 2008 56
Figure 4.2. Skills and Education of Labor as No Obstacle by Income Classification 57
Figure 4.3. Skills and Education of Labor as an Obstacle vs. Labor Productivity 58
Figure B4.3.1. Productivity and Wage Growth in Poland 2004–2008 60
Figure B4.3.2. Productivity and Wage Growth in Ukraine 2004–2008 60
Figure B4.4.1. Workers' Remittances (% of GDP), 2008 61
Figure B4.4.2. Skills and Education of Labor as No Obstacle vs. Remittances 62
Figure B4.4.3. Skills and Education of Labor as No Obstacle and Emigration of the Tertiary Educated 62
Figure 4.4. Skills and Education of Labor as an Obstacle vs. Unemployment 63
Figure 4.5. Skills and Education of Labor as an Obstacle vs. Unemployment of Tertiary Educated 64
Figure 4.6. Skills and Education of Labor as an Obstacle vs. Unemployment of Secondary Educated 64
Figure 4.7. Provision of Training by Region 66
Figure 4.8. Provision of Training by Income Classification 66
Figure 4.9. Skills and Education of Labor as an Obstacle vs. Provision of Training 67
Figure B4.6.1. Firms Planning to Downsize 68
Figure B4.6.2. Skills and Education of Labor as No Obstacle and Plans to Downsize 68

Tables

Table 2.1. Foreign Banks in ECA Countries during the First 10 Years of Transition 24
Table 4.1. Employment Elasticity of Growth 2004–2008......52
Table 4.2. Cross-Regional Comparison: Labor Regulations and Skills and Education of Labor as a Major or Very Severe Obstacle, 2008 (percentage of respondents)......53
Table 4.3. Skills and Education of Labor as an Obstacle to Doing Business (relative ranking among 14 obstacles)......56
Table A1.1. Regression Controls: Summary of BEEPS-Based Control Variables......86
Table A1.2. Results from Probit Regression of Firm Exit on Enterprise Characteristics......98
Table A1.3. Probit Models, Financial Constraints Analysis......99
Table A1.4. Comparison of Balanced BEEPS Panel and Full Sample, BEEPS 2002, 2005, and 2008......101
Table A1.5. Regressions on the Effects of Power Outage Costs on Labor Productivity Based on Varying Firm Characteristics......106
Table A1.6. Regressions on the Effects of Power Outage Costs on Productivity by Firm Productivity Quintile......107
Table A1.7. Regressions on the Effects of High-Speed Internet Access on Firm Productivity Based on Varying Firm Characteristics......107
Table A1.8. Regressions on the Effects of Email Use on Productivity by Firm Productivity Quintile......108
Table A1.9. Regressions on the Effects of High-Speed Internet Access on Productivity by Firm Productivity Quintile......108
Table A1.10. Regressions on the Effects of Power Outage Costs in Countries with Good Governance, Good Control of Corruption, and Good Government Regulation on Labor Productivity......108
Table A1.11. Regressions on the Effects of High-Speed Internet Access in Countries with Good Governance, Good Control of Corruption, and Good Government Regulation on Labor Productivity......109
Table A1.12. Marginal Effects of Generalized Ordered Logit Models of the Effects of Various Firm Characteristics on Electricity Perceptions......109
Table A1.13. Regression Results for World Governance Indicators on Power Outage Costs and Access to High-Speed Internet......110
Table A1.14. Estimated Power Outage Costs and Access to High-Speed Internet......110
Table A1.15. Marginal Effects of Primary Variables on Labor Regulations as No Obstacle and Major Obstacle (General Ordered Logit Models)......115
Table A1.16. Marginal Effects of Primary Variables on Skills and Education of Labor as No Obstacle and Major Obstacle (General Ordered Logit Models)......116
Table A1.17. Results of the Innovation and ICT Use Logit Models......117
Table A1.18. Regression Results of the Training Logit Models......118
Table A1.19. Regression Results of Labor Productivity Models......119
Table A1.20. Regression Results of the Professionalism of Labor Model......119

Table A2.1. Sample Summary 2005 and 2008 122
Table A3.1. Problems Doing Business: Ranking of Problems 2008 123
Table A3.2. Problems Doing Business: Ranking of Problems 2005 124
Table A3.3. Factors that are Not a Problem Doing Business, Percentage Point Changes and Statistical Significance 125

Acknowledgments

This report was prepared by Gregory Kisunko (Task Team Leader), George Clarke, Robert Cull, Kimberly Johns, Marc Schiffbauer, Erwin Tiongson, and Ricky Ubee under the overall guidance of Yvonne Tsikata and Roumeen Islam. Valuable contributions were made by Bryce Quillin, William Dillinger, Pedro L. Rodriguez, and Jan Rutkowski.

We are grateful for the advice and comments of the peer reviewers: Leora Klapper, Arvo Kuddo, James S. Moose, and L. Colin Xu. In addition we would like to thank Randi Ryterman, James Anderson, and John Giles, who advised on the concept. Comments provided by the Office of the Chief Economist, Europe and Central Asia Region of the World Bank are gratefully acknowledged.

This report uses data from the European Bank for Reconstruction and Development-World Bank Business Environment and Enterprise Performance Survey (BEEPS), and we wish to acknowledge those at Enterprise Surveys who worked to ensure the data were collected in a timely manner and were of high quality, including James Anderson, Jorge Luis Rodriguez Meza, and Veselin Kunchev of the World Bank and Helena Schweiger of the European Bank for Reconstruction and Development. Finally we wish to thank the more than 30,000 enterprise managers who have given their time to this survey over the years.

Acronyms and Abbreviations

AFR	Sub-Saharan Africa
BEEPS	Business Environment and Enterprise Performance Survey
BIS	Bank for International Settlements
CIS	Commonwealth of Independent States
EAP	East Asia and the Pacific
EBRD	European Bank for Reconstruction and Development
EC	European Commission
ECA	Europe and Central Asia
EPL	Employment Protection Legislation
EU	European Union
EU-10	European Union 10 Countries
FCS	Financial Crisis Survey
FDI	Foreign Direct Investment
FSU	Former Soviet Union
FSU-N	Northern Former Soviet Union Countries
FSU-S	Southern Former Soviet Union Countries
GDP	Gross Domestic Product
ICT	Information Communication and Technology
IMF	International Monetary Fund
KEK	Kosovo Energy Corporation
KILM	Key Indicators of the Labor Market
LCR	Latin America and the Caribbean
LCU	Local Currency Units
LME	Large and Medium-sized Enterprises
MNA	Middle East and North Africa
OECD	Organisation for Economic Co-operation and Development
SAR	South Asia
SEE	South Eastern Europe
SME	Small and Medium-sized Enterprises
WDI	World Development Indicators
WEF	World Economic Forum
WGI	World Governance Indicators

Country abbreviations used in figures and tables:

ALB = Albania
ARM = Armenia
AZE = Azerbaijan
BLR = Belarus
BIH = Bosnia and Herzegovina
BGR = Bulgaria
HRV = Croatia
CZE = the Czech Republic

EST = Estonia
MKD = FYR Macedonia
GEO = Georgia
HUN = Hungary
KAZ = Kazakhstan
KSV = Kosovo
KGZ = the Kyrgyz Republic
LVA = Latvia
LTU = Lithuania
MDA = Moldova
MNE = Montenegro
POL = Poland
ROM = Romania
RUS = the Russian Federation
SRB = Serbia
SVK = the Slovak Republic
SVN = Slovenia
TJK = Tajikistan
TUR = Turkey
UKR = Ukraine
UZB = Uzbekistan

Executive Summary

This report takes stock of enterprise sector performance in the Europe and Central Asia (ECA) region and its key drivers: access to finance, infrastructure, and labor. It is the second of two complementary reports that examine selected trends emerging from the Business Environment and Enterprise Performance Survey (BEEPS) data that are of immediate policy relevance to ECA countries.[1] Both reports draw primarily on information from data collected *prior* to the crisis. This report also uses data on employment and access to finance collected *during* the crisis in a subset of ECA countries.[2]

The global financial crisis has had enormous consequences for firms' access to finance, the availability of qualified workers, and the ability of governments to provide (and of private sector to obtain) reliable infrastructure services. The extent and impact of these constraints is yet to be determined—but their presence at a time of economic growth suggests they may re-emerge during the post-crisis economic recovery.

The BEEPS captures information on a number of aspects of the business environment. This report highlights the elements of firm finance, labor regulations and skills, and infrastructure that are covered by the BEEPS questionnaire. Where possible, the data are supplemented with data from other sources. The report covers a lot of ground, and several broad findings from the analyses stand out.

Access to Financial Resources

In the period just before the crisis, credit to the private sector grew sharply. In large part, the rapid growth of credit reflects many important reforms in the region's banking and financial sectors that were carried out during the first decade of transition. Increasing foreign bank participation also provided broader access to credit, and introduced new financial instruments on the eve of the crisis.

Firms who responded to the BEEPS questionnaire reported that access to finance was, on average, easiest in 2005. This reflects the significant change in financial market conditions that took place in the early 2000s, driven in large part by the restructuring of the banking sectors throughout the region in the 1990s and broadened access to credit made possible over time by increasing foreign bank participation. This access gradually tightened over time through 2008/09 on the eve of and during the global financial crisis. In 2008, access to finance was, on average, perceived as the 5th highest out of 14 obstacles measured by the BEEPS.

The data collected during the crisis in six ECA countries suggests that access to finance was a critical factor in a firm's ability to survive the beginning of the economic downturn. The analysis of these data shows that large, established firms with stronger ties to credit institutions tended to better weather the storm than smaller, newer firms. But not all forms of finance were equally beneficial. The presence of foreign-owned banks with well-established local networks, financed primarily from local deposits, and lending in local currency tended to have a stabilizing effect, whereas other forms of finance, including direct cross-border lending and local lending in foreign currency, did not.

Adequacy of Infrastructure

Although the region entered the transition with a relatively large transport and energy infrastructure endowment, over time it has not kept pace with growing demand. For a variety of reasons—the recession in the early transition period, pricing policies in the energy sector, and weak fiscal resources—governments in the region have generally not been able to provide adequate resources for the maintenance and development of infrastructure.

For example, of 14 obstacles measured by the BEEPS, electricity ranked 3rd in 2008 (behind only tax rates and corruption), up from 12th in 2005. While the electrical infrastructure constraints found in ECA are similar to those reported in other developing regions, the consequences to enterprise operation and sales are more substantial, especially in the lower-income countries of ECA. The magnitude of outages is much larger in the ECA region—32 hours per month, almost three times higher on average than in LCR, while for low and lower-middle income countries this difference is even more significant—58 and 16 hours in ECA and LCR, respectively. These outages are tied to losses in sales, which are particularly large among firms in lower-income countries with limited access to secondary sources of energy, such as generators. This is also, at least partially, the result of limited private investment (relative to other regions) in the electricity sector.

Further, firms in countries with weaker public sector governance experience shortages of and difficulties with access to electricity and information communication and technology (ICT) services that lead to higher losses as a share of sales, compared to firms in countries with more effective governance and regulatory frameworks. This finding suggests that reforms in the sectors may be more effective if coupled with other governance and administrative reforms.

Labor Regulations and Adequate Labor Skills

Throughout most of the region, firms report that labor regulations have become less of a burden since 2005. The rank of labor regulations as an obstacle to doing business fell from 9th place in 2005 to 13th in 2008. Only enterprises in Poland and Slovenia reported that labor regulations have become more of a burden. These improvements may be attributed to active labor market reform efforts, which increased flexibility and lowered the costs of employing workers.

During the same period, firms reported a growing dissatisfaction with the quality of labor. Dissatisfaction with the skill level of the labor force has risen in all but three countries in the region, becoming the 4th highest obstacle in the region. The inability of firms to find workers with adequate skills has been accompanied by sharp increases in wages exceeding the growth of labor productivity. This reflects a structural transformation in the labor markets in the region—the rising number of jobs with higher skill content—as well as the inability of education systems to respond to the growing demand for skills, and the migration of skilled workers to higher-income countries. The results of the analysis provide evidence of an emerging skills shortage in the region. A solution to the problem may lie in the development of marketable skills, rather than simply increasing the formal educational attainment of the workforce.

Are Obstacles to Doing Business Distributed Evenly?

The obstacles to doing business and the benefits of improvements in the business environment are not distributed uniformly across enterprises. Small firms, for instance, complained particularly about difficulties in accessing credit and because this problem is long standing, these firms were *less* affected by the sudden tightening of credit that accompanied the global financial crisis. At the same time, difficulties in accessing financing may have left them without the means to weather the lean years. As a result, many young and innovative enterprises failed to survive the crisis.

Large firms were more likely to complain about labor quality—although they were also more likely to have sufficient resources to mitigate it. In 2008, 80 percent of large firms were dissatisfied with the skills of the labor force, compared to only two-thirds of small firms. At the same time, while larger firms were more likely to provide training to their employees, the burden of internally developing their workforce may impact the productivity and efficiency of these firms.

The impacts of access to reliable infrastructure services vary both by country and across different types of firms. Firms in low- and middle-income countries appear to face higher costs for power outages than those in high-income countries. Certain firms are also more vulnerable to the electricity bottlenecks. For example, firms that innovate and low productivity firms appear to face higher constraints in terms of how power outage costs affect labor productivity than their counterparts. Similar trends appear when examining access to high speed Internet—increasing access to ICT may provide a comparatively higher productivity boost for smaller firms and those in lower-income countries.

What Does the Future Hold?

In the recovery period, a new round of emigration may further exacerbate skill and labor shortages, as younger and higher skilled workers are more likely to leave. Those who stay behind will be even less qualified to perform tasks required of jobs in a changing economy if proper training is not provided on an appropriate scale. At the same time, the fiscal condition, weakened by the crisis, may further constrain the ability of ECA countries to invest in education (including worker training) and infrastructure.

By the same token, the ample supply of financing available to the region prior to the crisis may not reappear, as banks attempt to recover from the crisis and central banks strengthen prudential requirements. ECA countries will have to compete for foreign investment with countries in other regions that have recovered earlier, faster, or were less affected by the global crisis.

On the eve of the crisis, enterprises in ECA complained about infrastructure bottlenecks and the lack of qualified workers, indicating limited reform progress on several fronts. In a weak recovery period and in an environment characterized by fragile fiscal balances, the ability of the ECA region to carry out needed reforms in these areas may be significantly constrained. The region will therefore have to explore alternative means to enhance labor skills and upgrade infrastructure. Further improvements in labor regulations will also be critical, despite notable achievements in regulatory reforms just before the crisis. Measures to further ease firm entry and the hiring of workers will also be warranted.

Notes

1. The first report, *Trends in Corruption and Regulatory Burden in Eastern Europe and Central Asia* was published in January 2011.
2. The BEEPS survey collects comparable firm-level data across countries in the ECA region to measure aspects of firm performance and the business and regulatory environment in which they operate. First conducted in 1999 and every three years thereafter, the 2008 round of BEEPS includes over 11,000 firms in 29 countries. A Financial Crisis Survey was conducted by the Enterprise Survey Unit of the World Bank in 2009 in six countries, to help assess the impact of the crisis on firm survival. BEEPS 2008 results were supplemented with results of this survey conducted in June and July 2009 in Bulgaria, Hungary, Latvia, Lithuania, Romania, and Turkey.

CHAPTER 1

Overview

Introduction

Owing to their tight linkages with international labor, trade, and financial markets, countries in the Europe and Central Asia (ECA) region, on average, experienced strong economic growth in the years just before the global financial crisis. Such rapid growth was underpinned by substantial inflows of funds, robust growth in exporting activity, and in some countries, large remittance inflows sent home by migrant workers in Western Europe and in the middle-income countries of the Commonwealth of Independent States (CIS), notably the Russian Federation.

What started as a crisis in the housing market in the United States in late 2007 quickly became a full-fledged global financial crisis. The financial crisis led to a massive worldwide economic slowdown, with gross worldwide product shrinking by 2.1 percent in 2009. Although all regions were affected, economies in the ECA region experienced some of the steepest declines. After growing at an annual rate of 7.1 percent in 2007 and 4.2 percent in 2008, GDP in the region contracted by 5.3 percent in 2009—a larger contraction than in any other region.[1] This was accompanied by a large drop in private inflows of capital. In 2007, $491 billion (16 percent of the regional GDP) of private capital came into the region. By 2009, this had fallen to $84 billion.

Regional Economic Developments and Prospects

Economies in the region are now embarking on a period of economic recovery, though at a much weaker pace than other emerging and developing countries. While developing economies in Asia are expected to grow at a rate of 8 percent per year through 2013, driven largely by China and India, the ECA region is projected to grow by about 4 percent a year over the same period.

Despite the prospect of growth, the jobless nature of ECA's economic recovery is a cause for concern.[2] Rates of joblessness remain high in much of Eastern Europe and are rising in some countries of the CIS. In the Russian Federation, for example, unemployment rates are currently projected to worsen before signs of improvement emerge. Meanwhile, fiscal resources in the region remain weak, thus constraining the ability of governments to provide social protection and support the recovery.

In this difficult, post-crisis economic environment, identifying constraints on the growth of enterprises will be critical to economic recovery. Understanding the nature of such constraints can help enterprises in ECA position themselves in what promises to be a more competitive, post-crisis economic environment.

While there is a large body of survey work on: government fiscal performance, household and individual consumption, labor market activity, and welfare covering the period just before the crisis and during the early stages of economic recovery;[3] relatively little is known about firms in the ECA region and their performance during this same period. There are several enduring questions regarding obstacles to business activity. What are the key constraints to enterprise growth in the ECA region after two decades of structural and policy reforms? Do enterprises have sufficient access to financial resources? Are firms able to find workers with the requisite skills and qualifications? And, are firms supported by adequate energy, telecommunications, and transport infrastructure? An understanding of these and other issues will have immediate implications for policy, particularly in a challenging post-crisis period.

The Scope and Rationale of this Report

In the period just before the crisis, a number of elements, such as access to finance, skills, and qualifications of labor, and the quality of infrastructure, remained or became important obstacles to enterprise growth. The relative importance of these obstacles has evolved over time, reflecting structural reforms and progress in improving the business environment, yet they were important constraints to growth, even in a period characterized by robust financial inflows and generally strong fiscal balances.

This report focuses on these key drivers of enterprise sector performance. It is the second of two reports that examine selected trends emerging from the BEEPS data, the first report being an analysis on governance and trends in corruption in the region. The selection of specific topics to be covered in this report was driven by the following considerations:

First, the report addresses the core components of enterprise activity, namely, the factors of production and the public infrastructure to support them, and seeks to assess the availability and accessibility of these inputs in the ECA region. Second, one can view these building blocks as major forms of capital—human capital, financial capital, and public, physical capital—which then leads to an assessment of how these factors impacted firm survival, productivity, and performance in the face of the financial crisis, and how these impacts vary across different types of firms. One key insight from the first generation of studies of enterprises is that obstacles to enterprise activity and access to key resources are *not* uniformly distributed across firms. Enterprises face varying levels of pressure depending on their characteristics and location, the resources directly accessible to them, and the quality of services and regulation provided by their governments.[4]

Third, the report presents an opportunity to evaluate progress made along these three key dimensions near the end of two decades of transition. Much of the transition period in the 1990s and the structural transformation associated with the period have consisted of efforts to promote broader access to capital, deregulate labor markets, and promote skills, and to maintain if not to upgrade infrastructure. In order for the recovery to be successful, it is critical to understand where the region stands now relative to these elements, especially as they are perceived by enterprises, the engine of private sector-led growth.

Main Issues Reflected in the Report

Trends in Firm Financing

In the period just before the crisis, credit to the private sector grew very sharply. In large part, the rapid growth of credit reflects many important reforms in the region's banking and financial sectors that were carried out during the first decade of transition. One of the most dramatic changes of the 1990s was a restructuring of the banking sectors in ECA countries from the state-run mono-banking systems inherited from the Soviet era to private ownership of banks occupying different market niches and drawing resources from internal and international financial markets. In fact, the defining feature of the restructuring of the banking sectors in ECA countries was the heavy involvement of foreign banks. By 1996, majority foreign-owned banks held 20 percent of banking sector assets in ECA, and by 2003, over 50 percent of ECA's banking sector assets were in the hands of foreign controlled banks. Increasing foreign bank participation provided much broader access to credit prior to the crisis. Not surprisingly, BEEPS data confirm that financial constraints were less binding in countries where foreign banks had been present for some time.

The most worrisome effect of the financial crisis on firms was the accompanying drop in demand for products and services. As a result, some firms did not survive. Using data from Enterprise Surveys on the financial crisis, which revisited the same BEEPS firms in six ECA countries, the impact of the crisis was visible. The results show that access to finance played a key role in keeping firms afloat by providing supplementary working capital during the crisis.

Deterioration of Physical Infrastructure and Growing Disparities in Access to New Infrastructure

At the beginning of the transition, many countries in the ECA region enjoyed better infrastructure, with respect to quality and quantity, compared to many other countries at a similar level of development. However, the supply and maintenance of infrastructure services did not keep pace with the rising demand for such services by firms, even in the wealthier economies of the region. Enterprises report that electricity is third among the major obstacles to business activity in 2008, after tax rates and corruption.[5] Overall, between 2005 and 2008, firms' views on the quality of electricity, telecommunication, and transport infrastructure deteriorated the most among all reported obstacles.[6]

Deterioration of firm perceptions of electricity may reflect in part the escalating energy prices worldwide during this period, rather than just the state of electricity infrastructure in the ECA region. However, BEEPS does not sufficiently cover the cost of energy to firms, therefore an analysis of the cost of electricity is outside the scope of this report.

Although the infrastructure constraints found in ECA are similar to those reported in other developing regions, the consequences for enterprise operation and profitability are far more pronounced for ECA firms. The cost of such bottlenecks is hefty, accounting for a loss of about 5.4 percentage points of annual output (measured by lost sales revenue) for ECA firms. These costs are disproportionately larger among firms in the low and lower-middle income countries of ECA (9.7 percentage points vs. 2.8 percentage points for higher-income countries).

Shortage of Skilled Labor and Easing of Labor Regulations

Until the global financial crisis, the ECA region experienced substantial improvements in labor market conditions along with steady economic expansion. After a number of years of stalled employment creation in the period following the 1998 Russian crisis, job opportunities grew rapidly in the period after 2004. For the new EU member countries, robust economic growth and job creation coincided with their EU accession. For other countries, job creation coincided with easing labor market regulations and the large inflow of capital. In this environment, BEEPS data suggest that firms' views regarding labor regulations and the availability of skills have generally evolved in opposite directions.

Firms' perceptions of labor regulations have steadily improved since 2005 throughout most of the region. One of the explanations offered in the literature[7] is that labor regulations become less binding in a period of strong labor demand and economic growth.

At the same time, firms reported a growing dissatisfaction with the quality of labor over this period. The average level of dissatisfaction with the skill level of the labor force has risen in all but three countries in the region, though the average level in ECA is comparable with those of other developing regions, such as LCR. These unfavorable views reported by respondents to BEEPS are consistent with other surveys of enterprise perception. Recent data and studies on labor market trends suggest that there are several drivers of the skills shortage, including the rising number of jobs with higher skill content associated with structural transformation, the inability of education systems to respond to the growing demand for skills, and the emigration of skilled workers (from EU-10 countries and some of the low-income countries of the CIS alike).

What Are the Prospects in the Post-Crisis Period?

Some obstacles to doing business may have been eased by the crisis as falling energy use alleviated the energy crunch and as retrenchments reduced the labor and skill shortages. Notwithstanding this partial relief, access to finance worsened, as is evident from data collected for selected countries through 2009. It is not clear whether such crisis conditions continue to hold during the recovery, or whether pre-crisis conditions will slowly re-emerge.

Will firms be more or less constrained in the recovery period, relative to finance, labor, and infrastructure obstacles? The answer is not obvious. For example, in the face of sustained joblessness in the region, labor shortages previously felt in the pre-crisis period may be temporarily relieved. At the same time, with recovery underway, workers from Eastern Europe may be compelled to find work in growth poles abroad, once again, as the crisis has widened income disparities across countries. In addition, as enterprises strive to be more productive during a period of weak recovery, the need for higher quality labor becomes even more urgent, thus boosting the competition for skilled labor. The net effect of all these developments is not clear.

In the post-crisis period, access to finance will be a much larger constraint than it was previously as banks recover from the negative effects of the crisis and consolidate their finances, as central banks strengthen prudential requirements, and as ECA countries compete for foreign investment with countries in other regions that have recovered earlier, faster, or were much less affected by the global crisis.

In this weak economic environment, policy measures to improve the business environment and promote job creation will be essential. An analysis of the region's policy options is beyond the scope of this report. However, some preliminary policy implications emerge from the analysis. First, further improvements in labor regulations will be critical, despite notable achievements in regulatory reforms just before the crisis. With job creation stagnant, economic activity still weak, and the recent loss of young, innovative firms, measures to further ease firm entry and increase the flexibility of employing workers will be warranted. Second, the region has to explore alternative means to upgrade infrastructure, in light of limited government resources. Public works and public-private partnerships aimed at the maintenance and the upgrading of infrastructure may be one way of employing jobless workers while addressing infrastructure bottlenecks in the region.

Data and Methodology

The 2008 round of surveys was administered to managers of over 11,000 firms in 29 ECA countries. For the first time, the BEEPS exercise included Kosovo and Montenegro as separate countries. The BEEPS project stands out from other private sector surveys done by the World Bank as the largest simultaneous survey of firms, virtually covering an entire region. The BEEPS has been undertaken every three years since 1999.

The 2008 BEEPS questionnaire and sample design were modified[8] from previous rounds to enhance comparability of indicators with similar firm-level surveys in other regions. These changes, however, make it more difficult to track progress over time between 2005 and 2008. Changes in the sample design make it necessary to drop some firms from the 2005 and 2008 samples, so they are sufficiently similar in composition by firm size and industry. Resulting reductions in sample size make it somewhat less likely that a change over time of a given magnitude will be statistically significant.

Another notable change is that many of the questions included in 2005 (and in earlier BEEPS surveys) were dropped. Many other questions, from the World Bank's Enterprise Surveys conducted in other regions, were added. One benefit of, and the main driver for the changes in the survey, is an enhanced ability to draw comparisons between ECA countries and countries in other regions.

Each chapter in this report uses a subset of BEEPS questions and supplemental data sources; therefore each chapter has a specific section dedicated to explaining the methodological approach, caveats, and data sources used.

The Structure of This Report

The rest of the report is organized as follows: Chapter 2 focuses on access to finance as an obstacle to doing business. Chapter 3 examines infrastructure bottlenecks confronting enterprises in the region and Chapter 4 explores the evolution of labor regulations and skills constraints.

Notes

1. World Bank (2010).
2. See, for example, World Bank (2010b, 2010c), IMF (2010a and 2010b).
3. See, in particular, EBRD (2002 and 2005). The ECA regional report on productivity (Alam et al., 2008) includes enterprise data through 2005. Relatively little is known about enterprises in the region in the period after 2005, except for the initial analysis of the 2008 BEEPS data in Chapter 5 of the *Turmoil at Twenty* regional report (Mitra et al., 2009) and Chapter 5 of the recent Transition Report 2010 Recovery and Reform (EBRD, 2010).
4. See, for example, EBRD (2002).
5. Due to changes in the survey instrument, it is not possible to make robust conclusions about trends in absolute terms. The relative change, however, is valid. It is derived by using the mean response across firms as the basis to evaluate the severity of 14 individual problems doing business

asked about in the survey, which include tax administration, corruption, customs regulations and labor regulations and skills and education of labor among others. Each obstacle is ranked by severity, 1 for most severe, 14 for least severe.

6. See Appendix 3.

7. See Rutkowski (2007) as an example.

8. A detailed discussion of these differences is presented in Appendix 2.

CHAPTER 2

Access to Finance

What started as a crisis in the subprime mortgage market in the United States in late 2007 quickly became a full-fledged global financial crisis. The financial crisis led to a massive worldwide economic slowdown, with gross worldwide product shrinking by 2.1 percent in 2009. Although all regions were affected, the Europe and Central Asia Region (ECA) was hit harder than others. After growing at an annual rate of 7.1 percent in 2007 and 4.2 percent in 2008, GDP in the region contracted by 5.3 percent in 2009—a larger contraction than in any other region.[1] This was accompanied by a large drop in private inflows of capital. In 2007, $491 billion (16 percent of GDP) of private capital came into the region. By 2009, this had fallen to $84 billion. The combination of a drop in demand and a drop in the availability of external financing affected firms throughout the region.

Because the crisis started out in the financial sector and inflows of capital slowed, it should have been more difficult for firms in the region to maintain access to financing. Although this was the case, access to financing, surprisingly, was not what concerned firms' managers most during the crisis.[2] When firm managers were interviewed, most said that the biggest problem that their firms faced *during the crisis* was a drop in demand—between 70 and 80 percent of the surveyed firms in each country identified this as the most serious problem. By comparison, less than 10 percent said reduced access to credit was the most serious problem (Ramalho et al., 2009).[3] This does not mean that access to financing was unimportant: empirical results in this chapter address this issue along with several other important questions.

The first question addressed in this chapter is: what firm characteristics affected their access to finance and consequently their chances to survive the crisis? Some early answers are:

- Relative to non-crisis periods, larger and older firms were less likely to have stopped operating by mid-2009 than similar smaller, younger firms.
- Controlling for firm performance, firms that had access to financing were better able to weather the crisis than those that did not. In particular, firms that had loans and overdraft facilities were less likely to have stopped operating, which is consistent with the hypothesis that firms that lacked access to external funds were most vulnerable to the drop in demand.
- If, in the same analysis, financial access and firm performance are controlled for, the difference in survival rates between large and small firms is substantially reduced. Because informational asymmetries between borrower and lender are less severe for larger, older firms, lenders find it easier and cheaper to extend credit to them. Thus it is not firm size and age, per se, that reduced the likeli-

hood that a firm stopped operating, but rather the relationships between those characteristics and access to credit.

The second question addressed in the chapter is: what types of firms and countries were most affected by the crisis in terms of financial constraints? The analysis is done mostly along two dimensions: differences in foreign participation in the banking sector and differences in exchange rate regimes.

- First, given the high foreign bank participation rates in many countries in the region—and that the financial crisis started in developed economies—it is plausible that foreign banks could have contributed to a contraction in credit. Foreign bank participation might, therefore, have contributed to problems with access to financing during the crisis. Despite this possibility, the empirical results in this chapter suggest otherwise.
  - Having a well-established foreign bank presence helped to ease financial constraints during the crisis. That is, firms were less likely to report that access to financing was a serious problem in countries with high foreign participation in the banking sector.
- Second, relative to local lending in local currency, both direct cross-border flows to ECA and local lending in foreign currency had been growing much more rapidly, and the latter grew especially quickly relative to other regions. The large decline in direct, cross-border inflows of capital and local lending in foreign currency during the crisis affected access to financing.
  - In contrast to the stabilizing influence of foreign-owned banks with a strong local presence, direct, cross-border capital flows appear to be destabilizing. Those flows fell substantially after the onset of the crisis.[4]
  - This was especially true in countries with pegged exchange rates, where capital inflows contributed to the pre-crisis lending boom and the severity of the drop in access when the bubble burst.
  - Countries with large current account deficits, especially those with pegged exchange rates had lending booms in the middle of the decade, but became most vulnerable when the situation unraveled by 2008–2009.

The rest of this chapter is organized as follows. The next section provides a brief overview of relevant developments in the financial sector in ECA over the last 10–15 years. The second section discusses the two sources of data used in the chapter. The third section provides an analysis of financial constraints while the fourth section addresses the 2009 Financial Crisis Survey and provides a concrete indicator of the effects of the crisis, therefore complementing the constraint analysis with a "survival" analysis (for six countries where the follow-up survey was conducted). The fifth section provides the main conclusions.

Financial Sector Developments in the Eastern Europe and Central Asia Region

When ECA countries began transitioning from planned to market-based economies the very notion of private banks was all but alien to many policy makers there. Therefore, one of the most dramatic changes of the 1990s was a restructuring of the banking sectors in ECA countries from the state-run mono-banking systems inherited from the Soviet era to private ownership of banks occupying different market niches and drawing resources from internal and international financial markets.

Among ECA countries, the average ratio of liquid liabilities in the financial system relative to GDP stood at just 27 percent in 1996, almost as low as levels in Sub-Saharan Africa. The ratio of liquid liabilities to GDP climbed steadily, more than doubling to reach almost 50 percent by 2008 (Figure 2.1). Although other regions also experienced gains in this ratio during the same period, none was as dramatic as the gains in ECA, and thus the region had moved well past Africa and closed the gap in financial development relative to the rest of the developing world.

Indeed, these averages hide even bigger country-level changes. For example, the ratio of liquid liabilities to GDP has almost quadrupled over this period in Georgia—from the region's lowest (6 percent) in 1996 to almost 24 percent in 2008. The largest relative increase was seen in FYR Macedonia—from 11 percent in 1996 to almost 55 percent in 2008. Among ECA countries, Albania had the highest liabilities to GDP ratio in 2008—over 80 percent. The only country in the region where this ratio went down was the Slovak Republic—from 59 percent in 1996 to 56 percent in 2006.

Perhaps the defining feature of the restructuring of the banking sectors in ECA countries was the heavy involvement of foreign banks. Lacking capital to begin with and often faced with banking sector instability in the early phase of the transition to private ownership, many ECA countries turned to foreign investors.[5] The transformation was remarkable—prior to the fall of the Berlin Wall there was no foreign ownership of banks. By 1996, majority foreign-owned banks held 20 percent of banking sector assets in ECA (Figure 2.2). Though that figure continued to increase in regions such as Latin America and Sub-Saharan Africa, it skyrocketed in ECA. By 2003, over 50 percent of ECA's banking sector assets were in the hands of foreign controlled banks. Only Sub-Saharan Africa came close on that dimension.

Figure 2.1. Liquid Liabilities as a Share of GDP

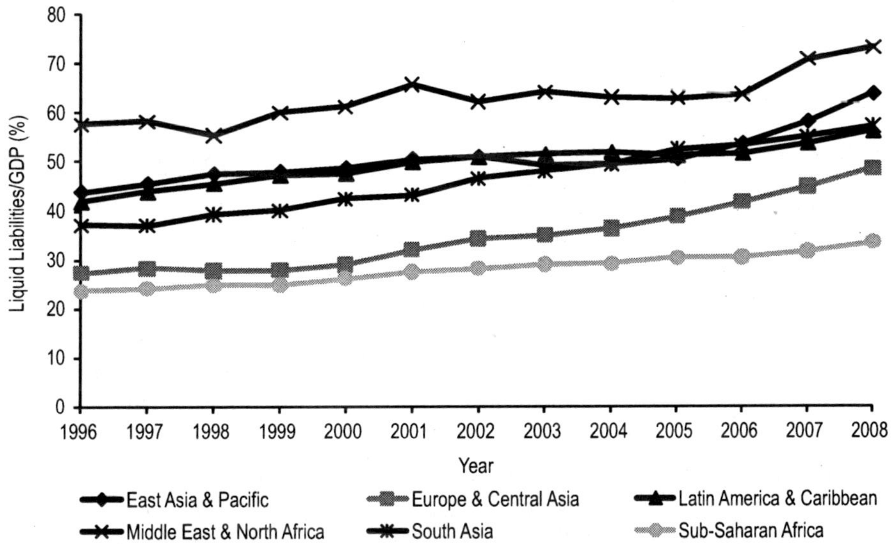

Source: World Bank Database of Financial Development and Structure.

Figure 2.2. Foreign Controlled Banking Sector Assets

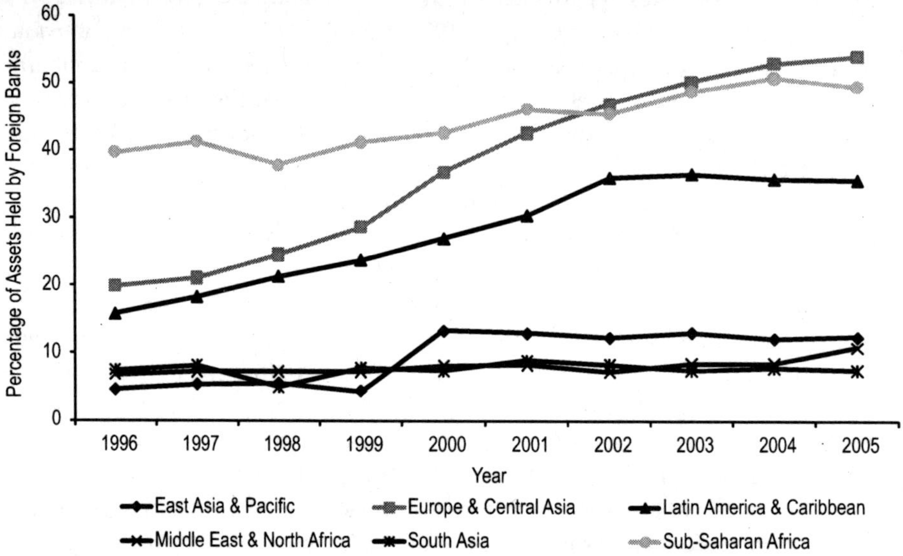

Source: Claessens, et al. (2008).

The diversity among ECA countries was stunning. Whereas just over 1 percent of banking sector assets was held by foreign-controlled banks in Uzbekistan in 2005, in countries as diverse as Albania, Bosnia and Herzegovina, Estonia, and the Kyrgyz Republic at least 75 percent of banking sector assets were controlled by foreign-owned banks. Overall, in 2005, among 26 ECA countries for which data is available, 15 countries had the majority of banking sector assets held in the hands of foreign controlled banks.

The empirical evidence shows that foreign banks in ECA were more efficient than domestic banks and the remaining state-owned banks with private ownership, especially with respect to minimizing their costs.[6] As the later firm-level evidence confirmed, lending by foreign banks during this period was associated with growth in firms' sales, assets, and leverage.[7]

Regarding the outreach of the banking sectors in the ECA region, the benefits of foreign bank participation were slower to develop. Foreign banks had long been accused of cream-skimming in developing countries, that is, lending only to top-rated clients. While granting that foreign banks had contributed to the overall development and stability of ECA's banking sectors, as late as 2005 some observers lamented that credit markets remained shallow and access to credit for SMEs limited.[8] Interviews with managers of foreign banks in the region revealed an intent to incorporate lending to small firms over time, and thus over the medium to long-term there was no intended bias toward lending to large multinational firms.[9] Evidence has also confirmed that the links between foreign lending and growth in firms' sales, assets, and leverage were less pronounced for small firms through 2002. At the same time, those links were more pronounced for young firms indicating that foreign banks were broadening access to finance for new (though not necessarily small) upstarts.[10] In that sense, they could be described as broadening access to credit.

The effects of expanded access to credit became evident late in the period, especially in the four years leading up to the recent crisis (Figure 2.3). As early as 2006, some observers had warned that the next major financial crisis would occur in Eastern Europe because the classic pattern—large current account deficits, large foreign debt, currency mismatches, and misaligned exchange rates—had already emerged.[11]

Between 1996 and 2008, in countries like Albania, Kazakhstan, and Latvia, the credit to private sector to GDP ratio increased more than tenfold. Only in the Slovak Republic was this increase less than 10 percent. The overall ratio went down only in the Czech Republic, from about 66 percent in 1996 to 48 percent in 2008.

The vulnerability of the ECA region and the early effects of the crisis were apparent in data reported by the Bank for International Settlements (BIS) on the gross claims of foreign banks on the financial and non-financial sectors of developing countries.[12] From 1996 to 2004, the ratio of credit to the private sector relative to GDP rose modestly from 18 percent to 25 percent. From 2004 to 2008, that figure climbed from 25 percent to 50 percent (Figure 2.3). Although other regions experienced increases on this measure, none were as dramatic as ECA's and, unlike for liquid liabilities, the region stood on par with or ahead of other developing regions on this measure by 2008. Of course, the rapid growth in credit late in the period ushered in a new set of concerns about foreign banks and their impact on stability. At the same time, the ratio of foreign claims to GDP in ECA grew two-fold between 2004 to 2007 when it peaked, and had already begun its decline in 2008 (Figure 2.4). Box 2.1 illustrates effects of "easy money" on selected ECA countries.

Figure 2.3. Access to Credit

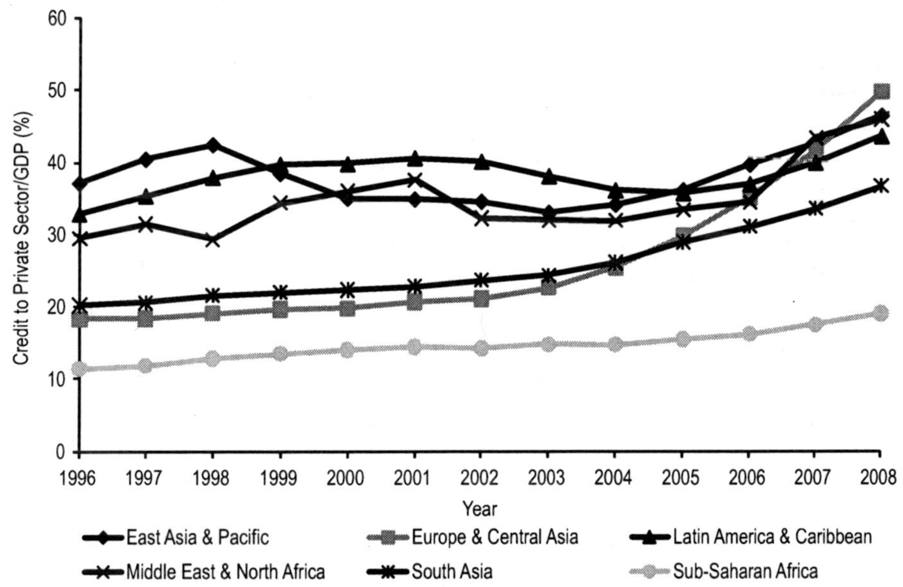

Source: World Bank Database of Financial Development and Structure.

Figure 2.4. Foreign Claims as a Share of GDP

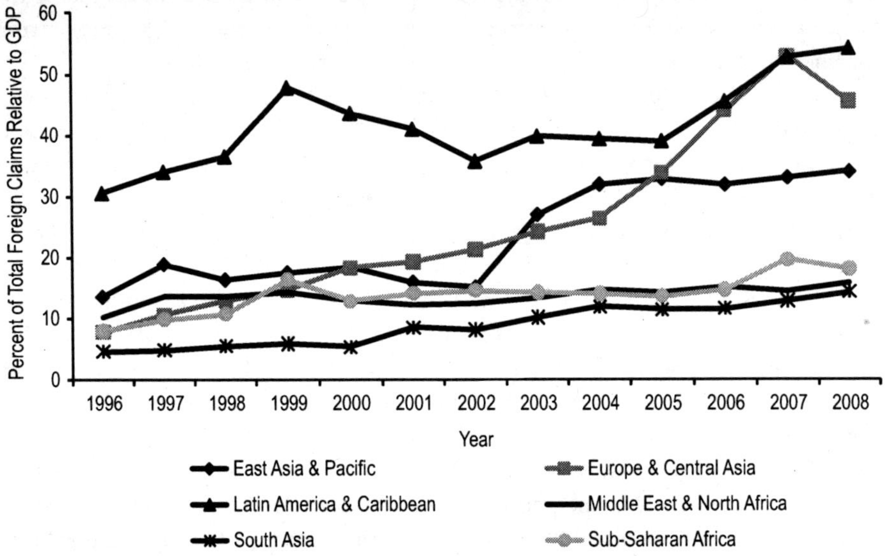

Source: Bank of International Settlements.

Box 2.1. Effects of Easy Money

The averages presented in Figure 2.4 do not show the dramatic diversity of the specific country conditions. There is a strong connection between the increase of credit to the private sector, foreign bank claims, and the effect of the financial crisis on economic growth (Figures B2.1.1 and B2.1.2).

Figure B2.1.1. Private Credit/GDP Change (2004–2007) vs. 2009 GDP Growth

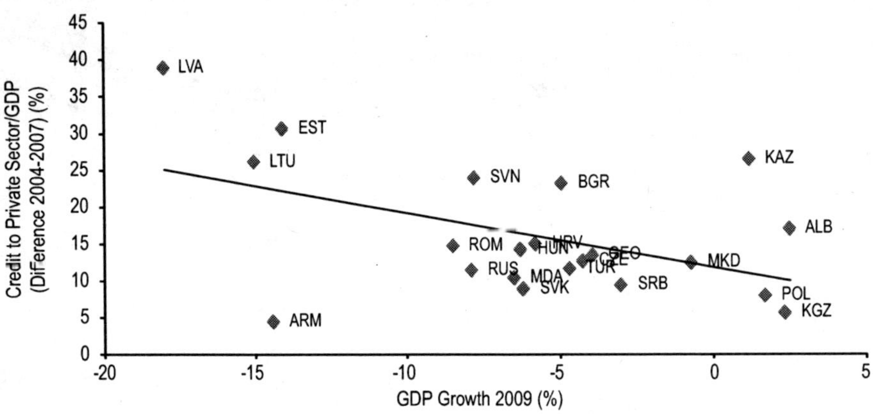

Source: World Bank Database of Financial Development and Structure, World Development Indicators.

(Box continues on next page)

Box 2.1 (continued)

Figure B2.1.2. Change in Foreign Bank Claims to GDP Ratio (2004-2007) vs. 2009 GDP Growth

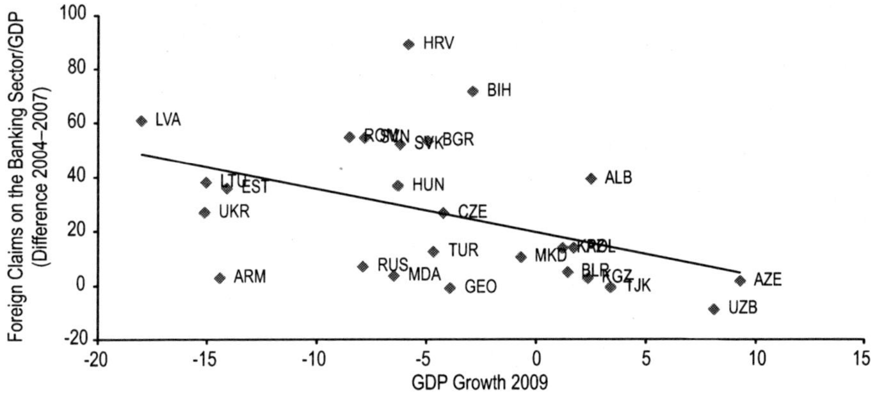

Source: Bank of International Settlements, World Development Indicators.

Latvia, Lithuania, and Estonia experienced the largest increase of credit to the private sector over the 2004 to 2007 period and the largest economic contraction in 2009. There are only two countries that do not fit this relatively clear pattern—Armenia and Kazakhstan. The former had a very modest increase in credit, but a very significant contraction, while the latter had a credit expansion at the level of Lithuania, and maintained positive economic growth.

The situation was about the same with the foreign bank claims, although the two countries with the highest increase of foreign bank claims in 2004-2007—Croatia and Bosnia and Herzegovina—managed to contain their economic contractions within single digits, while Latvia, Lithuania, and Estonia experienced double-digit drops in GDP.

Source: Authors' calculations based on World Bank data.

When foreign claims are separated into direct cross-border flows (i.e., overseas lending by the parent of a multinational bank) versus local lending in host markets by the subsidiaries and branches of foreign-owned banks, it becomes clear that the decline in 2008 was attributable to reductions in cross-border flows and local lending in foreign currency. Local lending in foreign currency in ECA had been growing much more quickly than in other regions, and substantially more quickly than local lending in local currency. As in other regions, especially South and East Asia, direct cross-border flows to ECA had also grown robustly prior to the crisis.[13] The analysis of financial constraints that follows will try to distinguish the rapidly growing direct cross-border flows and local lending in foreign currency from the relatively more stable long-term local lending in local currency by subsidiaries and branches of foreign banks.

The effects of the crisis generally were more muted in countries where: (i) foreign banks conducted a larger share of their lending in local currency, (ii) a larger share of the funding of foreign-owned affiliates came from expanding the domestic deposit base rather than from the parent bank or from wholesale funding, and (iii) the roster of foreign banks was not dominated by banks from the United States and Europe.[14] For all of these reasons, LCR, which had over half of total lending in local currency and where domestic deposits equaled 105 percent of all loans, has emerged relatively unscathed. Conversely, ECA, with only a third of its lending in local currency and domestic deposits equal to 75 percent of all loans, has suffered. Similarly, Sub-Saharan Africa was also less affected by the crisis than ECA, though foreign banks in Africa also did not extend credit as widely as in ECA or in LCR prior to the crisis.

Observers remained seriously concerned about the effect of foreign banks on the stability and outreach of banking sectors throughout the region. One concern was that foreign banks might shift capital away from affiliates in response to real sector shocks that affect the profitability of lending in a host country. While there was evidence of some funds being pulled back to the home country when profitable lending opportunities were prevalent there,[15] multinational bank lending did not slow during systemic crises in the host countries, while lending by domestic banks did. Domestic banks in ECA contracted their credit bases during crises, whereas greenfield foreign banks did not.[16] In addition, parent banks were in a stronger position to assist affiliates when their other affiliates were performing well.[17]

The evidence also indicated that lending relationships for foreign banks tended to be more stable than those of domestic banks. Foreign banks were less likely to drop their clients, even in the aftermath of an acquisition, and over time, competition from foreign banks produced changes in the lending policies of domestic banks, making their lending relationships more stable and generally improving access to credit for all firms.[18] The analysis in this chapter will show that foreign bank participation is in fact associated with less severe obstacles to finance as reported by firm owners.[19] In that sense, foreign bank participation could be seen as a stabilizing force during difficult times, in part due to the stable lending relationships highlighted in the empirical literature.

Data and Methodology

The BEEPS[20] survey covers a broad range of issues about the business environment, including questions about access to, and use of, financial services and thus provides an excellent vehicle for studying the effects of the dramatic structural changes in banking described in the previous section.

The analysis undertaken for this chapter required an indicator of "access to" or "use of" financial services that is comparable over the survey rounds. The best candidate comes from the response to the following question:

> *"Is access to finance, which includes availability and cost, interest rates, fees and collateral requirements, no obstacle, a minor obstacle, a moderate obstacle, a major obstacle, or a very severe obstacle to the current operations of this establishment?"*

A variable equal to one if the manager of the firm responded that access to financial services was no obstacle is the dependent variable in the analysis of financial constraints that follows.[21]

An advantage of this question is that it provides a comprehensive measure of the firm managers' perceptions of financial constraints. The second advantage of using this question is that responses to questions about perceptions of financial constraints (or other topics that affect firms' operations) are likely to be forward looking.[22] Thus, concerns that the final round of the BEEPS survey coincided with the onset of the crisis are less worrisome than they would be for other types of questions.[23]

One potential concern in using this question was a change in the number of response categories between the 2005 and 2008 rounds of the survey: the category "very severe obstacle" was added. Since the statistical analysis in this chapter is focused on relative movements in the "no obstacle" indicator for different types of firms rather than on absolute levels and the wording of the question was identical for all firms in a given round, the relative changes across rounds provide a reliable comparison of the severity of financial constraints over time.

Another potential concern with the comparability of BEEPS results across different rounds of the survey was the changes in sampling methodology between 2005 and 2008. In order to mitigate this concern, the analysis of financial constraints presented in this chapter utilized the balanced panel of firms that responded to all three rounds of the survey. Inferences drawn from tracking responses to the same questions by the same firms over time are likely to be more reliable than those that could be drawn from the full BEEPS samples.[24]

While panel data provides for good cross-period comparability, using it narrows down opportunities to discuss the specifics of individual countries as country samples dwindle. Therefore, this chapter offers a limited number of country-specific examples.

The results of BEEPS 2008 were supplemented with results of the Financial Crisis Survey (FCS) conducted in June and July 2009 by Enterprise Surveys in six countries: Bulgaria, Hungary, Latvia, Lithuania, Romania, and Turkey. These follow-ups permit an investigation of the determinants of firm survival during the crisis in which the dependent variable indicates that the firm was no longer operating—either because it had closed, had filed for bankruptcy or insolvency, or was temporarily shut—at the time of the second survey. This occurred in 296 of 2,501 possible cases (11.8 percent).[25]

Financial Constraints

The BEEPS data indicate that financial constraints eased from 2002 to 2005 and then tightened, in 2008 (Figure 2.5). Of course, these averages mask wide variations in financial constraints reported by firms participating in the surveys. Some firms reported no constraints, despite the crisis, while others were constrained across all three waves of the BEEPS. The main results that emerge from the financial constraints analysis revolve around three themes: the relative reliance on external finance by large versus small firms, the effects of foreign bank participation, and the impact of exchange rate regimes.[26] Each is discussed in turn.

Large and Small Firms

Informational asymmetries between borrower and lender tend to be more severe for small, young firms, and thus lenders charge them higher interest rates or do not extend credit to them at all. Small firms therefore use less external finance than others. Protection of property rights helps mitigate these informational asymmetries, and increases external financing for all firms but more so for small firms, mainly due to its effect on bank finance.[27] The World Bank's Investment Climate Surveys reveal that access to finance ranks high among constraints to firm growth as reported by firm managers, and relaxing financial constraints has a proportionately greater effect on sales growth for small firms than for others.[28] Overall, recent findings indicate that larger firms find it easier to trade off between internal funding and external borrowing than small firms.

Figure 2.5. Firm Perceptions of Access to Finance

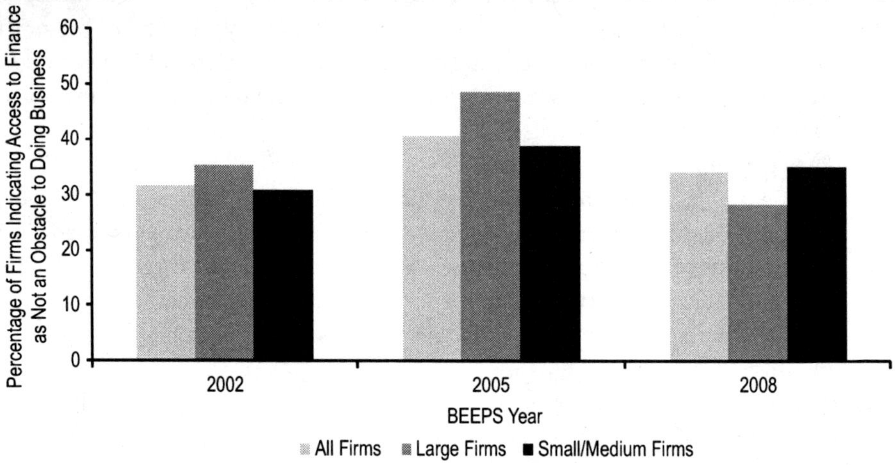

Source: BEEPS panel data, 2002, 2005, 2008.

Figure 2.5 shows that financial constraints eased for firms from 2002 to 2005, but then tightened again in 2008.[29] It also shows that large firms were four percentage points more likely to report that finance was no obstacle to their operations than small or medium-sized firms in 2002. Firm size categories are defined in the BEEPS as small, medium, and large; firms having 19 or less workers, 20–99 workers, and 100 or more workers, respectively.

By 2005, that gap had widened. Although all firms reported less severe financial constraints, nearly half of the large firms reported no constraints compared to less than 40 percent of the small and medium-sized firms. In 2008, the share of large firms that reported finance was no obstacle plummeted to 28 percent, a level slightly *below* that of the smaller firms.[30] The regressions described in Appendix 1, which control for a host of firm and country characteristics, confirm the same pattern. In 2002, large firms were 15 percent (4.5 percentage points) more likely to report access to finance as no obstacle, a gap that widened slightly by 2005. By 2008, the share of large firms that were financially unconstrained had fallen, and was no longer statistically distinguishable from that of smaller firms.

Greater reliance on external finance, however, also makes firms more vulnerable to sudden stoppages in funding. In normal times, larger firms find it easier to access external financing than small firms,[31] but the severity of the current crisis makes it likely that demands for finance from large firms exceeded the available supply.

Foreign banks in developing countries tend to lend less to SMEs, and thus large firms in the panel sample are the ones most likely to have received loans from foreign banks (though the BEEPS data do not permit this to be checked directly). Moreover, large firms were much more likely to rely on funding from foreign banks based in developed countries.[32] Lacking external finance prior to the crisis, smaller firms' sources of funding were less likely to have been affected.

Figure 2.6. Demand for External Funding

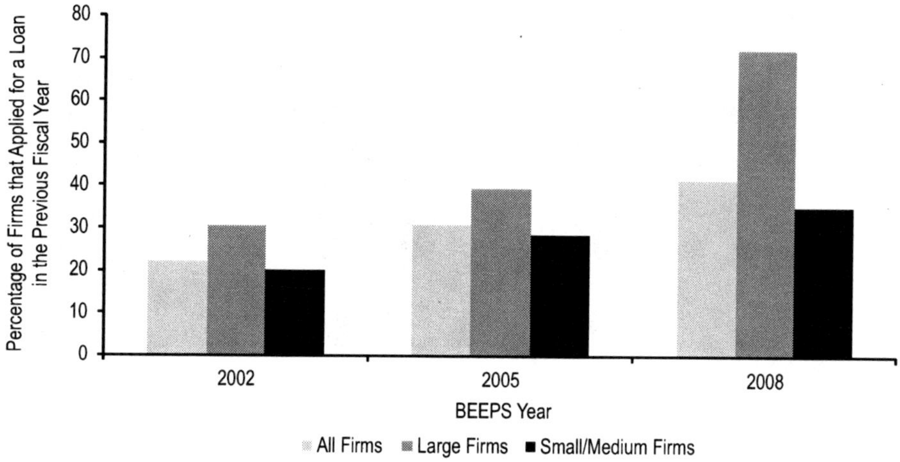

Source: BEEPS panel data, 2002, 2005, 2008.

Though it is not certain what motivated loan applications during the crisis, large firms were much more likely than others to apply for external sources of funding in response to the dramatic drop in demand in the ECA region (Figure 2.6).[33] Whereas large firms had been about one-third more likely to apply for a loan than small and medium-sized ones in 2002 and 2005, they were twice as likely to do so in 2008. The share of small and medium-sized firms that applied for a loan also increased, but much less sharply.[34]

Taken together, the steep decline in the share of large firms that reported finance was not an obstacle to their firms' operations in 2008 and the sharp increase in the share of large firms applying for loans suggests that large firms were able to ride out the crisis by relying on external financing; certainly more so than smaller ones.

Foreign Bank Participation

The extent of foreign participation in bank ownership varies widely among ECA countries. A high degree of foreign bank ownership was associated with relative difficulty in accessing credit at the outset of the decade, but less so at the end. The BEEPS data reveal a distinction between countries that had a well-established foreign bank presence by 1999 and those that did not in terms of reported financial constraints (Figure 2.7). In 2002, an estimated[35] one-third of the firms in countries with low levels of foreign bank presence (in 1999) reported that finance was not an obstacle to their operations. In the same year, in countries with medium and high levels of foreign bank participation, even fewer firms reported facing no obstacle accessing finance—27 percent and 19 percent, respectively.[36] But by 2008 the scales tipped in favor of countries with relatively high levels of foreign bank participation. About half of firms in these countries reported that finance was not an obstacle to their operations, whereas only a third of the firms in countries with low levels of foreign participation reported the same. These results suggest that foreign banks entered relatively credit-starved countries in the first part of the decade and substantially succeeded in addressing this constraint as the decade proceeded.

Figure 2.7. Predicted Probability of Access to Finance Being No Obstacle

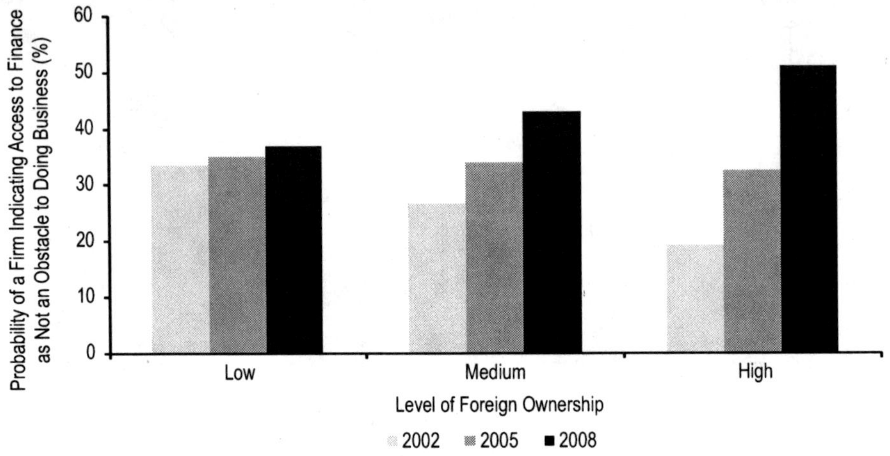

Source: BEEPS panel data, 2002, 2005, 2008.

Figure 2.8. Predicted Probability of Applying for a Loan

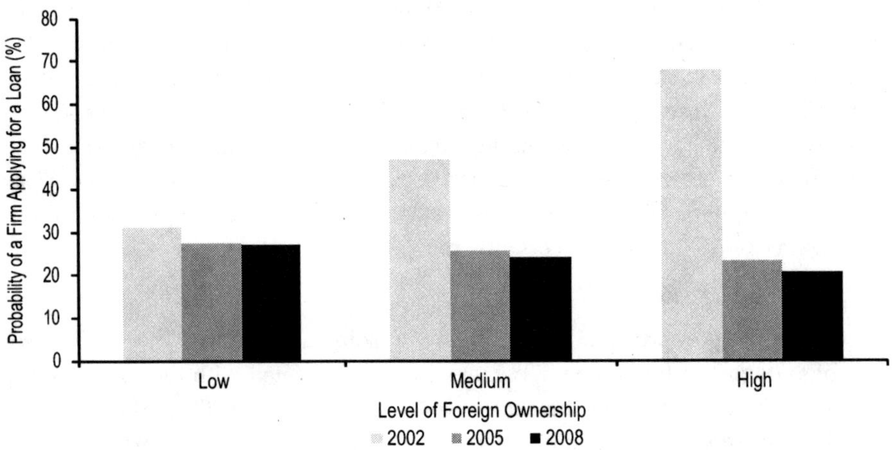

Source: BEEPS panel data, 2002, 2005, 2008.

Data on the share of firms that applied for loans also suggest that foreign banks were instrumental in meeting demands for credit at the beginning of the decade. In 2002, loan demand was highest in countries with a high level of foreign participation (Figure 2.8). It then dropped to levels prevalent in the region in 2005 and 2008. Overall, the results suggest that well-established foreign banks contributed both to the growth of firms prior to the crisis and were a stabilizing force, or at least an element of more stable banking environments, during the crisis.

Current Account Deficits and Exchange Rate Regimes

While foreign banks were instrumental in providing finance to firms in credit-starved countries at the outset of the decade, the role of foreign capital during the recent crisis has been more complex. The earlier discussion of the ratio of credit to the private sector relative to GDP (Figure 2.3) makes it clear that there was a steep decline in foreign lending in 2008, and that most of the reduction was in direct cross-border lending and local lending in foreign currency. In that sense, the rapid increase in certain types of foreign lending prior to the crisis was destabilizing.

The current crisis was in fact triggered by banks in developed countries, though its manifestation in the ECA region and the lead-up to it shared many features of other crisis episodes. Accumulation of foreign debt, excessive borrowing and lending, and a mismatch in the maturities and currency denomination of assets and liabilities of financial institutions and corporate firms are elements common to many recent crises, and all were evident in ECA.[37] These pressures came to be reflected in large current account deficits, which were further exacerbated by pegged exchange rates. As described in Aslund (2009), "the illusory safety of the pegged exchange rate attracted large inflows of short-term lending from European banks.... The temptation for international banks was irresistible. They could lend to consumers in Ukraine for 50 percent per annum with minimal financing costs." As foreign exchange inflows accelerated imports and balance of payments deficits increased, inflation soared, thus pricing countries with fixed exchange rates out of international markets. The situation was not sustainable and eventually resulted in large devaluations in a number of countries, although others such as Latvia chose to maintain its peg by implementing a program of deep austerity measures and wage adjustments.

The following analysis, therefore, will distinguish the rapid, ultimately destabilizing increase in some types of foreign lending from the steady, gradual growth in lending through the subsidiaries and branches of foreign banks. Due to lack of detailed, bank-level data on the nature and currency composition of foreign banks' loans, country-level proxies are used to capture these two effects. The literature on crisis episodes suggests readily available proxies for capturing destabilizing lending: the current account deficit and the exchange rate regime. As noted, overheating in the banking sector was most pronounced in countries with pegged exchange rates (i.e. fixed and crawling exchange rate regimes) and it came to be reflected in large current account deficits. Those variables are used as proxies for the "hot" destabilizing lending that was occurring prior to the crisis, while foreign bank participation in 1999 is a proxy for the more stable, rooted lending by foreign banks.[38]

The results of the analysis summarized in Figures 2.9 and 2.10 indicate that early on, i.e. up until 2005, reported financial constraints were substantially less severe in countries with exchange rates determined by a fixed or a crawling peg that also had high current account deficits.[39] This finding is consistent with the notion that the pre-crisis lending boom was largest in countries that had pegged exchange rates and large current account deficits, as was noted by many observers.[40]

So, too, is the finding that in 2005 the share of firms that applied for loans was much higher in countries with pegged exchange rates and large current account deficits (Figure 2.11). In countries with a peg and a current account deficit greater than 8 percent of GDP, over 60 percent of firms applied for a loan. In those with relatively small current account deficits (0–4 percent of GDP), only about a quarter did so.

Figure 2.9. Predicted Probability of Access to Finance Not Being an Obstacle, by Current Account Deficit (Fixed Exchange Rate Regime)

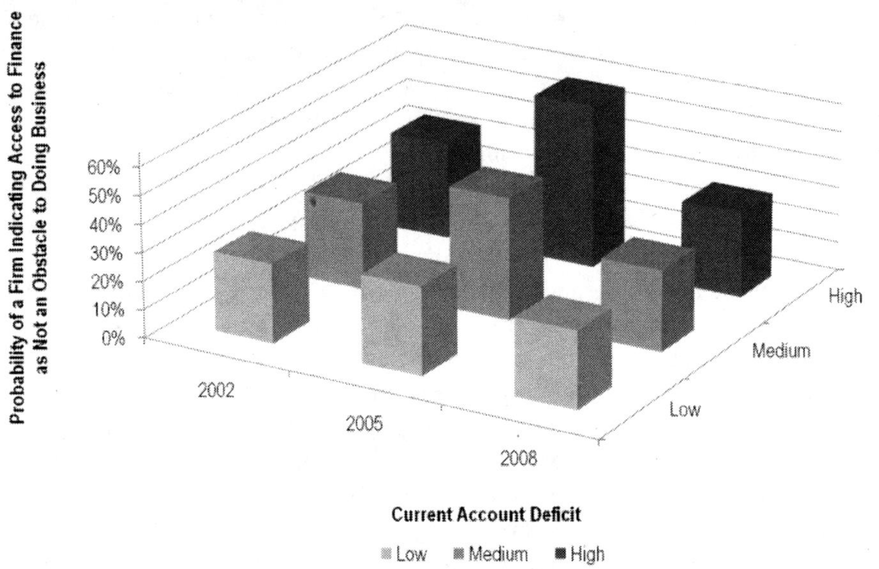

Source: BEEPS panel data, 2002, 2005, 2008.

Figure 2.10. Predicted Probability of Access to Finance Not Being an Obstacle, by Current Account Deficit (Crawling Exchange Rate Regime)

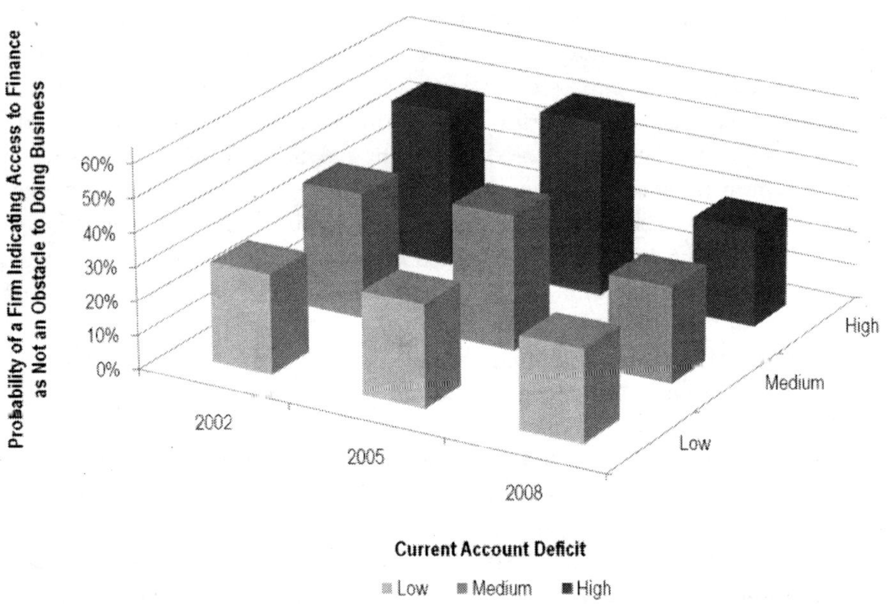

Source: BEEPS panel data, 2002, 2005, 2008.

Figure 2.11. Predicted Probability of Applying for a Loan by Current Account Deficit and Exchange Rate Regime

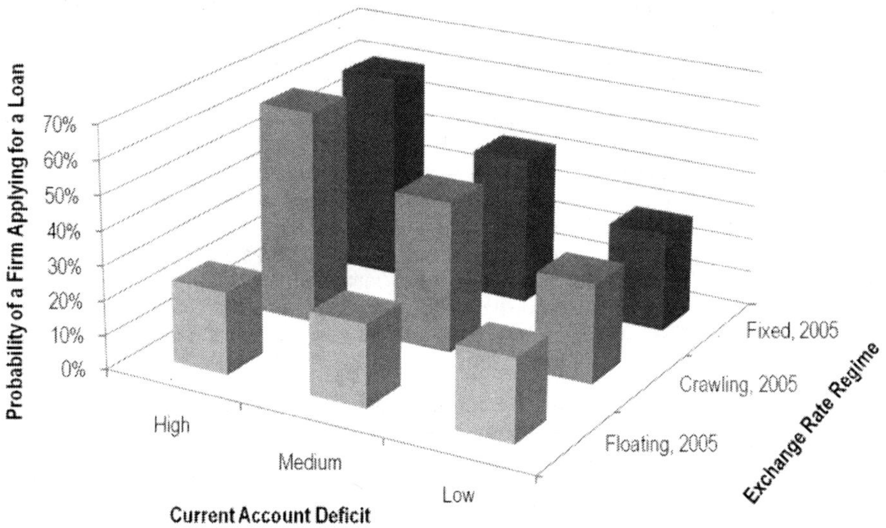

Source: BEEPS panel data, 2002, 2005, 2008.

By 2008, there were no longer statistically significant differences in reported financial constraints for firms in countries with pegs, regardless of the size of their current account deficit. The mechanism that brought about the lending boom in countries with pegged exchange rates and high current deficits had unraveled.

The lending boom as reflected in the BEEPS data on financial constraints and loan applications coincides with the increase in foreign claims depicted in Figure 2.4, an increase that was fueled by direct, cross-border lending and local lending in foreign currency by the parents of multinational banks. This suggests that the beneficial aspects of foreign bank participation summarized in Figure 2.7 reflect the relatively more stable lending in local currency by the subsidiaries and branches of the multinational banks in the ECA region. This is consistent with the conclusions of other observers about the volatility of cross-border flows and the severity of the crisis.[41]

In other words, countries that kept their exchange rates pegged and borrowed heavily directly from the parent foreign banks might have benefited in the run-up to the crisis when funding was plentiful, but were hit harder when the crisis arrived and cross-border flows and local lending in foreign currency dried up.

The regression models estimate the effects of fixed and crawling exchange rate regimes relative to the reference category, countries with floating exchange rate regimes. The effects of current account deficits for floating exchange rate countries are negligible, as reflected in the insignificant coefficients for the yearly dummies and a predicted probability of reporting that access to finance was no obstacle near 25 percent for all three waves of the BEEPS survey (not shown in a figure).

Box 2.2. Fixed vs. Floating—Example of Bulgaria and Poland

To illustrate, in Bulgaria, which maintained a fixed exchange rate, only 13.5 percent of BEEPS respondents indicated that access to finance was no obstacle in 2002 and the current account deficit stood at 2 percent of GDP. In 2005, 65.8 percent of those *same* firms responded that finance was not an obstacle as the current account deficit grew to 12.3 percent of GDP. By late 2008, the share of those firms (that participated in all three rounds of survey) indicating finance was not an obstacle had plummeted to 31.6 percent and the current account deficit stood at 25.2 percent. In contrast, in Poland, which maintained a floating exchange rate, the share of firms that reported finance was no obstacle went from 25 percent in 2002, to 22.2 percent in 2005, and increased to 33.3 percent in 2008. Poland's current account deficit remained relatively stable at 2.8 percent of GDP in 2002, 1.2 percent in 2005, and 5.5 percent in 2008. In other words, the Bulgarian current account deficit grew steadily between 2002 and 2008; a sample of the same Bulgarian firms went from reporting relatively severe financial constraints in 2002, to much less severe constraints in 2005, and then back to relatively severe constraints in 2008. In Poland, where the current account deficit has grown at a much slower pace, there were no such fluctuations in reported financing constraints.

Bulgaria was also somewhat slower to embrace foreign bank participation than Poland, and this might have contributed to the relative mildness of the crisis in Poland, in line with the results from the previous section. In 1999, foreign owned banks controlled 59.6 percent of banking sector assets in Poland compared with 41.4 percent in Bulgaria.

Source: BEEPS 2002, 2005, 2008, World Bank data and author's calculations

Firm Survival

As mentioned earlier, the BEEPS 2008 survey was followed up by the Financial Crisis Survey conducted in six ECA countries in June-July 2009. The results of the latter survey show that most firm managers saw the contraction in demand to be the most important effect of the crisis on their business rather than the credit crunch. It also shows that the sales growth of innovative and young firms was significantly more adversely affected by the crisis than that of other enterprises.[42] It was these firms that tended not to survive the crisis.

As shown in Figure 2.12, firms with five or fewer employees were 63 percent more likely to fail than those with 100 or more employees. The analysis shows that an increase in the number of workers from 1 to 10 reduced the likelihood that a firm was no longer operating at the time of the follow-up survey by about one fifth—from 14.6 percent to 11.6 percent.[43] By the same token, firms that had been in business for five years or less were three times more likely to fail than those that had been in business for over 25 years. While volatility among start-ups is high even in the best of times, the results for firm survival are consistent with the view that small, young start-ups suffered most as a result of the crisis.

But size and youth are not the most important explanation of firm failure. Empirical evidence found in the academic literature indicates that larger and older firms tend to have greater access to external finance than others.[44] Therefore, a close relationship between firm age, size, and access to external finance would be expected. BEEPS-based results suggest that one of the reasons why larger and older firms fared better in terms of survival was that they had better access to finance than smaller firms. When firm age, size, and access to external finance are all included in the firm survival regressions, the finance variable explains more variation than the two firm characteristics. In fact, firm

Figure 2.12. Predicted Probability of Firm Exit Based on Firm Size

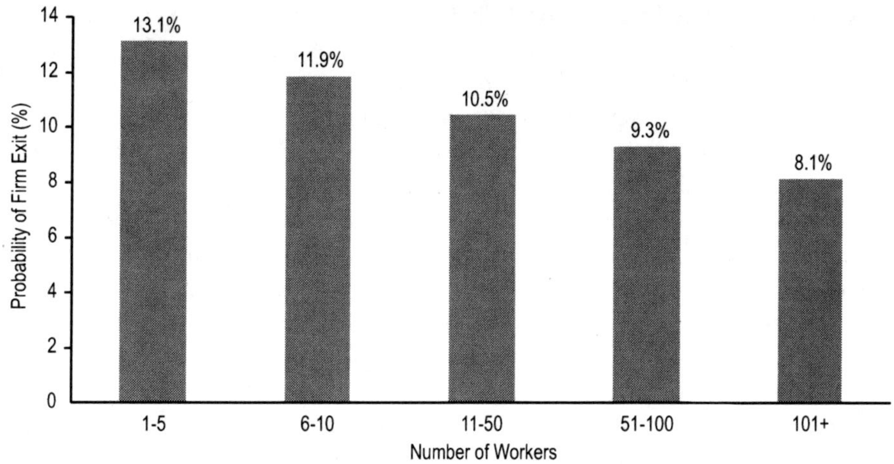

Source: BEEPS 2008, Financial Crisis Survey 2009.

Figure 2.13. Predicted Probability of Firm Exit Based on Firm Age

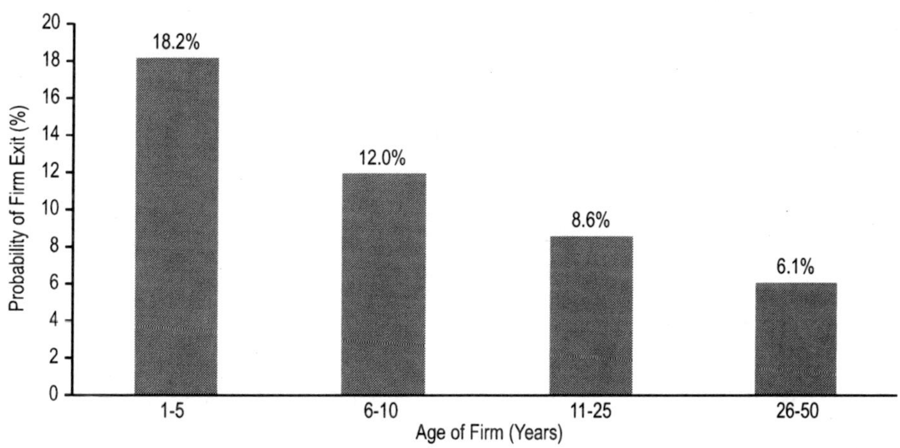

Source: BEEPS 2008, Financial Crisis Survey 2009.

size is no longer significant. The analysis therefore indicates that apart from influencing access to external finance, a firm's size did not exert a strong influence on its survival.

Everything else being equal, firms with loans or overdrafts were 3.8 percentage points more likely to still be operating in mid-2009 than firms without. In relative terms, their exit rate was about one third lower than for other firms.[45] Retaining access to financing was therefore important for firm survival. Given that the most common concern about the impact of the crisis on firm performance was the effect of a drop in demand, one plausible explanation is that firms with access to finance were better able to maintain access to working capital and manage the drop in demand.

Understanding Foreign Bank Presence

Results from the foregoing analysis strongly suggest that a well-established foreign bank presence helped to ease financial constraints during the crisis. This section examines the determinants of foreign bank participation levels in 1999 to better understand why this should be so. The WGI index, the measure of broad institutional development created by Kaufmann, Kraay, and Maztruzzi (2007), was substantially lower for low-foreign bank participation countries than for high ones from 1996 to 1998 (Table 2.1), while per capita income levels are similar for both groups.

However, other things being equal, foreign bank participation in 1999 was significantly higher in countries with low initial levels of per capita income.[46] Controlling for the level of institutional development using the WGI index, this pattern is consistent with foreign banks seeking out relatively underdeveloped banking markets.

Foreign bank participation was also likely to increase in the wake of financial crises, as local government officials sought to re-capitalize insolvent banking sectors.[47] Yet, Table 2.1 indicates that most countries in the ECA region experienced a systemic banking crisis at some point during 1990 to 1998, and thus crises explain little variation in

Table 2.1. Foreign Banks in ECA Countries during the First 10 Years of Transition

Country	% Assets Held by Foreign Banks (1999)	WGI, 1996-1998 (Avg)	GDP Per Capita, 1998 in Constant 2000 $US	Banking Crisis, 1990–1998	German Legal Origin	French Legal Origin	Socialist Legal Origin
Estonia	92.3	0.72	3,734.3	X	n.a.	n.a.	n.a.
Hungary	88.3	0.88	4,262.6	X	X		
Czech Republic	65.8	0.83	5,245.4	X	X		
Latvia	65.6	0.32	2,903.6	X	X		
Croatia	61.6	−0.21	4,673.5	X	X		
Kyrgyz Republic	59.8	−0.39	261.2	X			X
Poland	57.7	0.78	4,065.0	X	X		
Armenia	56.0	−0.53	562.0	X			X
Bulgaria	41.5	−0.11	1,415.2	X	X		
Moldova	39.7	−0.12	357.6				X
Romania	30.5	−0.05	1,632.3	X		X	
Bosnia and Herzegovina	28.4	−0.57	1,326.4	X	X		
Slovak Republic	17.4	0.49	5,250.7	X	X		
Uzbekistan	15.4	−1.12	528.5				X
Albania	13.5	−0.48	1,014.6	X		X	
Ukraine	13.2	−0.63	589.9	X			X
Russian Federation	11.4	−0.68	1,510.5	X			X
Kazakhstan	5.4	−0.71	1,076.3				X
Belarus	5.0	−0.91	1,156.3				X
Slovenia	3.5	1.09	9,120.2	X	X		
FYR Macedonia	1.4	−0.38	1,648.8		X		
Turkey	1.4	−0.36	4,021.6	X		X	
Lithuania	0.0	0.47	3,148.5	X		X	
Georgia	0.0	−0.87	600.2	X			X
Azerbaijan	0.0	−0.93	558.4	X			X
Top 13 (Avg)	54.2	0.16	2,745.4	0.85	0.58	0.08	0.33
Bottom 12 (Avg)	5.9	-0.46	2,081.1	0.75	0.25	0.25	0.5

Sources: WDI Database; Caprio and Klingebiel (2003)*; Claessens et al. (2008); La Porta et al (1999).
Note: *Caprio and Klingebiel define a systemic crisis as occurring when much or all of the capital of the banking system is exhausted. In the case of ECA, this situation often coincided with the breakup of the mono-banking systems inherited from the Soviet Era. Hence, many of those crises were qualitatively different from more recent ones.

foreign bank participation in 1999, though this was likely an important factor relative to other developing regions. Cultural similarity, as reflected in origin of legal code, also can explain variation in foreign bank participation levels. Countries of German legal origin tend to rank near the top of Table 2.1 (five of the top seven spots) while none of those of French legal origin rank higher than eleventh.[48]

With only 25 countries in the sample, it is difficult to draw definitive conclusions, but at least notionally, in the early stages of the transition, foreign banks were drawn to countries with better established institutions, greater potential for growth and development and closer cultural ties. All of these factors enhance the likelihood that these early entrants were committed to pursuing profit opportunities in these host markets over the long haul. Against this backdrop, it does not seem far-fetched that during the recent crisis, firms in countries with well-established foreign banks faced less severe financial constraints than those in countries where this presence was limited.

Conclusions

Analysis of the BEEPS data shows that, in line with predictions drawn from the literature, access to finance was a critical factor in a firm's ability to survive the crisis. As a result, large, older firms with their well established credit relationships tended to do better than smaller, newer firms. However, not all forms of finance were equally beneficial. Foreign-owned banks with well-established local networks, financed primarily from local deposits, and lending in local currency tended to have a stabilizing effect. Other forms of finance, including direct cross-border lending and local lending in foreign currency, did not.

Notes

1. World Bank (2010).
2. This is based on the 2009 Financial Crisis Survey implemented by Enterprise Survey Unit of the World Bank. Some caution is warranted in interpreting the results, as they mainly reflect the view of *surviving firms* and not the firms that failed to survive the crisis.
3. Note that comparisons of binding constraints are only valid for firms that survived the crisis. Information is not available on the most binding constraints for firms that are no longer in operation.
4. Cross-border capital flows reflect not only financial sector issues, but are endogenous to cross-border trade and sensitive to the economic performance of trading partners.
5. In some cases (particularly in Eastern Europe), foreign banks followed the entry and growth of large foreign corporates and thus had additional motivation to enter certain markets.
6. See Bonin et al (2005); Grigorian and Manole (2006); Kiraly, et al (2000): Nikiel and Opiela (2002); and Semih, Yildrim, and Phlippatos (2007). That evidence also indicated that pre-existing banks that were acquired by foreign owners performed worse than foreign banks that initiated greenfield operations. Both the greenfield operations and the relative efficiency of foreign banks overall suggested banking competition had improved as a result of their entry. Had the ECA countries just sold their pre-existing banks without permitting greenfield entry, it is likely that banking sector outcomes would have been worse. See Bonin et al. (2005).
7. Giannatti and Ongena (2009a).
8. See Marton and McCarthy (2008).
9. De Haas and Naaborg (2006).
10. Giannatti and Ongena (2009a). One might be concerned that foreign banks will revert to lending primarily to blue-chip clients in response to the crisis. However, evidence from other parts of the developing world indicates that credit growth rates were higher and lending volatility lower for foreign banks than for domestic banks during recent crisis episodes, especially in Latin America.

See, for example, Dages et al. (2000) and Crystal et al. (2001, 2002).
11. The warning came from Morris Goldstein and is reported in Aslund (2009).
12. Claims include not only bank loans, but also financing through debt securities and equity. Bank loans are by far the largest component, however.
13. Detailed breakdowns of the foreign bank claims data are available in Cull, Martínez Pería, and Teplitz (2011) and Kamil and Rai (2010).
14. See analysis in Kamil and Rai (2010).
15. The evidence comes from a study of 45 of the largest multinational banks from 1991 to 2004 (de Haas and van Lelyveld, 2010).
16. The evidence comes from 1993 to 2000 (de Haas and van Lelyveld, 2006).
17. De Haas and van Lelyveld (2010). Of course, this also means that credit growth slows when other affiliates are less profitable.
18. The evidence comes from a study of banks and firms in 13 countries from 2000 to 2005 (Giannetti and Ongena, 2009b).
19. Foreign banks also contributed to increased financing through new techniques. For example in Turkey, until recently, there was very limited project financing; the Turkish banks, for the most part, only loaned to the Government. Local banks were reluctant to finance infrastructure and when they did they usually required collateral or other bank guarantees, which were in excess of the amount loaned. It was only after exposure to competition from foreign banks using project financing that they have been moving in that direction.
20. The first round of the BEEPS was conducted in 1999 but the coverage of firms and format of questions was not sufficiently similar to later rounds to include that data in this analysis. In what follows, the 2002 survey is referred to as being the first round.
21. Although the response categories vary slightly across the rounds of the BEEPS (see Appendix 1), the "No Obstacle" category appears in all three.
22. For example, Clarke (2010) shows that concern about the long-term viability of the power sector in South Africa led to a rapid and sharp deterioration in views during the first weeks of a power crisis. Before the first blackouts, about 10 percent of firms said power was a serious problem. Shortly thereafter, almost 50 percent of firms said it was a serious problem. The decline was so rapid and steep that it seems unlikely to be attributable to only one week of blackouts but rather to predictions of years of future problems. Similarly, respondents to the final rounds of the BEEPS survey had likely received enough signals about the impending financial crisis (indeed some responded to the survey after Lehman Brothers had failed) that it seems likely that their views regarding financial constraints would reflect their predictions about the severity of the crisis.
23. The main concern is that the BEEPS 2008 occurred too early to be a useful tool for studying the effects of the crisis. The focus on relative changes over time in responses to the same question mitigates these concerns, even if respondents to the 2008 survey could not perfectly forecast the severity of the crisis. A secondary concern is that the 2008 round of the BEEPS occurred at different times across countries, some completed by mid-2008, others in spring 2009 when the effects of the crisis had become more evident. Therefore, a variable is included in the regression indicating whether firms were surveyed prior to the Lehman Brothers failure in August 2008, viewed by most observers as the defining moment of the recent crisis. That variable (and other variants on survey timing) was not significant and its inclusion did not alter the results of the analysis.
24. However, Appendix 1 shows that the characteristics of the balanced and the full sample (i.e., any firm that responded to a BEEPS survey in 2002, 2005, or 2008) are very similar and regression results from the full sample tend to be very similar to those for the balanced panel.
25. See Appendix 1 for a more detailed description of the construction of the dependent variable for the firm survival analysis.
26. A regression analysis was used to better understand the types of firms that were constrained, and how those constraints evolved over time. The regressions are described in detail in Appendix 1. Note that the regressions control for a host of factors including firm characteristics (number of employees, the age of the firm, its sector, exports as a percent of sales, the shares of foreign and private ownership, and a variable indicating whether the firm was privatized) and country characteristics (GDP per capita, measures of institutional development, inflation, GDP growth, popula-

tion and population density). All of the results described in the chapter are derived holding all of these factors constant.
27. Beck, Demirgüç-Kunt, and Maksimovic (2008).
28. Beck, Demirgüç-Kunt, and Maksimovic (2005).
29. A skeptic might argue that the changes in question format are driving these changes in reported financial constraints. However, since all respondents in each wave answered the same question, changes in their reported obstacles measured *relative to each other* are meaningful, even if the question format produced slightly higher (or lower) reported obstacles in a given BEEPS wave.
30. Many of the differences in reported financing obstacles across years are statistically significant in Figure 2.5. For example, the share of large firms that reported access to finance was no obstacle decreased significantly from 2005 to 2008 (from 48.5 to 26.5 percent, t-statistic 2.65, p-value 0.01). By contrast, the decline for small and medium firms was not significant (from 38.8 to 33.5 percent, t-statistic 1.34, p-value 0.18).
31. Beck, Demirgüç-Kunt, and Maksimovic (2008).
32. See Cull and Martinez Peria (2010) for an overview of that literature.
33. See Correa and Iootty (2009, 2010).
34. These patterns are again confirmed in the regressions in Appendix 1. While all firms faced a decline in demand due to the crisis, the hypothesis is that large firms were better able to access finance from external sources to make ends meet. This hypothesis is tested below in the analysis of firm survival rates. Since interest rates on loans were increasing at the time of the crisis, they cannot account for the steep increase in loan applications by large firms.
35. Based on the regression models in Table A1.3 of Appendix 1.
36. Low foreign bank participation is defined as 0–20 percent of banking sector assets in the hands of majority-foreign-owned banks, medium as 20–60 percent, and high above 60 percent.
37. See Corsetti, Pesenti, and Roubini (1999) for a review of crises.
38. Since the crisis was triggered by banks in Europe and the United States, a series of regressions was run to estimate separate coefficients for the foreign participation variable for different regions of origin (Europe, North America, rest of developed world, developing world). The coefficients for European and North American foreign bank participation were significant and very similar. Those for the rest of the world were not. Therefore only those regressions with the aggregate foreign bank participation variable are presented.
39. However, the evidence also suggests that these effects were already present in 2002 in countries with crawling pegs.
40. Regression models used for this analysis estimate the effects of fixed and crawling exchange rate regimes relative to the omitted reference category, countries with floating exchange rate regimes.
41. Again, see Kamil and Rai (2010) for comparisons across regions.
42. See Correa and Iootty (2010) for comparisons of the severity of different types of constraints.
43. Based upon the regression models in Table A1.2 of Appendix 1 evaluated at the sample means for the explanatory variables.
44. The literature traces its origins back to the pecking-order theory of financial services (Myers and Majluf, 1984). This theory holds that internal funds are less costly than external funds, because borrowing firms have better information about the quality of their investment opportunities than lenders do. The lender, therefore, requires compensation in the form of a higher interest rate. Because external funds are more costly, firm owners first exhaust internal funds to support investment before turning to credit markets, leading to a pecking order with respect to the two sources of finance. Informational asymmetries between borrower and lender tend to be more severe for small, young firms, and lenders, therefore, charge them higher interest rates or do not extend credit to them at all. As a result, small, young firms use less external credit than others. Analysis of the 2008 BEEPS shows, in ECA, 65 percent of large firms in the region had loans or lines of credit, while only 38 percent of small firms did. The data are from www.enterprisesurveys.org based upon BEEPS data. These are unweighted averages of the weighted country averages (i.e., all countries are weighted equally but weighted averages are used for each country).
45. The regression that produces this estimate controls for other factors that could affect firm survival.

46. The regression model is:
Foreign Bank Asset Share (1999) = 0.453*** + 0.342**WGI Index (1996-1998) − 0.0001**GDP Per Capita (1990–1998) − 0.0018 GDP Growth + 0.248*** German Legal Origin, where ***, ** represent the 1 and 5 percent significance levels, respectively. The WGI measure of institutional development is positive and significant, as expected. Controlling for that variable, the level of per capita GDP is *negative* and significant in the regression. The regression therefore indicates that, for a given level of institutional development, foreign banks were more likely to enter lower income countries.
47. Cull and Martinez (2008).
48. Regressions confirm that the differences in foreign bank participation across countries of German and French legal origin are significant. Additional factors including geographic proximity to London and GDP growth were also included in the regressions, though none proved significant.

CHAPTER 3

Infrastructure Bottlenecks

Since the 1950's there have been numerous examples of how infrastructure impacts economic development in both OECD and developing countries. The construction of highways, electricity, and telecommunications infrastructure has been linked to economic growth and positive productivity gains.[1] Recent studies show that in the ECA region, in contrast to the early transition years, infrastructure is becoming a bottleneck for productivity.[2] These studies show that quality rather than the quantity of transport and infrastructure services is a binding constraint in ECA (for example, see Calderon, 2007)[3] and this affects both economic development[4] and intra-regional trade.[5]

Since the beginning of the 2000's, productivity has been increasingly identified as by far the most important source of growth around the world.[6] The role infrastructure plays in productivity is not trivial. As firms move into the knowledge economy and use more energy and ICT services such as email, websites, and the Internet as avenues for sales, procurement, and communication, a reliable energy and telecommunications infrastructure is key to keeping these firms productive and growing.

This chapter analyzes the trends in infrastructure constraints that are covered in the 2008 BEEPS, including electricity and telecommunications, and provides a discussion of the factors that may partially explain the increase in the number of firms indicating electricity as an obstacle to doing business. It also discusses how these emerging infrastructure bottlenecks constrain firm productivity in the ECA region.[7]

The results of the 2008 BEEPS analysis showed that infrastructure bottlenecks such as power outages and limited access to information technology have a significant impact on firm productivity in ECA, in both the manufacturing and service sectors. The 2008 BEEPS also revealed:

- Electricity became the 3rd most severe obstacle to doing business across the ECA region. Only 39 percent of firms stated electricity posed no obstacle to doing business in 2008, down from 66 percent in 2005.
- Electricity bottlenecks have a significant negative impact on productivity, particularly for lower-productivity firms, although results show these negative impacts do not necessarily stem only from service outages.
- Electricity bottlenecks primarily affect small and medium-sized firms. Larger firms seem to be able to use their capacity and resources to mitigate electricity shortages with second best solutions, e.g. by acquiring power generators.
- For service firms, telecommunications became a greater constraint. Telecommunications became the 8th greatest obstacle overall in 2008, up from 14th in 2005. Access to new information technologies such as email, high-speed Internet, and websites has increased since 2005, and greater reliance on ICT may be causing lagging infrastructure to be a greater constraint.

The rest of this chapter is organized as follows. The next section provides a brief overview of relevant developments in ECA over the last 10–15 years. The second section discusses the sources of data used in the chapter. The third section explores changes in perceptions of electricity as an obstacle using BEEPS data over time; examines the cost of outages on firms in terms of lost sales, and the impact on productivity by focusing on country and firm level factors; and discusses the means to mitigate the effects of electricity constraints. The fourth section presents a discussion on ICT bottlenecks and the impacts on productivity. The fifth section provides a discussion of complementary factors highlighting the role of governance and regulation. The final section provides the main conclusions from the analyses.

Infrastructure in the Eastern Europe and Central Asia Region

The capacities of many infrastructure facilities, especially in the former Soviet Union and Yugoslavia, were large as they were designed to meet the demand of subregions rather than the demand of each republic. When these republics became independent countries, they had to rely on trade with neighbors to meet their needs. In CIS countries such as Russia, Kazakhstan, and others, key infrastructure facilities were constructed during Soviet times to provide universal access. Prices were seldom related to the true cost of infrastructure supply, which was generally considered an entitlement at little or no cost. As a result, artificially low energy prices induced an inefficiency of energy use and promoted output with high-energy intensities.

When output contracted in the 1990s, the demand for infrastructure services declined steeply, rendering the existing stocks excessive. Nonpayment for infrastructure services became severe and shortages in government budgets could no longer finance the deficits of utilities. As funds for maintenance decreased, the deterioration in the quality of assets severely reduced the quality of service. Thus, while most other regions of the world have to invest considerably to expand systems and increase access, the challenge in ECA has been to find resources to rehabilitate, operate, and maintain existing assets. This situation was exacerbated further by tariffs set too low by the government or by the regulator, thus distorting prices and consumption. The tariffs also constrain the utility companies' ability to maintain and invest in infrastructure.

Efforts to modernize infrastructure across ECA countries have differed over the last decade. Countries investing in ICT[8] over 2000–2006 were more often low-income countries: the largest increase took place in Moldova where 13.2 additional telephone lines per 100 people were added over the period. Transmission and distribution losses (as a percentage of output) were substantially reduced in poorer countries such as Armenia, as well as in richer countries such as Latvia and Turkey. The countries where electricity services did not improve or deteriorated were Russia, the Balkan countries and the countries of Central Asia. It is important to notice, though, some countries in the latter two groups were affected by war or ethnic conflict.

Infrastructure is one area that also benefits from private investment. In ECA, private investment rates are lower than other regions but have increased in recent years. The private investment in ECA[9] infrastructure accumulated to $246 billion[10] from 1990–2008 ($39 billion specifically in electricity).[11] This is lower than other regions. Private investment in LCR was $515 billion ($142 billion in electricity), while investment in EAP was $294 billion ($92 billion in electricity) in the same period. However, yearly private investment in ECA increased substantially in recent years: from $22 billion in 2006 to $46 billion in 2008, exceeding LCR ($40 billion). Over two-thirds of private infrastructure investment in ECA was concentrated in three countries: Russia (33 percent of total investment), Turkey (21 percent), and Poland (16 percent).

There is evidence that these findings are still relevant in the aftermath of the financial crisis. Other studies show that infrastructure gaps in emerging markets may expand in times of macroeconomic crises due to scarce public investments associated with budget deficits (e.g. Latin America from 1980–2000).[12] In addition, Mitra, Selowsky and Zalduendo (2010) identify bottlenecks in electricity infrastructure as one of the two main factors (together with education) that are most likely to distort the post-crisis recovery in ECA.

Data and Methodology

The analysis in this chapter is primarily based on the 2008 BEEPS survey. The analysis considers infrastructure services as an input to the production process. Firms producing or distributing electricity and telecommunication services are not included. The comparisons of 2005 and 2008 values—such as regional changes in perception of infrastructure constraints—are based on modified samples, maximizing comparability.

The following BEEPS infrastructure variables form the foundation for the analyses presented in this chapter:

- *Power outage* is a dummy variable representing a manager's response to the survey question: "Over fiscal year 2007, did this establishment experience power outages?"
- *Duration of power outages* only considers a subset of firms that experienced power outages. It is a compound variable multiplying the responses to the following questions: "In a typical month, over fiscal year 2007, how many power outages did this establishment experience?" and "How long (hours) did these power outages last on average?"
- *Cost of power outages* when used in regressions, considers all firms and is equal to zero if a firm did not experience power outages. When presented in terms of regional or country averages, only firms that have experienced power outages are considered. It is expressed as a percentage of total annual sales and refers to the following survey question: "Please estimate the losses that resulted from power outages?"
- *Generator* is a dummy variable representing a manager's response to the survey question: "Over the course of fiscal year 2007, did this establishment own or share a generator?"
- *Email* is a dummy variable corresponding to the following question: "Does this establishment use email to communicate with clients or suppliers?"
- *High-speed Internet* is a dummy variable representing a manager's response to the survey question: "Does this establishment have a high-speed Internet connection on its premises?"[13]

All regression analyses control for a variety of other firm and country characteristics listed in Table A1.1 of Appendix 1. A detailed discussion of regression analyses and model-specifications can also be found in Appendix 1.

The survey provides firm-level information on power outages, the use of ICT infrastructure, and managers' perceptions of infrastructure constraints. The BEEPS data are supplemented with infrastructure measures from the World Development Indicators, data collected by the World Bank Doing Business project, data from the World Bank Enterprise Surveys (for countries outside of ECA), selected World Bank country reports and other sources. The review of trends observed in the data is complemented with regression analysis where appropriate.

Electricity: A Growing Concern

Electricity Becomes a Top Business Constraint

One of the most noteworthy results regarding infrastructure was the emergence of electricity as a top constraint to doing business. Results of the 2008 BEEPS show that firms report electricity as the third biggest obstacle to business operations (out of 14 measured factors), behind only tax rates and corruption. Perceptions of electricity as a problem increased in all 27 countries participating in both the 2005 and 2008 BEEPS.[14] The greatest drops in satisfaction with electricity are seen in the FSU countries, including Belarus, Kazakhstan, the Kyrgyz Republic, and Russia. See Figure 3.1.

Some of the countries in Southeastern Europe also faced hefty electricity constraints. For example, only 2 percent of firms in Kosovo and only 8 percent of firms in Albania stated that electricity was not a problem, yet the results for the latter country, may have been aggravated by a spell of dry weather that seriously affected hydropower production, a significant source for electricity generation in Albania and some other SEE countries.

As expected, the perceptions of electricity as an obstacle are significantly affected by the number of power outages experienced, percentage of sales lost as a result of power

Figure 3.1. Electricity as No Obstacle, 2005 and 2008

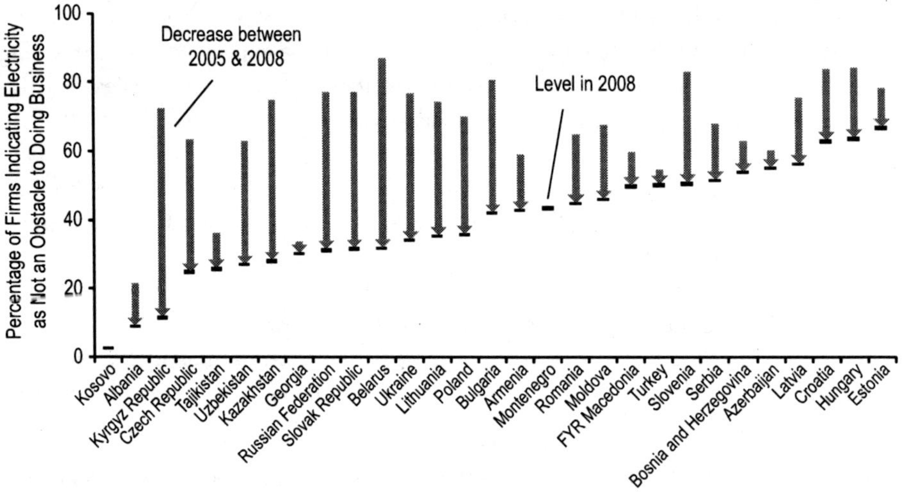

Source: BEEPS 2005, BEEPS 2008.

outages, and generator ownership. As each of these values increases, the likelihood that a firm will find electricity to be a major or very severe obstacle to doing business rises.[15] The analysis also shows that a similar relationship holds for firms expanding their labor force in the past three years: these firms were less likely to indicate electricity as not an obstacle to their business operations. Furthermore, the results point at the interdependence of infrastructure services; as access to high-speed Internet rises, electricity is more likely to be perceived as a major or very severe obstacle.

The electricity constraints seen in ECA are not unique compared to other regions. In fact, ECA firms have more positive perceptions of electricity as an obstacle than firms in other regions (Figure 3.2). While on average, about 39 percent of ECA firms stated electricity is not an obstacle, only 15 percent firms in SAR, 20 percent in AFR, 29 percent in LCR, and 30 percent in EAP have agreed with this statement. Though, this should not be used to understate the gravity of electricity as an obstacle, as outages carry a substantial cost to firms in terms of both sales and productivity.

Figure 3.2. Electricity as No Obstacle by Region

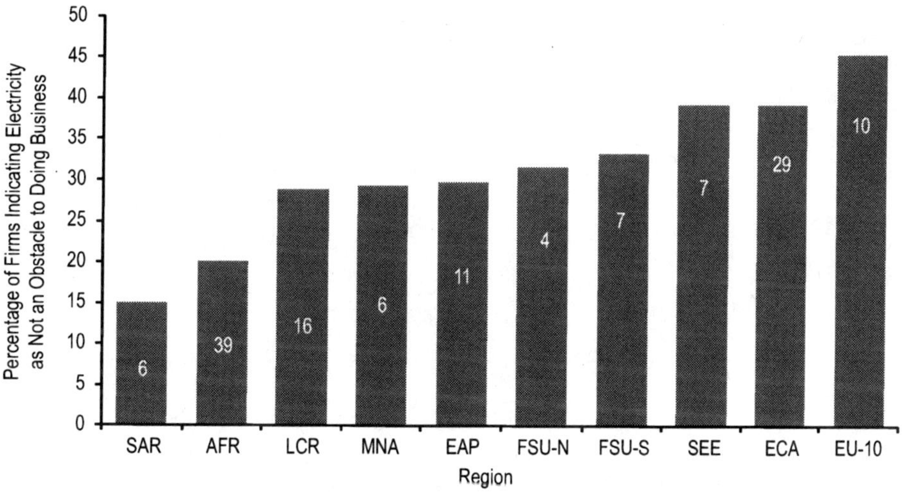

Source: BEEPS 2008, Enterprise Surveys 2006–2010.
* The number indicated within the bars represents the number of countries in each region.

Power Outages—Frequency and Cost to Business

The BEEPS results show a substantial variation in electricity bottlenecks across individual countries. On average, firms in poorer countries suffer more from electricity shortages. For example, 97 percent of firms in Kosovo and 90 percent of firms in Albania experienced power outages in a typical month, although, as it was mentioned earlier, results for Albania may have been affected by a particularly dry year that exacerbated hydro-power shortages in the SEE subregion. More than half of all firms suffered from power outages in Tajikistan and Uzbekistan. In contrast, Hungary, Belarus, and Poland together averaged only around 20 percent of all firms reporting outages. Of these, Belarus is a noticeable outlier: its GDP per capita puts the country in the middle of the pack, while at the time of survey, the country was benefiting (and still benefits) from special prices for energy resources and electricity deliveries from neighboring Russia. This favorable arrangement is perhaps a reason Belarus has a significantly lower than expected level of power outages.

Figure 3.3 below illustrates the relationship between the percentage of firms experiencing power outages and GDP per capita. It shows that electricity constraints are most severe in lower income countries. The reference line represents the linear relationship between these two variables. Countries falling above the line experience greater electricity constraints than predicted by their income level. The trend is visible even when extreme cases such as Kosovo and Albania[16] are not taken into consideration.

Figure 3.3. Power Outages vs. GDP Per Capita

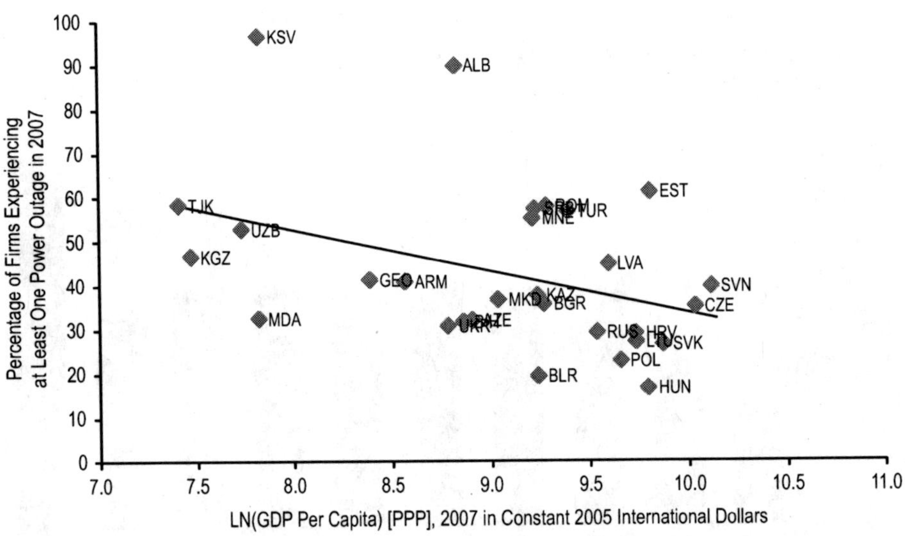

Source: BEEPS 2008, World Bank World Development Indicators.

On average, electrical service outages were experienced by 43 percent of all firms in ECA in 2007. In comparison to other Bank regions, ECA firms experienced the lowest percentage of power outages. Data from Enterprise Surveys shows that over 50 percent of firms experienced outages in the LCR, EAP, MNA, AFR, and SAR regions. Figure 3.4 below shows the percentage of firms experiencing outages over the year prior to the survey.

What really makes ECA different from other regions is the length and, consequently, costs of power outages to the firms. Power outages average 32 hours per month and account for 5.4 percent of output losses relative to annual sales among firms in ECA (while losses are 4.0 percent in EAP). The difference in losses is more pronounced when lower income countries are compared. For example, according to Enterprise Surveys and BEEPS respondents, power outages account for 6.7 percent and 9.7 percent of output losses in low- and lower-middle income countries in LCR and ECA, respectively. Losses

Figure 3.4. Breadth of Power Outages

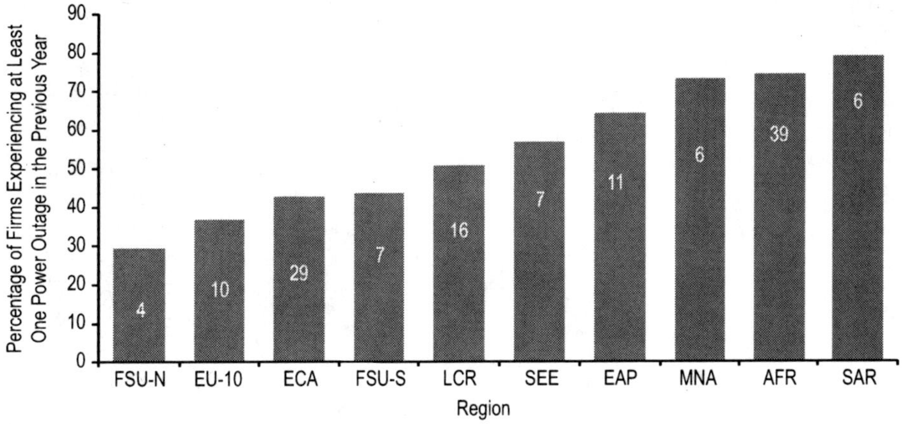

Source: BEEPS 2008, Enterprise Surveys 2006-2010
* The number indicated within the bars represents the number of countries in each region.

are also greater for comparable higher income countries[17]—4.2 percent and 5.3 percent in LCR and ECA, respectively. The impact of power outages is particularly high in the three low-income Central Asian countries and in the countries of Southeastern Europe. For example, the cost of power outages accounted for more than 10 percent of annual sales in FYR Macedonia (11.8 percent), the Kyrgyz Republic (13.7 percent), Albania (13.8 percent[18]), Kosovo (17.7 percent), and Tajikistan (18.4 percent). See Figure 3.5.

Similarly, firms in higher income countries perceive electricity to not be an obstacle more often than their counterparts in lower income countries (see Figure 3.6). This may be partly due to better quality infrastructure, the ability to invest in infrastructure maintenance and upgrades, and a better governance and regulatory environment in higher

Figure 3.5. Losses Due to Power Outages

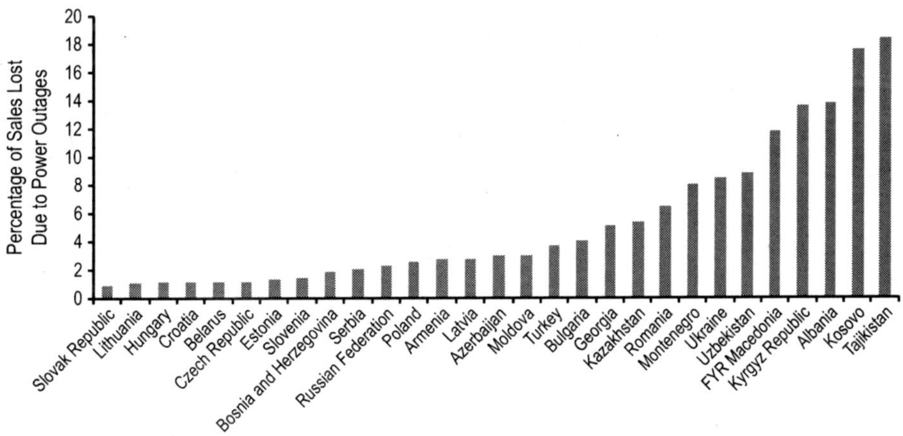

Source: BEEPS 2008.

Figure 3.6. Losses Due to Power Outages by Income Classification

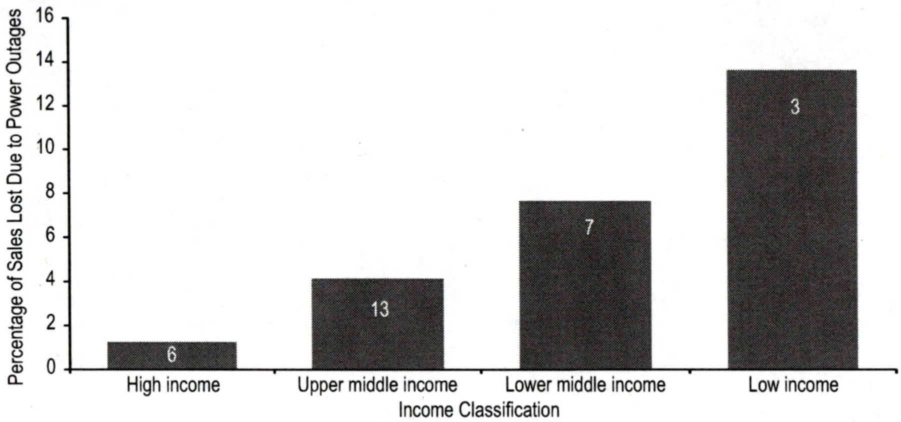

Source: BEEPS 2008.
* The number indicated within the bars represents the number of countries in each region.

income countries. Furthermore, certain firms[19] in these countries may have a greater ability to respond to outages by using generators as a secondary power source.[20]

Electricity Outages as a Constraint to Firm Productivity[21]

One important implication of infrastructure quality is its impact on firm productivity. The analysis of the BEEPS data shows that electricity shortages are a productivity constraint primarily for small and medium-sized firms.[22] The percentage of firms experiencing power outages is higher for small and medium-size firms than for large firms, as are the losses incurred from those power outages as a share of annual sales. Further analysis shows that the productivity costs incurred due to power outages are significant and comparable for small and medium-sized firms, whereas those of large firms are not statistically different from zero (after controlling for the effect of various other firm and country-specific factors).

The analysis shows that some firm-level factors appear to make certain firms more vulnerable to electricity bottlenecks.[23] For example, firms that innovate, low productivity firms, and firms with greater access to finance[24] appear to face higher constraints in terms of power outage costs' effects on labor productivity than their counterparts.

Large firms, firms that are part of a larger organization (i.e. subsidiaries), and high-productivity firms, on the other hand, suffer less from electricity shortages in terms of productivity. The analysis shows that labor productivity is not as constrained by power outages for the latter types of firms since they have superior capacities to address these shortages by themselves. For instance, buying or sharing a generator is an option, albeit an expensive one—and the analysis shows that large firms are significantly more likely to own a generator (fully or partially).[25]

Box 3.1. Cost of Power Outages in Kosovo

Managers in Kosovo consider the poor quality of electricity supply as the biggest obstacle to their businesses. Thirty-four percent of all managers perceive electricity as the biggest obstacle followed by corruption (21 percent). Eighty-three percent of all managers consider electricity as a major or very severe obstacle, which is by far the highest fraction in ECA. Kosovo is the country with the second highest reported cost due to power outages, accounting for 17.7 percent of annual sales. Moreover, 97 percent of all firms in Kosovo experience power outages and, on average, face 105 hours per month without power.

The poor quality of electricity supply originates from capacity shortages, poor management, low tariffs, and high distribution as well as commercial losses. The Kosovo Energy Corporation (KEK) is the sole producer and distributor of electric power in Kosovo. It operates the two old and poorly maintained power plants, Kosovo A and Kosovo B. Only 60 percent of their aggregate capacity is available, well below the peak capacity demand needed during the cold season. The distribution network has also suffered from many years of underinvestment. As a result, technical losses in the distribution system are very high, averaging 17 percent. Moreover, the operational and financial performance of the power sector is poor due to low billing and collection rates. In the last two years, commercial losses constituted about 35 percent of energy entering the network (about €96 million per year).

While the rehabilitation of generating capacities and the distribution system require major investments, reducing commercial losses requires institutional reforms. The investments required to rehabilitate the two power plants and the distribution network are estimated at about €80 million per year from 2010 onwards. In addition, a new power plant will be constructed to replace Kosovo A. Nevertheless, without policy measures improving the competence of KEK to enforce collections and reduce theft, there is limited scope for improving electricity services.

Improving the performance of the power sector requires complementary institutional reforms and good governance. In April 2010, the Parliament of Kosovo approved the Government's Energy Strategy 2009-2018 to address the problems. It is focused on rehabilitation and privatization efforts. In particular, the government plans to privatize KEK Distribution to improve payment discipline. This requires, however, the implementation of supporting measures; e.g. (i) making electricity theft a criminal offense and prosecuting offenders vigorously, (ii) providing funding to the courts to deal expeditiously with cases of theft and nonpayment of bills, and (iii) allowing a program of regular tariff increases as warranted, provided that customer service and quality of supply improve hand-in-hand.

Source: BEEPS 2008 and Kosovo Country Economic Memorandum 2010.

Innovative firms, which have introduced a new product or service in the last three years, experience slightly lower sales losses due to outages than non-innovative firms. However, the productivity of these firms is more constrained by electrical-infrastructure bottlenecks; and this occurs despite innovative firms being more likely to be larger firms (they have, on average, 55 percent more employees than non-innovative firms).

Low-productivity firms face greater productivity costs due to electricity bottlenecks than high-productivity firms. These findings are consistent with previous ones since less productive firms are less likely to be large or subsidiaries. This suggests that low-productivity firms might lack the capacity to address electricity shortages and are, as a result, more vulnerable to low quality infrastructure services. Thus, poor electrical infrastructure services tend to contribute to the gap between low-productivity and high-productivity firms.

Firms located in fast-growing low and medium income countries are particularly vulnerable to electricity bottlenecks.[26] One would expect to find inadequate electricity supplies in poorer countries. This conclusion is supported by the World Development Indicators (WDI), which show that stocks of infrastructure services are highly correlated with GDP per capita. In the survey year, productivity losses are particularly large in Kosovo, Albania, and Tajikistan.

Firms in countries with rapid economic growth[27] such as Azerbaijan, Belarus, Latvia, Russia, Tajikistan, and others appear to suffer more from electricity bottlenecks. This is because rapidly increasing demand makes it difficult to maintain a timely and effective supply of services.[28] Thus, anticipating infrastructure bottlenecks and planning ahead is particularly important for policy makers in fast-growing countries.

Mitigating the Effects in the Manufacturing Sector[29]

Some manufacturing firms are able to balance or offset the effects of power outages through the use of power generators. Use of generators is naturally prevalent in lower income countries with less reliable electricity systems. However, the use of generators is less widespread in low-income ECA countries than in comparator countries outside of the region. Partially and fully foreign owned firms and firms that innovate are more likely to use and/or own generators. Figure 3.7 shows that foreign manufacturing firms make extensive use of generators (24 percent) relative to domestic manufacturing firms (14 percent). Likewise, 16 percent of firms that invest in R&D or innovate use generators compared to 14 percent for those who invest in neither.[30]

Figure 3.7. Generator Use

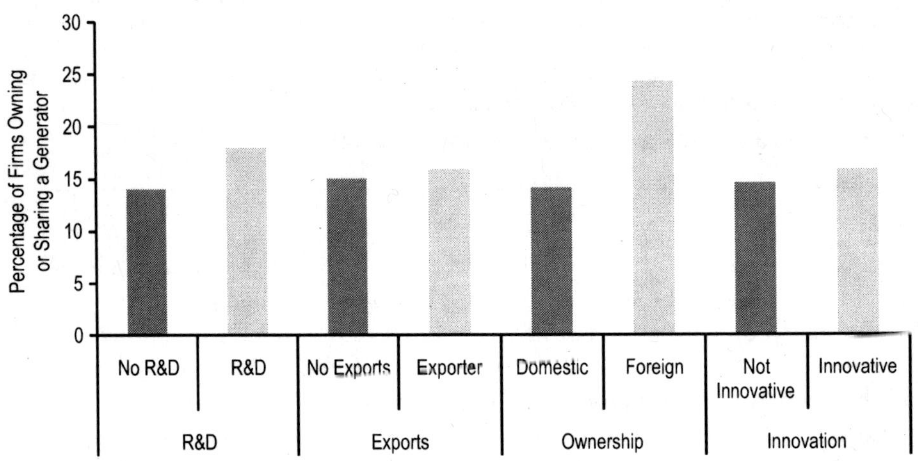

Source: BEEPS 2008.

Acquiring or sharing generators has a positive impact on productivity.[31] But generators are an inefficient means of mitigating power outages. The use of power generators indicates a poor quality or inefficiency of country-level institutional arrangements to guarantee a reliable electricity supply rather than an efficient solution. Thus, this costly firm-level intervention should be regarded as a second-best solution to address electricity shortages.

Why do firms that operate conventional technologies choose not to acquire or share generators? There are two factors that may potentially explain this: (i) limited access to finance, and (ii) lack of pressure to improve competitiveness by acquiring generators. Analysis of BEEPS data suggests that firms are more likely to use generators if they have access to credit.[32] This result suggests that firms in countries with better access to credit can better protect their businesses against power outages by financing generators. However, the cost of funding these generators can offset the reduction in productivity losses from power outages. Therefore this is always a second-best solution as compared to improving the quality of the public grid.

Telecommunications Usage on the Rise, but Access and Reliability Remain Issues[33]

The BEEPS results also point to bottlenecks in information and communications technology (ICT) infrastructure. Telecommunications became a greater obstacle to doing business, ranking 8th overall in 2008, up from 14th (the last among obstacles being measured) in 2005. Telecommunications became a bigger obstacle in 25 of 27 countries participating in both the 2005 and 2008 BEEPS. Of these, the decline in firms indicating telecommunications is not an obstacle to doing business was statistically significant in 22 countries. The most dramatic declines are seen in Bulgaria, the Kyrgyz Republic, Russia, the Slovak Republic, and Ukraine. See Figure 3.8 below.

Figure 3.8. Telecommunications as No Obstacle, 2005 and 2008

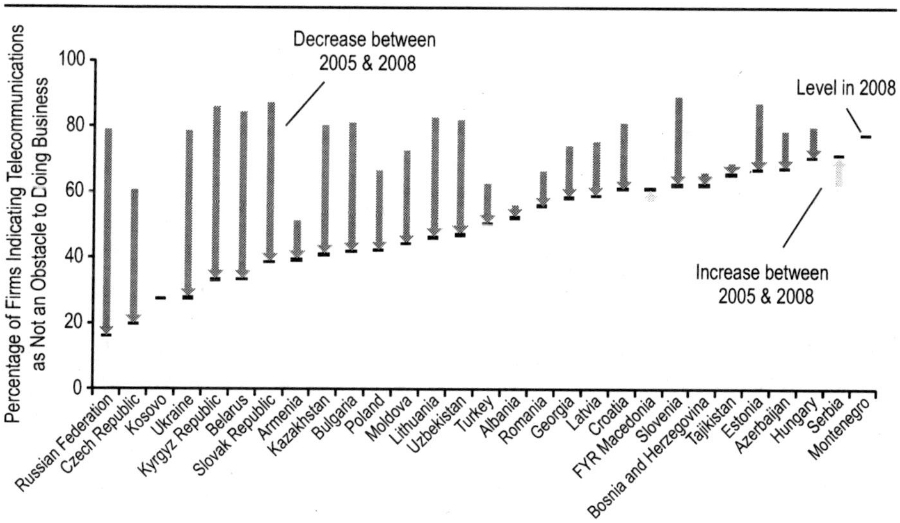

Source: BEEPS 2005, BEEPS 2008.

The emergence of telecommunications as an obstacle coincides with a period of greater access and use of email and other ICT technologies by firms. On average, 73 percent of firms across ECA in all sectors used email to communicate with customers or suppliers in 2008. Firms that participated in the 2005 and 2008 rounds of BEEPS reported a significant increase in the use of email communication.[34] While use has increased, access and reliability of services are still serious issues.

Usage of high-speed Internet is lower in ECA than other regions. Only 57 percent of firms across ECA use high-speed Internet, compared to 61 percent of firms in LCR.[35] The gap is narrower (and comparison to LCR more positive) in the EU-10 countries, where 72 percent of firms were connected to high-speed Internet in 2008. Of those firms with high-speed Internet, 37 percent of firms experienced Internet service interruptions, on average 4.6 times per month lasting an average of 2.7 hours each.

As with electrical infrastructure, the gap in telecommunications access is partially explained by country wealth. Poorer countries have less access to email and other ICT technologies; only about 40 percent of firms use email communication in Tajikistan and the Kyrgyz Republic compared to nearly 100 percent in Slovenia and the Czech Republic. Figure 3.9 below depicts the relationship between email use on the vertical axis and GDP on the horizontal axis. As would be expected, countries with a higher GDP per capita also have a greater percentage of firms using email. Countries falling above

Figure 3.9. Email Use vs. GDP Per Capita

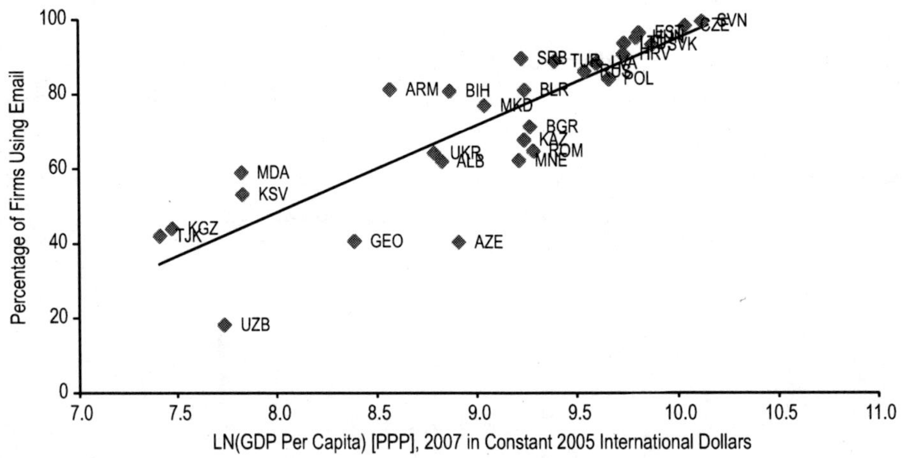

Source: BEEPS 2008, World Bank World Development Indicators.

the reference line have a greater percentage of users than would be predicted based on country income. Armenia seems to be the most distinguishable positive outlier[36] having significantly more email users than would be expected for a country at its income level (see Box 3.2). Firms in neighboring Azerbaijan and Georgia, however, report lower email penetration than one would expect based on the country's income level. Uzbekistan has the lowest percentage of email users in the region.

Some firms have greater access to email communication and high-speed Internet. Firm size, in particular, is a good predictor of broadband access.[37, 38] Small and medium-sized firms are less likely to use email communication (63 percent, 79 percent, and 93 percent for small, medium, and large firms, respectively) or have access to high-speed Internet[39] (49 percent, 68 percent and 84 percent, respectively) than their larger counterparts. Even though large firms make more use of the ICT infrastructure (measured as use of high-speed Internet), the regression analysis shows the gains to productivity

> **Box 3.2. Progress in Armenia's Telecom Sector**
>
> The telecom sector in Armenia has been improving rapidly after a long period of stagnation caused by a monopoly. As a result, mobile penetration and broadband subscribers have increased significantly since 2008. Full liberalization triggered several large investment deals, including the full acquisition of the former monopoly, Armentel, by Russian Vimpelcom; the acquisition of local leading mobile operator, Viva Cell, by Russian MTS; and the entry of France Telecom under the brand name Orange. Increased competition has resulted in new investments in advanced technologies and in better telecom infrastructure overall. The Internet services sector is also growing rapidly. iCON, a company established in 2007 with Diaspora originated investment, and Cornet (a recent acquisition by a Russian company), introduced WiMAX technologies in Armenia. Both companies provide broadband and high-quality wireless services. Furthermore, ADC, an Armenian-Norwegian joint venture continues to expand the fiber optic network in Yerevan and the Marzes.
>
> *Source:* World Bank.

from the ICT usage are not much larger than those of small and medium-sized firms.[40] Hence, ICT investment could induce across-the-board productivity gains and possibly give small and medium-sized firms a better competitive edge through higher email usage and better access to high-speed Internet (i.e. since large firms are already more likely to use email and Internet, such investment would implicitly favor small and medium-sized firms and allow them to close the gap).

The country where a firm is located in also plays a significant role in determining the gains from ICT access. The results of the BEEPS show that the productivity effect is significantly stronger in low-income countries and in fast-growing countries. Although this does not allow for much in the way of policy recommendations, it may give firms in these countries incentives to invest in their own ICT networks.

A similar pattern holds when examining email use. Figure 3.10 below depicts the relationship between email use and labor productivity. The graph shows that in general, firms in countries with a greater percentage of email use are also more productive firms, which is confirmed by statistical analyses controlling for other factors.

Figure 3.10. Email Use vs. Labor Productivity

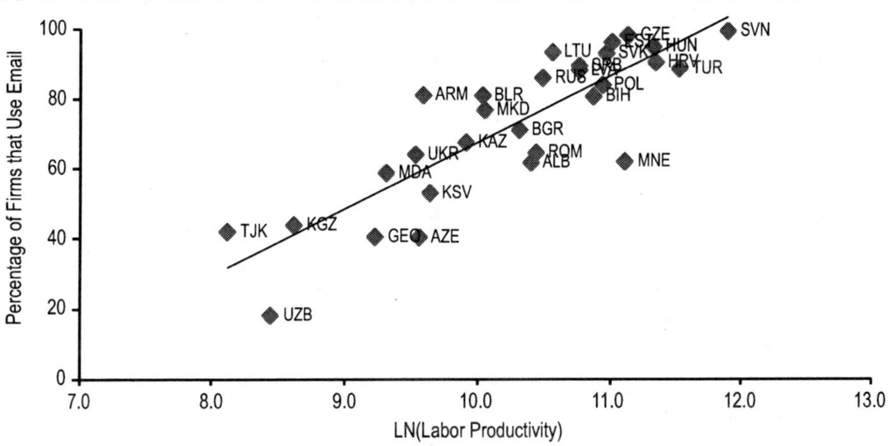

Source: BEEPS 2008.

The results of the analysis of individual firms show that in contrast to the electricity constraint, ICT access is more strongly correlated to productivity for lower productivity firms. When considering firms below the 75th percentile of productivity, the results show that the lower a firm's productivity level, the stronger the positive correlation between the use of email and productivity (access to high-speed Internet yields comparable results).[40] This shows that low-productivity firms benefit more from ICT in terms of productivity, and that email and/or high-speed Internet access would result in greater productivity gains for these firms.

As mentioned earlier, the findings show that access to ICT has a larger impact on productivity in fast growing countries. For example, the percentage of firms using email increased from 56 percent to 88 percent from 2002 to 2008 in Latvia and from 69 percent to 94 percent in Lithuania while both countries grew annually by 8 percent from 2000–2008. The second fastest growing country in the sample was Armenia (with Azerbaijan being the fastest), which experienced an annual growth rate of 11 percent from 2000–2008. At the same time, the percentage of firms using email to communicate with clients and suppliers increased from 40 percent in 2002 to 81 percent in 2008. Reportedly, the productivity in the service sector improved substantially in Armenia during this period and improvements in access to ICT infrastructure are likely to have at least partly contributed to this development.

The Role of Regulation and Governance

The Effect of Regulation

As shown in Figures 3.2 and 3.4, ECA is outperforming other regions in terms of perceptions of electricity as a problem and the breadth of power outage occurrences. Despite this, accumulated outages average 32 hours per month and cost firms 5.4 percent in annual sales (as opposed to 4.0 percent in EAP). Excessive regulation may be partly to blame for lackluster performance in specific electricity-related services, and results from the World Bank Doing Business Report offers some evidence to that end.

The World Bank's Doing Business Project, an annual exercise assessing business regulations in countries around the world captures *de jure* measures of the business environment. The methodology is constructed to provide comparable indicators of 10 aspects of the business environment. It uses a standard business case in order to ensure comparability across countries and regions. The BEEPS meanwhile, focuses on *de facto* firm-level perceptions and interactions. The difference in methodologies can lead to wide variation in values across indicators capturing similar aspects between the two data sources (see for example, Hallward-Dreimer, Khun-Jush, and Pritchett, 2009).

The Doing Business indicators on "Getting Electricity" suggest that the ECA region is the most underperforming region with respect to the number of procedures required to obtain an electricity connection and the median amount of time necessary to complete these procedures. In 2010, eight ECA countries were among the 15 weakest performers (out of 140 countries) in terms of *number of procedures* (Armenia, Azerbaijan, Russia,[42] Tajikistan, Ukraine, Bosnia and Herzegovina, Uzbekistan, and the Kyrgyz Republic). In terms of *median duration of time to complete procedures*, seven ECA countries (Russia, Ukraine, Czech Republic, the Kyrgyz Republic, Belarus, Hungary, and Romania) are also among the 15 weakest performers. An example of how the regulatory framework may affect access to electricity is shown in Box 3.3.

The true costs of regulations, i.e. how far they diverge from the "on paper" costs, and what relationship exists, if any, between them and the results from the BEEPS are, however, outside the scope of this report.

Box 3.3. Weak Governance and Infrastructure Services: Getting Electricity in Ukraine

Governance indicators and electricity services are below average in Ukraine. Ukraine is ranked in the lowest quartile among ECA countries in all three categories from the World Governance Indicators. For example, it has the sixth lowest score on regulatory quality among the 29 ECA countries. Similarly, the Doing Business indicators for 2008 report the highest costs to enforce contracts (42 percent of claim) in the region.

The Doing Business Report on Getting Electricity (2010) outlines how weak governance in the form of poor regulatory quality restricts firms' access to electricity services in Ukraine. The report outlines the steps necessary for a firm to obtain electricity services, with the procedures taking 306 days to complete at a cost of $8,419 (or 262 percent of Ukraine's income per capita) (see Figure B3.3.1). The preliminary steps required include the submission of a service application to the local distribution utility, securing a specialized project design from a private firm, and the hiring of an electrical contractor. The documentation required is cumbersome, as over 20 technical documents must be prepared for submission to different agencies before inspections occur. Three rounds of external inspection follow by the State Energy Inspectorate, the utility, and by the State Inspectorate for the Protection of Workers. Upon signing a supply contract, the firm is subjected to another inspection from the supplying utility. Once inspections have taken place, signatures from 14–15 different departments of the distribution utility are needed in order to turn the electricity on.

Figure B3.3.1. Duration of Procedures for Getting an Electricity Connection in Ukraine

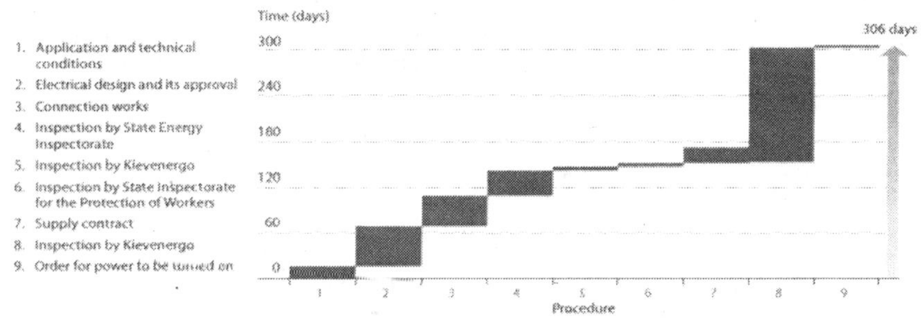

Source: Doing Business (2010).

Governance and Infrastructure Services

The effectiveness of governance and quality of regulations have both been shown to affect infrastructure services. Thus, good governance is a complementary factor to infrastructure services.[43] An approximation of a country's institutional capability can be made using data from the World Governance Indicators (WGI). Three variables from this dataset are considered: government effectiveness, regulatory quality, and control of corruption.[44] The first indicator primarily captures the capacity and independence of civil servants, the second the government's ability to provide sound regulation, and the third the extent to which public power is exercised for private gain as well as the capture of the state by elites.[45]

The results show that costs due to outages (measured by sales lost) is higher in countries with relatively weak governance. Figure 3.11 depicts the relationship between the losses of sales due to power outages and the WGI indicator of government effectiveness categorized into low, medium, and high effectiveness levels. The graph shows that the value of losses is greater in countries with less effective governments.[46] Figure 3.12 tells a similar story for outage costs compared to the WGI indicator on control of corruption.

In terms of productivity, the analysis shows[47] that firms in countries with relatively effective or uncorrupt governments are less affected by electrical outages than firms in countries with governments that are ineffective or corrupt (when controlling for per capita GDP and other country and firm characteristics).[48] In addition, the decreases in firm productivity from power outages are significantly less in countries with good regulation than in countries without.[49]

Figure 3.11. Outage Costs and Government Effectiveness

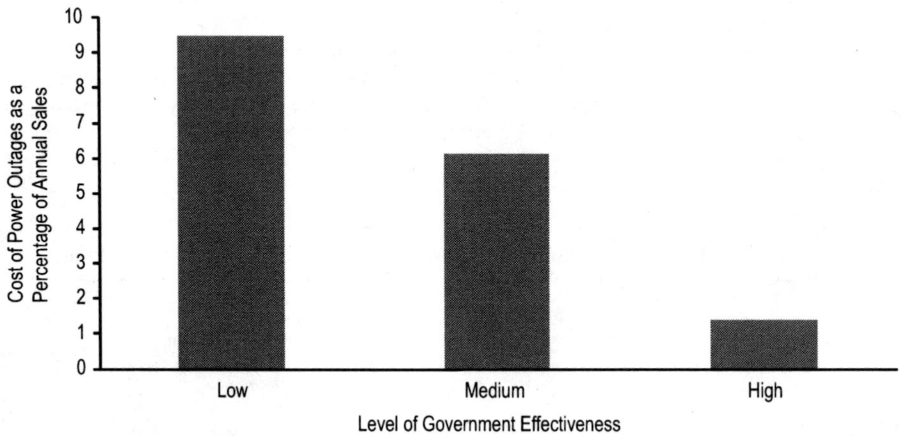

Source: BEEPS 2008, World Governance Indicators.

Figure 3.12. Outage Costs and Control of Corruption

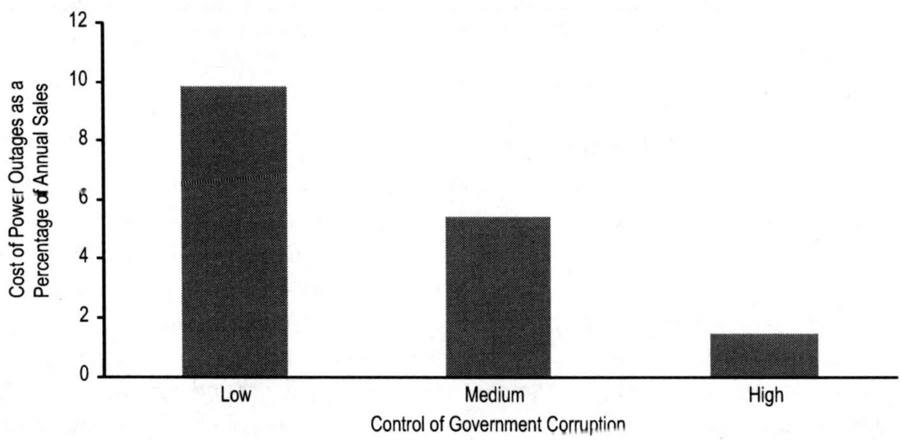

Source: BEEPS 2008, World Governance Indicators.

Weak governance also distorts the impact of ICT bottlenecks. Figures 3.13 and 3.14 below show that firms in countries with relatively non-effective governments and governments where the level of corruption is high are less likely to have access to high-speed Internet.[50] This lack of access to ICT constrains labor productivity.[51] The results are similar for the regulatory quality indicator. Thus, firms in countries with weak governance are relatively more constrained by ICT bottlenecks.

These findings suggest that institutional capabilities that provide credible and effective government policy, if enacted, may provide positive support to meet the need for high-quality infrastructure services. Thus, cross-country variations in governance and institutions (rather than variations in individual firms within a country) also influence the effectiveness of infrastructure services in ECA. The results are consistent with previous work (e.g. Fay and Estache, 2009). In other words, improving the quality of services depends also on institutional reforms that go beyond the design of infrastructure projects.

Figure 3.13. Internet Access and Government Effectiveness

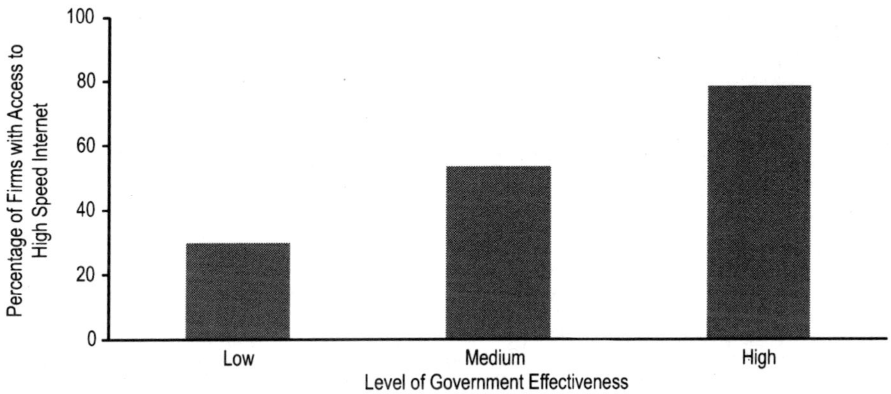

Source: BEEPS 2008, World Governance Indicators.

Figure 3.14. Internet Access and Control of Corruption

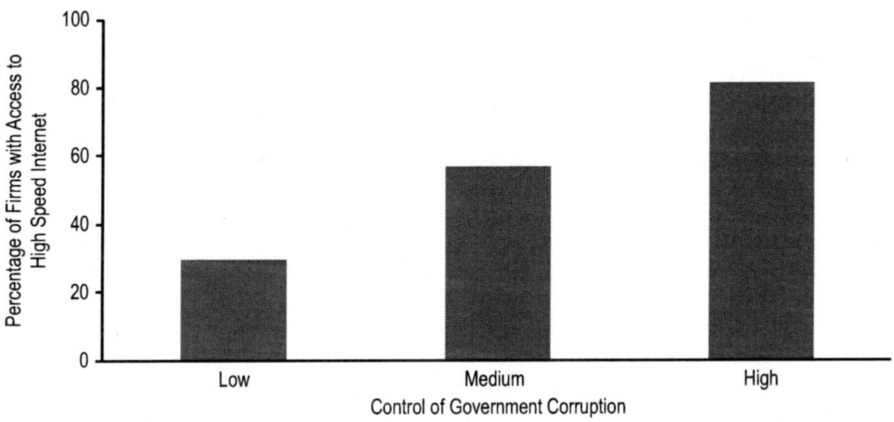

Source: BEEPS 2008, World Governance Indicators.

Box 3.4. Transport Constraints Tighten Across ECA

The results of the 2008 BEEPS show a decline in positive perceptions of transport by respondents. Overall, transport is ranked 12th of 14 obstacles doing business in 2008, however, the country level analyses show steep declines in countries such as Belarus, Kazakhstan, Kyrgyz Republic, Russia, Slovenia, and Ukraine among others. See Figure B3.4.1. These results may signal that transport will become a greater obstacle to firms in the coming years.

Figure B3.4.1. Transport as No Obstacle, 2005 and 2008

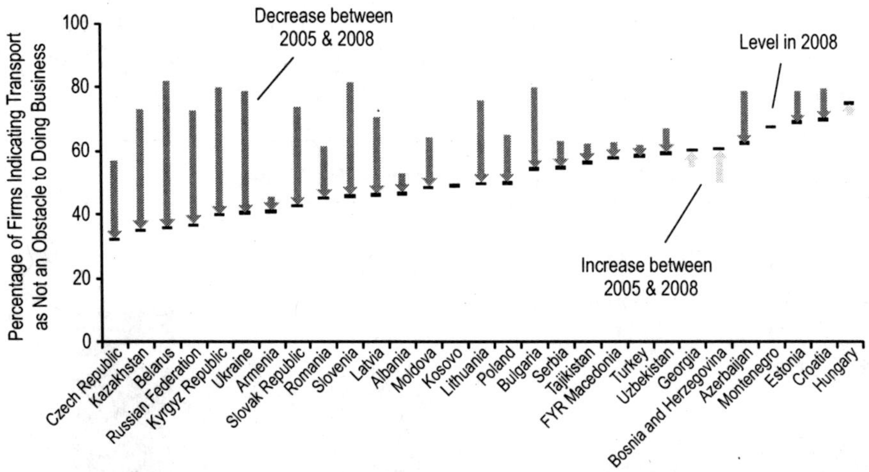

Source: BEEPS 2005, BEEPS 2008.

Managers' perceptions of transport constraints do not differ between countries with high or low rates of trade growth since the start of this decade. Averages (from 2000-2008) of the sum of export and imports relative to GDP (and FDI inflows relative to GDP) from the WDI are used as a measure of changes in trade liberalization.[a] It is expected that firms in countries with fast recent trade-growth are more constrained by transport bottlenecks. However, the results suggest that higher growth in trade volumes do not influence managers' perceptions of transport constraints in ECA.[b] Yet, this might simply reflect that access to foreign markets is limited to a few larger firms.

Comparing the data from the WEF Tourism and Transport Competitiveness Report to BEEPS, results show no distinct correlation between perceptions of transport being no obstacle and the quality of ground transport network indicator. One aspect of infrastructure that appears to impact perceptions of transport is the cost of transport approximated by fuel costs. The EBRD 2010 Transition Report: Recovery and Reform notes that fuel costs are closely linked to firm's perceptions of the transport constraint. This finding is important as it shows that costs are a greater driver of perceptions, however, it is also more difficult for governments to respond with policies other than tax reductions or subsidies that can reduce the cost of oil.

Sources: BEEPS 2005, BEEPS 2008, WEF Tourism and Transport Competitiveness Report 2009, EBRD Transition Report 2010, Recovery and Reform

Notes: a. There is no information available on Kosovo in the WDI.

b. This conclusion does not change if alternative measures of openness such as the share of FDI are used.

Conclusion

The results of the 2008 BEEPS show a significant increase in perceptions of infrastructure (electricity, telecommunications, and transport) as a problem doing business. The greatest deterioration is seen in electricity, where across ECA, only 39 percent of firms stated that electricity posed no obstacle doing business in 2008, down from 66 percent in 2005. Overall, electricity rose to the third ranked problem doing business in 2008, behind only tax rates and corruption. Similarly, deterioration is also seen in perceptions of telecommunications and transport. These infrastructure issues, while becoming more problematic, also have the potential to impact the growth and competitiveness of ECA firms during the recovery from the recent financial crisis.

At the firm level, electricity bottlenecks constrain the productivity of small and medium-sized firms while ICT bottlenecks constrain firms regardless of size. Certain firms with characteristics that are generally seen as desirable, e.g. innovative firms, end up being more constrained by these bottlenecks relative to the firms that do not have these characteristics. The firms that are able to avoid the negative productivity effects of electrical outages are either large, part of a larger firm, or highly productive. This indicates that such firms have the capacity and resources to ameliorate infrastructure issues that others cannot avoid, such as by taking full or partial ownership of a generator.

Results of the analysis show improving the quality of electricity services and increasing access to ICT services have significant productivity effects in low and medium income and fast-growing ECA countries. Thus, policy makers in these countries should anticipate and remove electricity and ICT bottlenecks in order to catch up with richer ECA countries. Further efforts to remove electricity or ICT bottlenecks could substantially boost firm productivity.

In order to improve infrastructure services, countries need not only invest in physical infrastructure projects but also in institutional capabilities that provide credibility and effectiveness. Findings show weak governance augments the effects of electricity constraints and access to ICT bottlenecks. Firms in countries with weaker government effectiveness experience higher losses as a share of sales due to service outages as do those in countries with less effective regulation.

Overall, better governance at the country level is required to prevent productivity slowdowns due to infrastructure bottlenecks. That is, improving the quality of infrastructure services goes hand-in-hand with institutional reforms, including governance reforms reaching beyond the design of individual projects in sectors.

Notes

1. Roeller and Waverman (2001) and Belaid (2004) find large positive productivity effects of telecommunication infrastructure in OECD and developing countries, respectively. Fernald (1999) shows that the construction of the interstate highway system in the U.S. from 1953-1973 induced strong productivity growth. Calderon and Serven (2005) estimate positive causal effects of different infrastructure measures on GDP-growth for a panel of 121 countries. Hulten et al. (2006) find that disparities in electricity-generating capacity across Indian states accounted for almost half the productivity growth of registered manufacturing firms.
2. Kessides and Khan (2009).
3. The World Bank report on Infrastructure in the ECA region (2006) and Iimi (2008) also emphasize the role of the quality of infrastructure services to reduce business costs.
4. Byrd and Raiser (2006).

5. The World Bank EU-10 Report (2010) underlines the importance of energy and transport infrastructure to promote productivity. In addition, Shepard and Wilson (2006), Grigoriou (2007), and Molnar and Ojala (2003) show that transport infrastructure is crucial to promote intra-regional trade in ECA.
6. See the World Bank report on Productivity Growth in ECA (2008).
7. The data are available for all ECA countries except for Turkmenistan. The country samples are designed to be nationally representative. The data are limited, however, to the formal economy.
8. Investors in ICT services, measured by the difference in telephone lines between 2000 and 2006.
9. According to the World Bank Private Participation database.
10. All amounts are presented in US$.
11. The database covers commitments by private investors to investments associated with management, concession, greenfield, and divestiture contracts that reached financial closure. Data on actual disbursements is not available.
12. See for example, Calderon, Easterly, and Serven (2003).
13. This question was included only on the Service Module of the BEEPS Survey.
14. It should be noted that Figure 3.1 does not capture how far countries have come along. For example, Georgia's power sector bottomed out in the 1990s and has improved substantially since then, as communicated in most energy reports from the region.
15. See Table A1.12 in Appendix 1 for regression results.
16. Result based on data from the 2007 Enterprise Surveys. Due to the small universe of firms coupled with "survey fatigue" in Albania, it was not possible to conduct the full BEEPS survey on a large sample of firms in 2008.
17. These numbers are for counties at the same income level, i.e. the ECA average does not include countries with incomes higher than those in Latin America.
18. Result based on data from the 2007 Enterprise Surveys. See note 16.
19. The questions on generator use and ownership were included only on the Manufacturing Module of the BEEPS Survey.
20. However, these generators are typically very expensive and inefficient. The power they generate is much more expensive than power from the grid. As a result, firms in higher-income countries also suffer financially from unreliable electricity supplies.
21. Conclusions in this section follow from the regression results presented in Tables A1.5 and A1.6 in Appendix 1.
22. Small firms are defined as having 5–19 employees, medium size firms 20–99, and large firms more than 100.
23. Electricity bottlenecks are the negative effects of a rise in the costs from electrical outages on labor productivity.
24. Level of access to finance is determined from Doing Business' "Getting Credit" indicators, with groups defined as follows: good access to credit: ALB, AZE, BGR, CZE, HUN, KGZ, KSV, LVA, MDA, MKD, MNE, POL, ROM, SRB, SVK, UKR; bad access to credit: ARM, BEL, BIH, EST, GEO, HRV, KAZ, LTU, RUS, SVN, TJK, TUR, UZB.
25. The question on generator ownership was included only on the Manufacturing Module of the BEEPS survey.
26. For the purposes of this analysis, the country income groups are as follows: high income: SVN, CZE, SVK, EST, HUN, LTU, HRV, POL, LVA, RUS; middle income: TUR, ROM, BGR, BLR, KAZ, SRB, MNE, MKD; low income: AZE, BIH, ALB, UKR, ARM, GEO, KSV, MDA, UZB, KGZ, TJK. Thresholds are 8,000 and 13,000 GDP per capita at PPP in 2007 in constant 2005 international dollars.
27. A country is defined as fast-growing if its average growth rate from 2000–2008 exceeded six percent. Fast-growing are: AZE, ARM, KAZ, BLR, GEO, LVA, UKR, LTU, MDA, RUS, TJK, EST, BGR, ROM.
28. The fast-growing countries have an average GDP per capita at PPP in 2007 (in constant 2005 international dollars) of 9,500 relative to 12,500 in slow-growing.
29. Questions about generator ownership were primarily asked to firms within the manufacturing sector, hence analysis in this section is limited to this set of firms.
30. Levels of generator use are based on simple, non-weighted averages of firm-level data. Both differences are statistically significant at $p=0.10$ or better.

31. See Table A1.5 for results.
32. The difference between generator usage in countries with good access to credit and those without is statistically significant at p=0.10.
33. Questions pertaining to access to high-speed Internet and telecommunications as an obstacle were primarily asked to service-sector firms. Email usage questions were asked of all firms.
34. Based on the panel dataset.
35. The data for LCR is based on results from Enterprise Surveys. The countries used are listed in Appendix 1. Firms in República Bolivariana de Venezuela were not asked this question; hence it is not included in the average.
36. While Armenia lagged considerably in ICT reforms through the year 2000, recent reforms such as liberalization of the telecommunications sector has led to significant improvements since 2008. The introduction of competition has resulted in new investments in advanced technologies and in better telecom infrastructure overall.
37. Arbore and Ordanini (2006).
38. Duffy-Deno (2003).
39. See notes 13 and 33.
40. See Table A1.7 in the Appendix 1 for regression results.
41. See Tables A1.8 and A1.9 in Appendix 1 for regression results.
42. The results of the Doing Business Project for Russia are somewhat misleading, as they measure cost and duration in the capital of Moscow, which has a very particular set of rules. Other Russian regions have significantly lower costs and durations for this procedure.
43. Esfahani and Ramirez (2003), Cadot et al. (2006), and Fay and Estache (2009) reveal that the impact of infrastructure investments depends on good governance and political economy considerations. Basu and Fernald (2007) find that ICT capital investments require complementary investments in human capital to generate productivity growth. Agenor and Moreno-Dodson (2006) highlight the effect of infrastructure on education and health outcomes (e.g. access to clean water, hospitals, and schools).
44. The World Governance Indicators cover Montenegro only since 2006. Kosovo is covered from 2006, 2008, and 2003 for the government effectiveness, regulatory quality, and control of corruption indicators, respectively.
45. All three indicators are highly correlated among the 29 ECA countries. In particular, splitting the sample according to government effectiveness or control of corruption yields almost identical country groups.
46. Regression analyses that control for GDP and other characteristics show similar conclusions. Regression results and estimated power outage costs are shown in Tables A1.13 and A1.14 in Appendix 1, respectively.
47. Shown in Table A1.10 in Appendix 1.
48. The coefficient for government effectiveness is nearly significant at p=0.12 and the coefficient for control of corruption is nearly significant at p=0.11.
49. The coefficient for regulatory quality is significant at p=0.06.
50. Regression results and estimates for the percentage of firms with Internet access (Tables A1.13 and A1.14 in Appendix 1, respectively) show similar results.
51. See Table A1.11 in Appendix 1 for regression results.

CHAPTER 4

Labor: Challenges Ahead of the Crisis

During the last twenty years, labor markets across countries in Europe and Central Asia (ECA) have undergone considerable changes. Global conditions boosted growth and labor demand, and domestic policy and regulatory reforms have had an impact on employment and wages. More recently (between 2004 and 2008), overall unemployment rates fell across ECA with dramatic decreases seen in countries as diverse as Croatia, Estonia, Poland, and Moldova. Higher growth has led to an overall increase in demand for labor. However, structural transformations have also boosted demand for workers with a specific set of skills, which appears to have led to a skills shortage in many economies across the region. The BEEPS and other sources provide evidence that firms are indeed having more difficulty locating workers with desired skill sets to fill vacancies.

This development is particularly important as the results of BEEPS show the skills constraint is having a negative impact on the productivity of firms in ECA countries. However, unbundling the factors that drive the rising perception of the skills constraint is a challenging task, as there may be multiple explanations for this phenomenon. Firms may perceive a rising skills constraint due to the general increase in labor demand and rise in wages, which has increased competition for quality workers or because certain types of skills shortages are indeed emerging. This chapter provides evidence of a rising skills shortage and discusses related trends seen in ECA, including wage growth, characteristics of the unemployed, and migration patterns.

The analysis in this chapter also shows that:

- Skills and education of labor became the 4th highest obstacle to firms behind tax rates, corruption, and electricity. Only a third of firms in the 27 countries covered by the BEEPS in both 2005 and 2008 indicated that skills and education was not an obstacle to doing business in 2008. The declines are most severe in Azerbaijan, Belarus, Russia and Uzbekistan.
- Labor regulations are less of a constraint to enterprises, especially in countries implementing labor market reforms. Recent labor market reforms have aimed to reduce the burden on firms and usher in more flexibility in labor management. Also, in times of economic growth, such as the period before the financial crisis, labor regulations such as redundancy and severance are less of an obstacle for firms.
- Evidence shows that increasing the formal educational attainment of the workforce may not be the most effective means to curb the skills constraint. Skills

constraints are larger in countries with greater unemployment among people with tertiary education, which may signal that the solution does not lie in a simple increase in the quantity of educated workers, but in the development of relevant skills.

- Some firms, such as large firms, are able to mitigate the effects of the skills constraint on productivity by providing training to their workers. Firms in higher income countries, such as those in the EU-10, appear more able to train their employees than those in lower-income countries.

This chapter presents key BEEPS results regarding features of the labor market in the ECA region, including trends in firms' perceptions regarding the characteristics of the labor force in the business environment, in the period just before the global financial crisis. Where available, benchmark comparisons are made between ECA countries and countries at similar levels of development outside the region using the World Bank Enterprise Surveys data.

The chapter is organized as follows: first, an overview of recent labor market trends and a discussion of the BEEPS results on labor indicators are presented. A summary of the data and methodology for analysis follows. Next, the results on skills and education of labor are discussed in-depth, with an emphasis on the emerging skills shortage and potential contributing factors, including the role of emigration, characteristics of unemployed workers, and firm level factors that are shown to affect perceptions of labor quality. Firms' responses to the skills shortage are then discussed. A glimpse into the early effects of the financial crisis on labor follows. The last section concludes.

Recent Labor Market Developments in the Eastern Europe and Central Asia Region

Between 2004 and 2008, the region saw broad-based improvements in labor market conditions alongside robust economic growth. For many countries in Central and Eastern Europe, strong growth coincided with their EU accession. After a period of stagnant job creation in the early 2000s following the 1998 Russian crisis—giving rise to the "jobless growth" phenomenon particularly in the new EU member states and the Western Balkans[1]—the region saw substantial net job creation starting in 2004, lasting until the eve of the financial crisis.

Stronger labor market conditions are evident in falling unemployment rates, growing employment ratios, and rising employment elasticity of growth. In the early 2000s, employment growth associated with output growth (or the employment elasticity of growth) was insignificant at 0.07, indicating that each percentage point expansion in output was associated with close to zero employment growth. Between 2004 and 2008, the employment elasticity of growth rose sharply to 0.24 (see Table 4.1). In addition, for the region as a whole, unemployment rates fell, from close to 12 percent in the early 2000s to 8.5 percent over the same period. Very sharp reductions in joblessness were seen in the new EU member states. For example, between 2004 and 2008 the unemployment rate in Poland fell from 19 percent to 7.1 percent, and in Lithuania, it dropped from 11.3 to 5.3 percent. Nonetheless, there remain important distinctions across country groups in the region, with respect to employment and unemployment indicators that help explain some of the peculiarities noted in the next sections.

Table 4.1. Employment Elasticity of Growth 2004–2008

	2000–04	2004–08
ECA	0.07	0.24
CIS	0.18	0.20
EU-10	0.08	0.23
SEE	-0.35*	0.38

Source: KILM (6th Edition) and authors' calculations.
* The negative employment elasticity of growth in the SEE subregion is driven by FYR Macedonia. Other countries in the average such as Albania and Bosnia and Herzegovina have small but positive elasticities. Although negative elasticities can indicate a higher level of productivity without an increase in employment, it appears that in FYR Macedonia, per the World Bank FYR Macedonia Poverty Assessment for 2002–2003, higher productivity sectors such as trade and manufacturing were shedding labor in this period (World Bank, 2005).

The improvement in labor markets in ECA may be the result of rapid growth in labor demand.[2] Successful labor market reforms and improvements in the investment climate appear to have contributed to the rise in labor demand. Further, the rise in labor demand has been associated with rapid growth in wages. In the new EU member states, the average real wage growth in the period after EU accession and before the crisis was about 9 percent (based on the year-on-year four-quarter moving average).[3] See also Box 4.3.

Data and Methodology

The primary data sources for this analysis are the results of the BEEPS for 2005, 2008, and a panel of firms that participated in each of the 2002, 2005, and 2008 rounds of the survey. As mentioned in the introductory chapter, in 2008, the BEEPS underwent a series of changes to both the sampling methodology and the questionnaire. Although the changes in the survey and sample pose challenges to the cross-period comparability, steps have been taken to find an intersection between these two samples in terms of sector, firm size, age, and ownership, to make the samples from 2005 and 2008 as comparable as possible. Analyses also include data from other sources such as Doing Business, IMF, KILM, World Bank World Development Indicators, and others.

The two primary questions of interest in BEEPS regard labor-related obstacles to doing business: one measuring the severity of labor regulations as an obstacle to doing business, and the other measuring the severity of skills and education of labor as an obstacle to doing business. Both questions were asked in the context of current operations:

> *"Are labor regulations no obstacle, a minor obstacle, a moderate obstacle, a major obstacle or a very severe obstacle to the current operations of this establishment?"*

> *"Is an inadequately educated workforce no obstacle, a minor obstacle, a moderate obstacle, a major obstacle or a very severe obstacle to the current operations of this establishment?"*

Where it is possible to compare the 2008 results with those of 2005, the values are based on the adjusted samples to maximize comparability. Other results discussed in the context of the 2008 round are based on the full sample of firms. Similarly, the results of the panel dataset are based solely on the panel of firms participating in each of the 2002, 2005, and 2008 cycles. Readers will sometimes encounter different country-level figures for the same indicator for 2008. Both are correct, but for differing purposes.

In order to test hypotheses, econometric methods such as logistic regression analysis and generalized ordered logit models are employed. The generalized ordered logit models are based on the methodology of Pierre and Scarpetta (2004 and 2006). All models include control variables. More information on the methodology and the results can be found in Appendix 1.

Labor Constraints in ECA

Firms' responses to questions on labor regulations and skills and education of labor in BEEPS 2008 compared to 2005 reveal two distinct and opposite trends. Region-wide, firms' perceptions of labor regulations have improved since 2005 while at the same time, satisfaction with skills and education of labor has deteriorated. The improvements in labor regulations are significant in many countries (see Box 4.1). However, the declines in the perceptions of skills are more widespread—decreasing in all but three countries: Hungary, Latvia, and Slovenia.

The severity of these issues is not unique to the ECA region. Table 4.2 shows the percentage of firms in ECA and other regions[4] indicating that labor regulations and the skills and education of labor are a major or very severe obstacle. ECA outperforms all but Africa and the East Asia and Pacific regions in terms of the severity of labor regulations; however, the skills and education of labor constraint appears to be a problem for all regions.

Table 4.2. Cross-Regional Comparison: Labor Regulations and Skills and Education of Labor as a Major or Very Severe Obstacle, 2008 (percentage of respondents)

Region	Labor Regulations as major or very severe obstacle	Skills and Education of Labor as a major or very severe obstacle
Eastern Europe and Central Asia	18.7	43.2
EU-10	21.8	42.3
FSU-N	18.8	62.8
FSU-S	17.2	45.0
SEE	16.3	32.6
Africa	17.3	32.6
East Asia & Pacific	14.5	33.8
Latin America & Caribbean	29.5	42.5
South Asia	19.0	24.8
Middle East & North Africa	36.2	54.4

Sources: BEEPS 2008 and Enterprise Surveys 2006–2010

Skills and Education of Labor Becomes a Top Constraint

The results of BEEPS 2008 show skills and education of labor are a growing constraint to doing business compared to 2005. The skill-level of workers ranks 4th out of 14 obstacles to doing business in 2008, behind tax rates, corruption, and electricity, up from 7th in 2005. It is also among the top three obstacles in 11 countries in 2008, up from 4 in 2005 (see Table 4.3). The most dramatic changes in ranking (changing 5 rank positions or more) are seen in Albania, Azerbaijan, Bosnia and Herzegovina, the Czech Republic, Kazakhstan, Moldova, Poland, Tajikistan, Turkey, and Uzbekistan.

Box 4.1. Strides in Labor Regulations

The results of BEEPS 2008 show labor regulations are less of an obstacle to firms in ECA: the relative rank of labor regulations as a problem fell from 9th in 2005 to 13th in 2008. Only Estonia and Slovenia ranked labor regulations as a top-three obstacle to doing business in 2008.

In general, labor regulations tend to be viewed less favorably by firms in EU-10 countries which are more likely to enforce them (including through court challenges), and less of a problem in CIS economies where the capacity for enforcement is weaker. In practice, for many firms (especially the smallest firms), labor regulations tend to be bypassed, which then translates to a labor market that is virtually unregulated.

The percentage changes in perceptions of labor regulations are small across many countries (see Appendix 3), which points to labor regulations being a less important obstacle overall when compared to other aspects of the business environment. The results indicate that in times of greater prosperity, labor regulations such as redundancy or termination costs are not as much of a hindrance to firms as they are in periods when economies and firms are contracting.

The results may also reflect recent labor market reforms designed to ease the burden on firms. In recent years, new labor laws have been adopted in Estonia and Montenegro (2008), the Czech Republic and Georgia (2006), FYR Macedonia and Serbia (2005), and Armenia and the Kyrgyz Republic (2004). These reforms may have affected employers' perceptions.

For example, Estonia launched a comprehensive effort to deregulate Employment Protection Legislation (EPL), culminating in a new Employment Contract Act adopted by parliament in 2008 (implemented in 2009). The new legislation requires a shorter notice period for redundancy and reduced severance payments, among other changes (Brixiova, 2009; O'Higgins, 2010).[5] Although labor regulations remain a top obstacle, Estonian firms were already reporting more favorable views toward labor regulation in 2008. Meanwhile, in the Slovak Republic, there have been important reversals in regulatory reform: the 2003 Labor Code was amended in 2007 to introduce more rigidity in employment regulation. Not surprisingly, Slovak firms perceived labor regulations to be a greater obstacle in 2008 than in 2005.

The 2008 Doing Business Report shows Slovenia has the highest rigidity of employment index value of ECA countries, ranking at the 54th percentile, while Georgia has the lowest (7th percentile). Stricter EPL may minimize or smooth effects of economic shocks on the labor market at the macro level (Cazes and Mesporova, 2003), while at the micro level, there are mixed effects. Theoretically, stricter EPL benefits firms[6] through enhanced productivity (Scarpetta and Tressel, 2004)[7], however, it also increases the cost of labor. The results of the BEEPS analysis support those of previous studies (e.g. Pierre and Scarpetta, 2006) showing firms in countries with more stringent employment regulations are more likely to report labor regulations as a major or very severe obstacle when controlling for other factors such as GDP and unemployment.[8*]

Results also show:

- ***Income plays a role*:** Labor regulations are less of a problem in lower income countries, which may be a function of less stringent regulations or weaker *enforcement* of labor regulation. For example, Tajikistan, the poorest country in ECA, shows the greatest satisfaction with labor regulations. See Figure B4.1.1.
- ***Certain firms are more vulnerable to labor regulations:*** Large firms and firms that innovate are less likely to report labor regulations are not an obstacle.[9] For large firms, as the number of workers employed by a firm rises, labor regulations reflected in the cost of hiring would translate to higher overall costs. Likewise, innovative firms are more likely to see labor regulations as a major problem because the hiring and firing cost of workers may influence the magnitude of innovative activity (Scarpetta and Tressel, 2004).
- ***Labor regulations affect innovation:*** The rigidity of employment regulations has a significant positive effect on firm innovation.[10] See Figure B4.1.2. If labor regulations impose hiring costs, firms may implement workflow innovations to increase productivity of existing staff.

(Box continues on next page)

Box 4.1 (continued)

Figure B4.1.1. Labor Regulations vs. GDP Per Capita

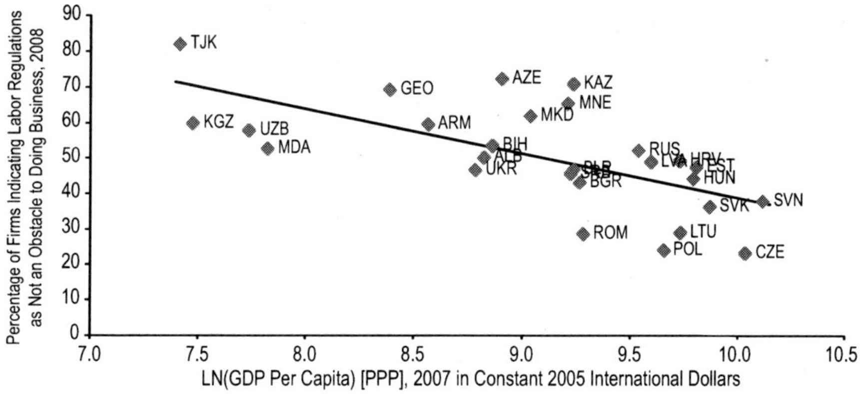

Source: BEEPS 2008, World Development Indicators

Figure B4.1.2. EPL Rigidity vs. Innovation

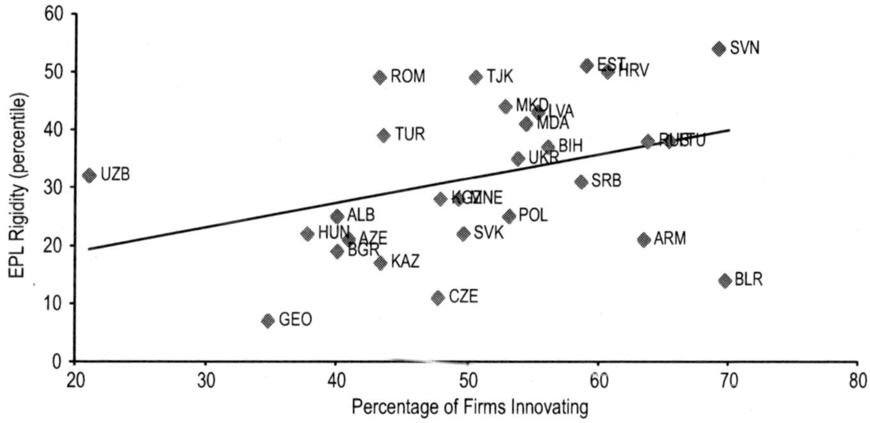

Source: BEEPS 2008, Doing Business 2008.

One of the most important implications of innovation is the impact on productivity. The results of BEEPS 2008 support the results of previous research—innovation has a significant and positive effect on firm level productivity when controlling for other factors[11] (see Ahn 2002; Janz et al 2003; Griffith et al 2006 as examples). The results of BEEPS also show that there is a reciprocal relationship between productivity and innovation.[12] This may be a function of aggregate productivity increases with successive innovations—that firms reaping the benefits of product or process innovations may be more likely to invest in additional innovative activity.

Source: BEEPS 2005, BEEPS 2008, Doing Business (2005-2008).

* However, there may be a threshold level of regulation that reduces the burden on firms while protecting the rights of workers. Moderate regulation may benefit firms as a higher percentage of firms in countries with more stringent EPL (from 45–60th percentiles) and those with less stringent EPL (ranging from the 0-14th percentile) report labor regulations to be a major or very severe obstacle.

Table 4.3. Skills and Education of Labor as an Obstacle to Doing Business (relative ranking among 14 obstacles)

Top Ranked		2nd Ranked		3rd Ranked	
2008	2005	2008	2005	2008	2005
Estonia	None	Belarus	Estonia	Albania	Latvia`
Kazakhstan		Latvia	Lithuania	Turkey	
Russia		Lithuania	Ukraine		
		Moldova			
		Poland			
		Uzbekistan			

Source: BEEPS 2005 and BEEPS 2008.

In all but three ECA countries, Hungary, FYR Macedonia, and Montenegro, more than half the firms reported that the skills and education of workers have at least marginally constrained their operations. The magnitude of the deterioration in the quality of skills is large: the percentage of firms reporting that skills and education of labor was not a problem declined in 24 of 27 countries, 17 of which were statistically significant (see Figure 4.1 below). The sharpest declines can be seen in Azerbaijan and Uzbekistan, and among the northern FSU countries of Belarus, Russia, and Kazakhstan.

The increase in the skills constraint appears to be a recent phenomenon. Looking at firms that participated in the 2002, 2005, and 2008 rounds of BEEPS, the results show a significant decrease in the percentage of firms indicating skills and education of labor is not an obstacle from 2005 to 2008. For the panel firms, 42 percent of firms stated skills and education of labor was not an obstacle in 2005, compared to 37 percent in 2008. The results for 2002 and 2005 show practically no change—44 percent of the panel firms stated skills and education of labor was not an obstacle in 2002, compared to 42 percent in 2005.

Figure 4.1. Skills and Education of Labor as No Obstacle, 2005 and 2008

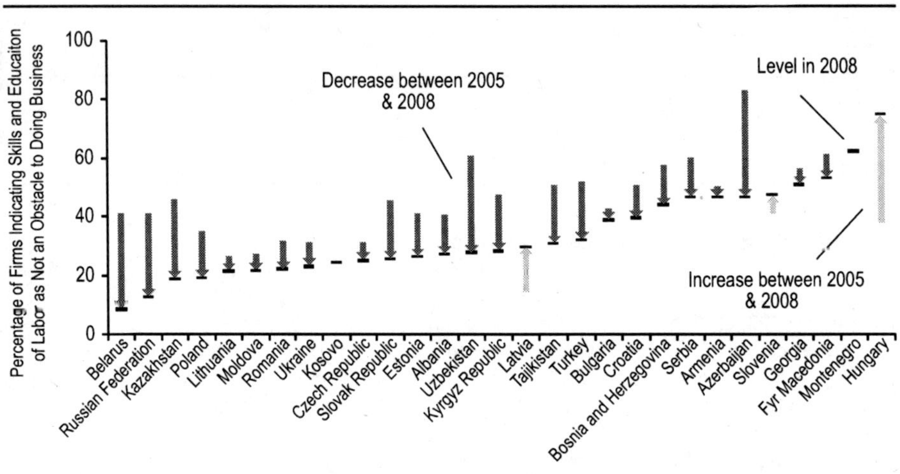

Source: BEEPS 2005, BEEPS 2008.

Box 4.2. Are the Trends Emerging from the BEEPS Data Consistent with Other Sources?

The BEEPS is unique in the fact that no other enterprise surveys are conducted as consistently in as many countries in the ECA region. However, there is a general consistency across BEEPS and other data sources. For example:

In Poland, some 60 percent of all enterprises surveyed by the National Bank of Poland in 2007 reported difficulties in finding workers, both skilled and unskilled (Rutkowski 2007). This was much higher than in 2006, when only about 40 percent reported such difficulties.

In Lithuania, some 12,000 unfilled vacancies were reported in 2005. The figures also suggest large labor shortages in the manufacturing and trade sector (Kahanec et al 2009).

In Russia, the Large and Medium Enterprise (LME) survey of 2005 showed firms reported that "the lack of skilled and qualified workforce" as one of the greatest constraints they face, second only to taxation. For these firms, shortages were reported across all skill categories, from management positions to skilled technical work. A longer time series suggests that the incidence of (self-reported) understaffing among firms started growing in 1998, during the recovery period, as output and labor use rates also grew (see Tan et al 2007a; and Tan et al 2007b).

In Moldova, a firm-level survey of 600 enterprises as part of a World Bank-assisted Competitiveness Enhancement Project (World Bank 2008a) revealed about a quarter of all firms felt that they do not have enough workers. There was a small increase in the number of enterprises reporting insufficient workers in 2005, potentially foreshadowing the skills constraint subsequently reported in the BEEPS.

Sources: Kahanec, et al 2009; Rutkowski, 2007; Tan et al (2007a); Tan et al (2007b);World Bank, 2008a.

Firms in ECA and other regions face serious skills constraints as shown in Table 4.2. Likewise, skills are problematic across income groups. Figure 4.2 shows that, comparatively, skills are a bigger problem for middle-income countries; however, the majority of firms in all income groups perceive skills and education to be at least a minor obstacle.

Figure 4.2. Skills and Education of Labor as No Obstacle by Income Classification

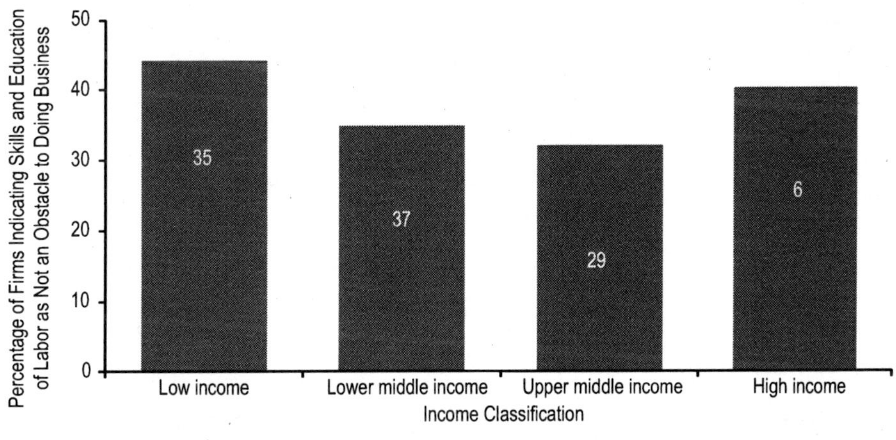

Source: BEEPS 2008, Enterprise Surveys 2006-2010.
* The number indicated within the bars represents the number of countries in each region.

Some Firms Are Hit Harder by Skills Constraints

Certain firm-level characteristics appear to make firms more vulnerable to the skills constraint including firm size, sector of the firm's primary activity, innovative activity, and ICT use.

Small firms view quality of labor more favorably than medium-sized and large firms.[13] In 2008, 38 percent of small firms (5–19 employees) stated skills and education was not an obstacle, compared to 29 percent of medium firms (20–99 employees) and 24 percent of large firms (100 employees or more). Secondly, firms in the manufacturing sector perceive skills and education of labor to be a greater obstacle than those in the service sector. Enterprises in the machine and equipment sector seem the least satisfied with the qualifications of available workers, followed by firms in construction, basic metals, and garments. Perhaps, these manufacturing sectors require more specialized skills than what is required for the majority of the service sector jobs.

Similarly, innovative firms, i.e. those introducing a new product or service in the last three years, are more likely to require workers with specialized skills, and thus are less likely to perceive skills and education as no obstacle.[14] Firms that use ICT, such as email to communicate with customers or suppliers, also see skills and education as a greater constraint. However, firms with these characteristics, at least in the manufacturing sector, may have found ways to mitigate the skills constraint via second-best alternatives, e.g. by providing additional training.

The skills constraint has measurable and significant negative impacts on firm productivity when controlling for other factors.[15] The impact is still negative but is not significant at the country level (Figure 4.3). Firms with higher productivity are also significantly more likely to state that skills are not an obstacle.[16] This offers evidence that more productive firms may be better able to overcome the productivity effect than lower productivity firms. Further, when controlling for the skills constraint, growing firms and innovating firms continue to have higher productivity.[17] This shows that more productive firms, growing firms, and innovative firms may be better able to locate and hire skilled workers, or mitigate the negative impact by providing training. The provision of training as a response to the skills constraint is discussed more fully later in the chapter.

Figure 4.3. Skills and Education of Labor as an Obstacle vs. Labor Productivity

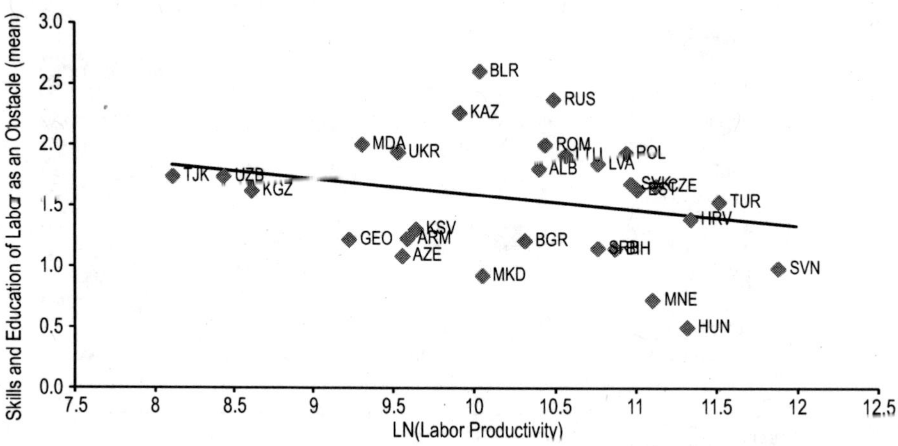

Source: BEEPS 2008.

Explaining Rising Skills Constraints: Evidence of a Regional Skills Shortage?

It is difficult to discern whether the rise in perceptions of skills as a constraint to business activity is the result of a general increase in labor demand and rising wages or because certain types of skills shortages are indeed emerging. Answering this definitively is outside the scope of this report. This section examines the characteristics of the regional skills shortage and assesses possible drivers of this trend to help explain why a skills shortage may be emerging in ECA.

First, developments associated with the transition process itself may have contributed to the rising skills shortage. At the beginning of transition, indicators of educational attainment suggested that these economies had higher stocks of human capital than countries at comparable levels of development. During the transition, the structure of employment shifted away from agriculture and industry into services, and jobs generally shifted from low to high skill content.[18] Even among high skill jobs, some highly specialized skills acquired during the central planning period quickly became obsolete, while at the same time, demand for other skills in emerging sectors was rising.

Unemployment was on the decline across many countries in ECA from 2004 to 2007. However, countries such as Georgia, Serbia, FYR Macedonia, the Czech Republic and the Slovak Republic still experienced unemployment rates of 10 percent or higher. FYR Macedonia had the highest unemployment rate of ECA countries (for which data are available) with nearly 35 percent unemployment, although it was unevenly distributed between two ethnic communities. The question becomes one of whether unemployment is due to a lack of job vacancies, an aggregate labor shortage, or a deficiency in the skill level of the available workforce, and it is a difficult one to answer. Skills shortages and unemployment can coexist: meaning there are pools of available labor but skills shortages remain (due to mismatches and the lack of regional mobility, among other reasons)—and this makes it difficult to explain labor market developments (Boswell, Stiller, and Straubhaar, 2004).

With many firms competing for quality workers with the desired skills mix, the issue may be one of supply. Earlier analytical work (e.g. Rutkowski, 2007) suggests that the former jobs shortage earlier in the transition period has been replaced by a skills shortage, and that in times of economic growth (i.e. the pre-crisis environment), the lack of skills in the available workforce becomes a bigger impediment to firms. During these times, the long-term unemployed often suffer from a qualitative skills shortage— they do not possess the skills or education to fill available jobs.[19] In 2007, the majority of unemployed and inactive workers in ECA were low skilled: close to two-thirds of inactive or long-term unemployed workers had, at best, completed only primary education. For countries which data is available, between 2004 and 2007, the unemployment rate for those with a tertiary education increased in Belarus, Georgia, and Ukraine, while over the same period, Armenia, Bulgaria, Estonia, Lithuania, Russia, and Tajikistan experienced a decrease in tertiary unemployment. Taken altogether, the evidence suggests that unemployed workers in ECA are typically less skilled.[20]

Data on recent vacancies also suggest that higher educational attainment is required. In Bosnia and Herzegovina, for example, between 2004 and 2008, the number of new vacancies that required a university degree outstripped the number of available workers with a tertiary education by several thousand.[21] The results of a survey of firms in Bosnia and Herzegovina also showed that over 80 percent of enterprises surveyed had unfilled vacancies, of which close to half required a university education.[22] Qualitative interviews with representatives of enterprises indicate that the inability to fill vacancies

Box 4.3. Wages and Productivity Increases: Do They Reflect Rising Skills and Labor Shortages?

All else being equal, the growth of skills shortages should be reflected in wage increases that exceed the growth of productivity. If the BEEPS results reflect broader labor market trends, then wage and productivity trends should be consistent with these perceptions as firms offer higher wages in search of suitably qualified workers.

In countries such as Bulgaria, FYR Macedonia, the Kyrgyz Republic, Latvia, Lithuania, Poland, Russia, and Ukraine, wage increases have outstripped productivity growth over the period from 2000 to 2007, or more recently from 2004 onwards. See Figures B4.3.1 and B4.3.2 as examples. Some of these developments may reflect institutional wage-setting arrangements. In Central and Eastern European countries, statutory minimum wages are a large fraction of average wages, and their frequent adjustment in turn pushes up average wages.

Figure B4.3.1. Productivity and Wage Growth in Poland 2004–2008

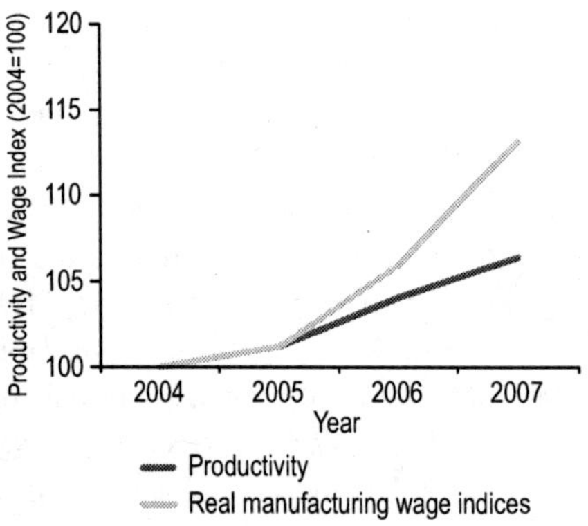

Source: KILM 6th Edition, 2009.

Figure B4.3.2. Productivity and Wage Growth in Ukraine 2004–2008

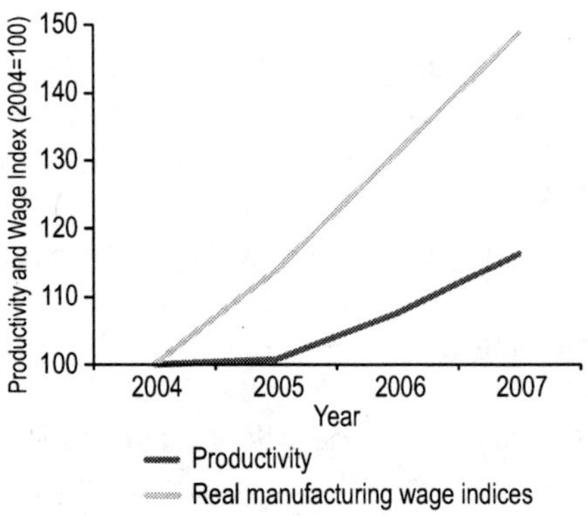

Source: KILM 6th Edition, 2009.

Such arrangements have been observed to hamper wage flexibility and employment growth, especially among workers at the lower end of the skills distribution. Meanwhile, in Slovenia, where wage growth has lagged behind productivity growth, collective bargaining agreements follow the principle of keeping wage increases just below growth in productivity.[23]

Most likely, these rapid wage increases reflect rising skills shortages, especially in recent years, as wage growth exceeded productivity broadly across countries in different sub-groups in the region.[24] Although minimum wages and centralized wage-setting mechanisms are relatively less common in the CIS, a number of CIS countries have also been experiencing very rapid increases in wages, such as Ukraine.

In addition, recent rapid increases were noted in Eastern European countries just as workers started migrating in large volumes to older EU member countries immediately following the 2004 EU enlargement, and as companies started complaining of labor shortages (see Wagstyl et al 2008 and Rutkowski 2007).

Sources: ILO (2009) KILM 6th Edition.

was largely due to the lack of the relevant skills among applicants, rather than reasons related to lack of mobility, labor market regulations, or wages.

Skills constraints are also known to be caused by regional mismatches characterized by the immobility of the workforce, among other reasons (Boswell, Stiller, and Straubhaar 2004). Internal geographic mobility is constrained in many of the countries in the region. In some cases, geographic immobility seems to reflect cultural preferences or ties to local communities; in other cases, underdeveloped rental markets and administrative controls help curb internal movements. For example, in Russia, an internal residence permit is required to get a job and switch residence. The lack of inter-regional movement may help explain the trends seen in BEEPS. Further, international emigration may also play a role as higher skilled workers seek opportunities in higher-income countries. See Box 4.4.

Box 4.4. Emigration and Brain Drain in ECA

The transition to market economies has been accompanied by generally poor domestic labor market outcomes in ECA (World Bank, 2008b). High levels of long-term unemployment, combined with large wage differentials, created powerful incentives for emigration, evidenced by the very large remittances to output ratios found in the low to lower middle-income economies in the region (Figure B4.4.1). Tajikistan is the most remittance-dependent economy in the world, and Moldova and Kyrgyz Republic are also in the top five countries with the highest ratio of workers' remittances to GDP.

Figure B4.4.1. Workers' Remittances (% of GDP), 2008

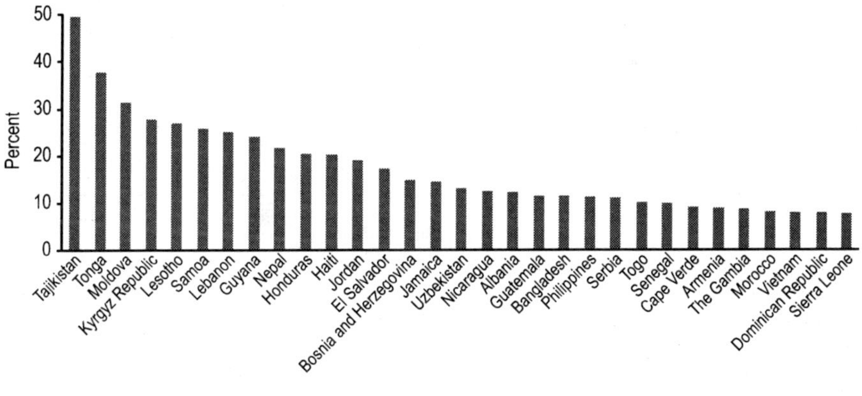

Source: IMF Balance of Payments, 2008.
Note: Remittances comprised of workers' remittances and compensation of employees.

If flows among developed economies are excluded, emigration among ECA countries and between ECA and industrial economies constitutes one-third of global immigration and emigration. Migration affects both the lower income ECA countries as well as higher income countries such as Russia, Kazakhstan, and Ukraine. The importance of emigration is not found solely in the CIS, but also in the EU as labor liberalization beginning in 2004 resulted in large emigration flows from new member states to Western Europe (World Bank, 2008c). For example, over 100,000 Poles registered to work in UK during its first year of EU membership. Over 60 percent of these emigrants were between ages 24 and 35 while 40 percent had a university degree.

Two mechanisms could link these high levels of migration with the emerging skills gap. First, the supply of skilled workers may have simply shrunk due to the prospect of higher wages abroad, particularly in the EU-10.[a] Second, demand for unskilled migrant labor may decrease the incentive to invest in education at home. Evidence from Albania finds that the opportunity costs of higher education may be too high when considering the significantly higher wages paid for unskilled work in Greece and Italy (Miluka and Dabalen, 2009). It is also possible that complications in having educational credentials recognized abroad results in so-called

(Box continues on next page)

Box 4.4 (continued)

'brain waste', where highly educated workers only qualify for low skilled jobs abroad, which increases the costs of pursuing higher education for students who may know that they want to emigrate (even if only on a temporary basis).

However, caution needs to be exercised in firmly drawing causal lines: the empirical relationships between the BEEPS 2008 results on skills constraints and various proxies of emigration intensity and 'brain drain' are mixed. The figures below reveal certain cases where there appears to be a relationship between emigration and the skills profile of migrants with perceptions of skills as no obstacle from BEEPS 2008, such as: Albania, Croatia, FYR Macedonia, the Kyrgyz Republic, Moldova, Poland, and Tajikistan. However, these relationships are not robust for the entire sample of ECA countries.

Figure B4.4.2. Skills and Education of Labor as No Obstacle vs. Remittances

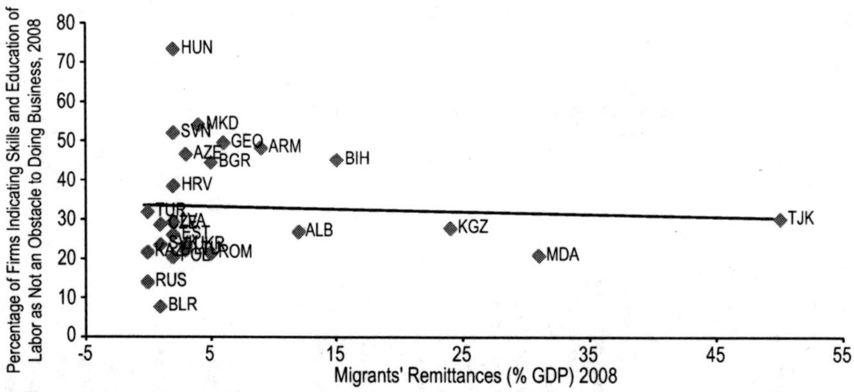

Source: BEEPS 2008, IMF Balance of Payments.

Figure B4.4.3. Skills and Education of Labor as No Obstacle and Emigration of the Tertiary Educated

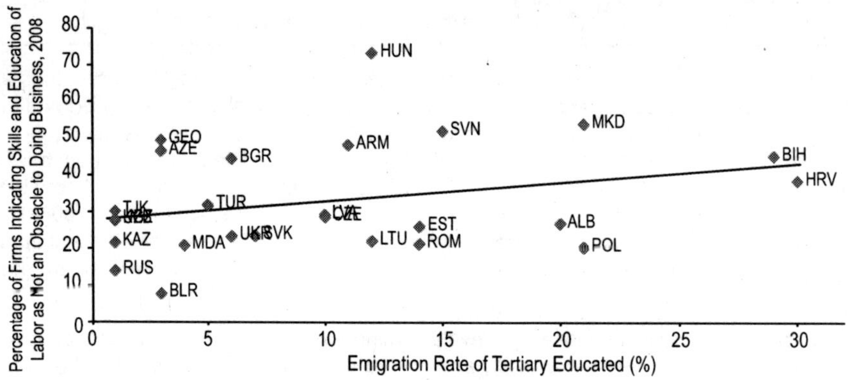

Sources: BEEPS 2008; World Bank (2008) Migration and Remittances Factbook.

Sources: BEEPS 2008; IMF Balance of Payments, 2008; World Bank Migration and Remittances Factbook, 2008.
Note: a. Kahanec et al (2009) summarizes recent papers on rising labor shortages in the new EU member states, suggesting that the emigration of workers from the EU-10 to some of the older EU member countries may worsen the weaknesses in labor markets. In the years immediately following the 2004 EU enlargement, large volumes of unfilled vacancies were reported in Lithuania, for example.

The Education Paradox

Without taking into account the educational attainment of unemployed workers, higher unemployment rates should have a positive effect on skills and education perceptions, as there is a larger pool of job applicants to fill vacancies. Comparing the average perceptions of skills and education as a problem and the unemployment rate in ECA countries (for which data are available), there is evidence that firms in countries experiencing high unemployment do indeed report a *lower* dissatisfaction with the education and skill of the labor force, on average. See Figure 4.4.

Figure 4.4. Skills and Education of Labor as an Obstacle vs. Unemployment

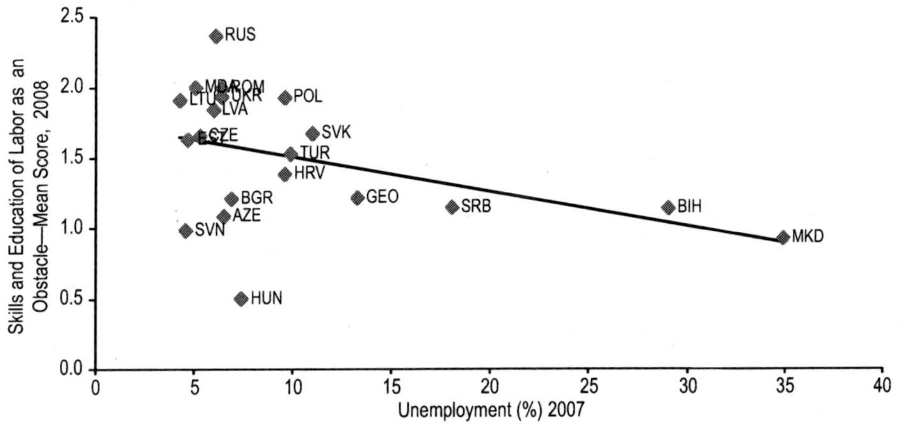

Source: BEEPS 2008, World Bank.

On the surface, this aggregate pattern may appear to contradict the discussion in the previous section on the links between unemployment and the skills constraint, i.e., how skills shortages may persist, despite growing pools of excess labor. However, the data on unemployment for the tertiary educated and secondary educated show very different patterns. Firms in countries with greater tertiary unemployment (a greater share of unemployed workers with tertiary education) report a *higher* level of dissatisfaction with the skills and education of labor than do those with unemployed workers consisting mostly of individuals with secondary school education. See Figures 4.5 and 4.6. One explanation is that at lower skill levels, unemployed workers can substitute for workers who do not have specialized skills. On the other hand, workers with tertiary education are not considered substitutes as they have specialized skills (e.g., engineers and lawyers). Thus, a larger pool of tertiary unemployed does not necessarily mean a larger pool of workers to draw from.

The graphs below suggest that the remedy to the skills constraint may not lie in formal education, but in relevant skills development. The BEEPS results follow this trend at the firm level: firms with a greater percentage of workers with university degrees are more likely to report that skills and education of labor is a major obstacle.[25] One explanation for this result is the degree of "over-education" among workers. In some cases, workers may possess a higher level of education or skill than the job requires, which

Figure 4.5. Skills and Education of Labor as an Obstacle vs. Unemployment of Tertiary Educated

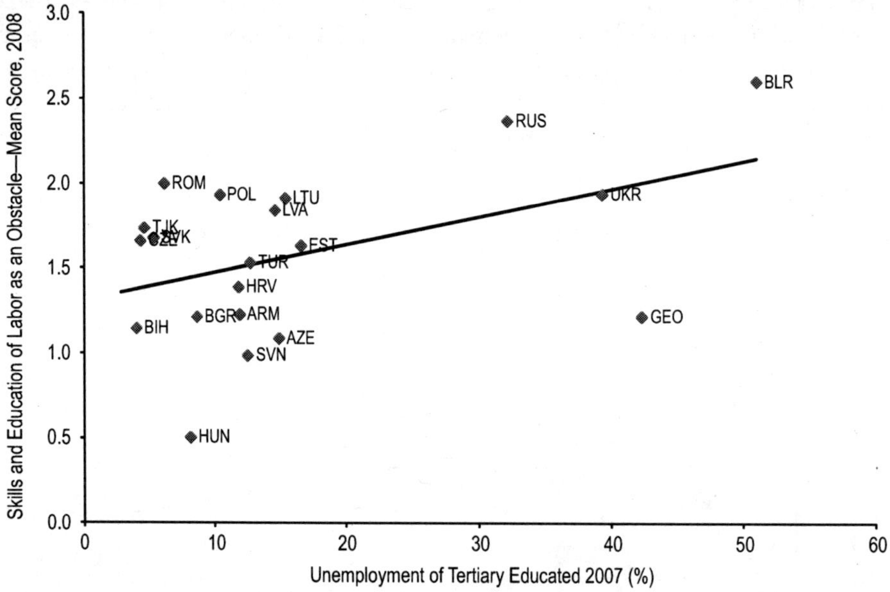

Source: BEEPS 2008, World Bank.

Figure 4.6. Skills and Education of Labor as an Obstacle vs. Unemployment of Secondary Educated

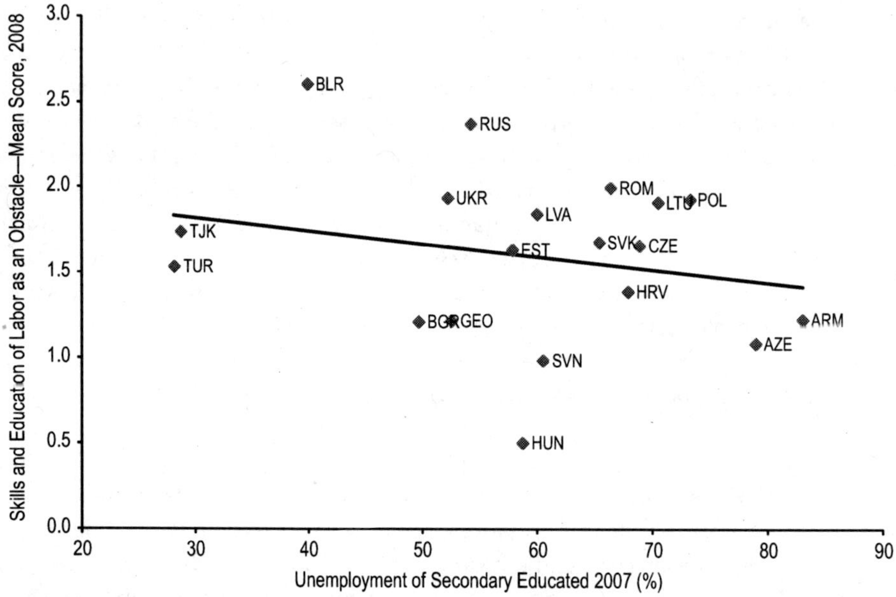

Source: BEEPS 2008, World Bank.

may lead to decreased productivity, the underutilization of skills, or skills mismatches within firms.[26] This relationship may also reflect an inability of formal training institutions to adapt to changing needs of the labor market, which is well documented.[27] This means that deficiencies in the educational system, which have been around for some time, may have become a greater obstacle as labor demand has grown stronger.

Box 4.5. Information Technology Use and Skills

ICT is becoming more pervasive in the business world globally, not just in the ECA region. Across ECA, the use of ICT has increased significantly from 2002–2008. The investment in ICT is best viewed using the panel dataset. Comparing the results from 2002, 2005, and 2008, the use of email communication increased significantly for panel firms between 2002 and 2005, increasing from 56 percent to 69 percent of all firms in the sample. In 2008, email use continued to increase, reaching an average of 74 percent.

ICT needs skills, or skills need ICT?

The increased use of ICT, and changes in organizational processes and products increase the need for workers to have a higher level of skills. Hence, labor demand has shifted toward skilled labor as firms become more innovative and adopt new technologies, the phenomenon referred to as *skills-biased technical change* (Bresnahan, Brynjolfsson and Hitt, 2002; Juhn, Murphy and Pierce, 1993).

Answering the question of causality, whether the use of ICT increases firm-need for skills, or vice versa is outside the scope of this report. However, the results of BEEPS provide evidence that they are complementary factors. Results of the multivariate regression support the hypothesis that firms that use ICT will use more highly skilled labor.[28] Similarly, firms with a higher percentage of workers with university degrees are more likely to use ICT, even when controlling for skills mix.[29]

In turn, the analysis shows that firms that use email are also more likely to provide training for their full-time workers.[30] Firms investing in ICT may complement this investment with other human capital investments. Results show that this practice pays off, as training has a significant positive effect on labor productivity at the firm level when controlling for other factors.[31] More on the role of ICT in productivity is found in Chapter 3.

Sources: BEEPS 2002, 2005, and 2008.

Responding to the Rising Skills Constraints

One way firms are responding to the rising skills constraint is by providing training to enhance the skills of those they hire. The provision of training is one means to increase the capacity of labor and develop a more functional and effective workforce. These firms that provide training are also more productive firms: training has a significant and positive relationship with productivity at the firm level when controlling for other factors.[32]

However, despite the productivity boost, only 35 percent of firms provided training in ECA, which places it in the middle of the pack compared to other regions. Based on comparable data from Enterprise Surveys, 29 percent of firms in AFR provided training to their full-time employees, as compared to 42 percent of EAP firms and 43 percent of LCR firms (see Figure 4.7). However, there is a wide variation across the countries within ECA—50 percent or more of the firms in Russia, Poland, Estonia, Bosnia and Herzegovina, and the Czech Republic offered training to their full time employees.[33] This is in sharp contrast to Azerbaijan, Georgia, and Uzbekistan, where 15 percent or less of firms offered training. There is not a discernible pattern across countries; however, there are significant differences across subregional averages.

Firms in the EU-10 train more than firms located in other ECA subregions. One explanation is that these countries tend to have higher incomes. Examining the provision of training by income classification confirms that more firms in high-income countries provide training than in lower income countries (Figure 4.8). Only 25 percent of firms in low-income countries on average provided training to their full time employees, compared to 44 percent of firms in high-income countries. The relationship is further confirmed by the results of statistical analyses that show GDP as a positive and signifi-

Figure 4.7. Provision of Training by Region

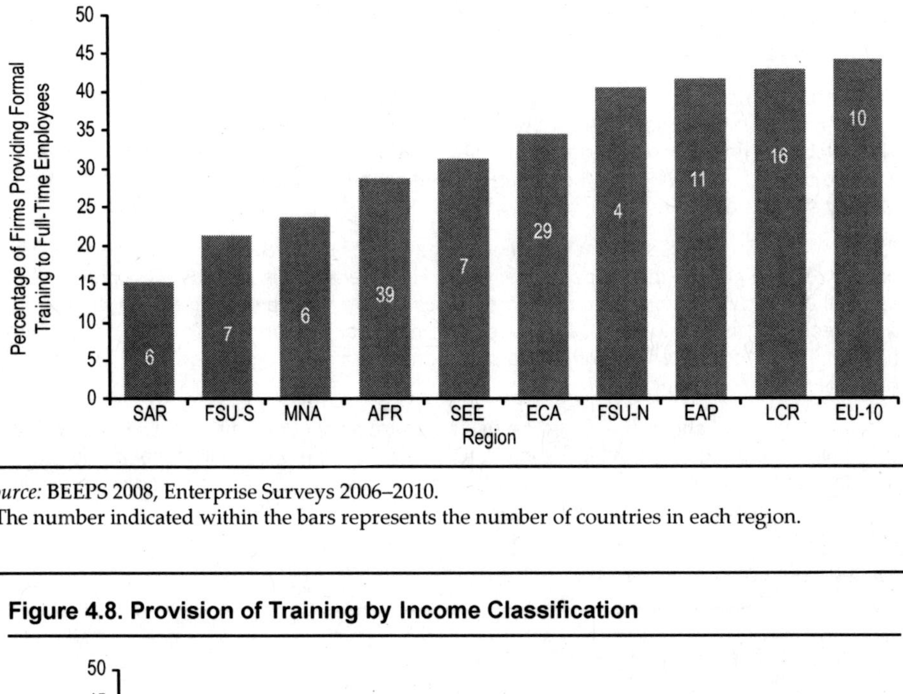

Source: BEEPS 2008, Enterprise Surveys 2006–2010.
* The number indicated within the bars represents the number of countries in each region.

Figure 4.8. Provision of Training by Income Classification

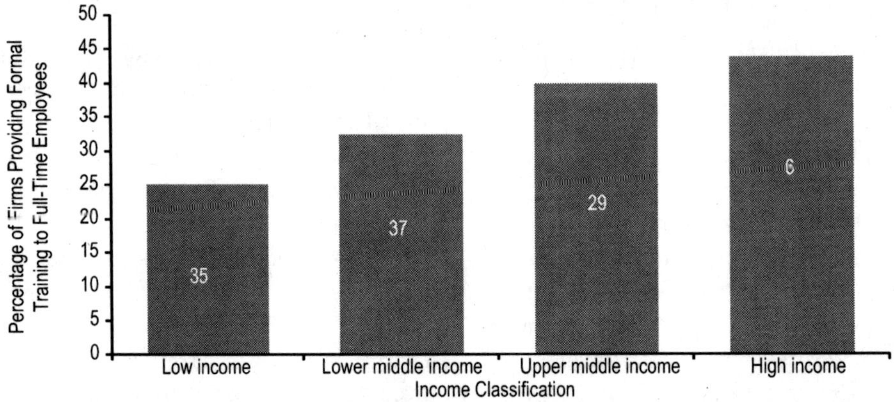

Source: BEEPS 2008, Enterprise Surveys 2006–2010.
* The number indicated within the bars represents the number of countries in each region.

cant predictor for provision of training, controlling for other factors.[34] One important implication of this finding is that although skills constraints are apparent across income groups, firms in richer countries appear better able to respond to the skills constraint.[35] Because firms in richer countries can provide more training and thus offset skills shortages, the gap in enterprise performance between rich and poor countries may widen further.

Differences in training patterns are also partially explained by firm characteristics, such as firm size. Small firms historically are less likely to provide formal training,[36] as they have fewer resources (Freel, 1999). This is visible in the BEEPS results: only 24 percent of small firms offered formal training to their employees, versus 39 percent of medium firms and 55 percent of large firms. The results of the analysis confirm that large firms are more likely to provide training than other firms (controlling for other factors).[37]

Firms that export or are partially foreign-owned are also more likely to provide training. In turn, these firms are also more likely to be innovative firms. Innovative firms may require a more specialized skill set of their employees, and therefore are more likely to provide training than their non-innovating counterparts. (See also Box 4.5). The results of BEEPS reflect this: 42 percent of innovative firms offered training programs compared to 26 percent of firms that did not innovate. Firms that increased their workforce between 2004 and 2007 were also more likely to provide training to their full-time workers. This may be a signal that new hires are lacking fundamental skills needed by firms. Thus, the training provided by growing firms may be aimed at equipping new hires with requisite skills to complete on-the-job tasks, rather than enhancing the existing skill sets of employees.

In summary, firms that are advancing in terms of adoption of technology, and innovating via the development of new products and services are more likely to provide training to their workers. However, this should not imply that firms that train are more satisfied with the quality of labor: in fact the opposite is true. Only 24 percent of firms that provided training reported that skills and education of labor is not an obstacle, compared to 33 percent of firms that did not train, and the difference is significant. See Figure 4.9 below.

Figure 4.9. Skills and Education of Labor as an Obstacle vs. Provision of Training

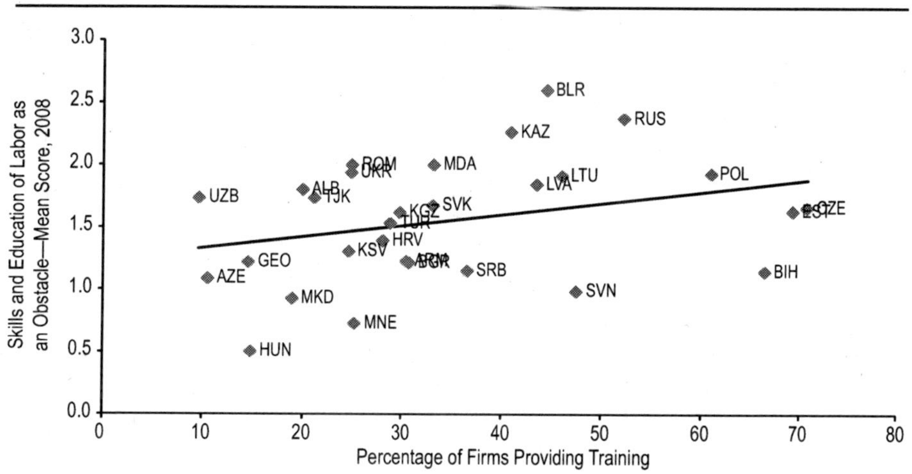

Source: BEEPS 2008.

The characteristics that make firms more likely to provide training are the same characteristics associated with a higher level of dissatisfaction with labor quality, particularly innovative activity and ICT use. These firms may be providing training to equip their workers with basic, requisite skills, instead of enhancing the skills of high-skilled workers. The negative relationship between training and labor satisfaction may be a function of the cost to the firm to provide these programs. If firms cannot find qualified labor, investing in training to meet internal needs may place an undue burden on these firms to stay competitive.

Box 4.6. Early Effects of the Financial Crisis

The financial crisis had a distinct effect on firms' management of human capital. The 2009 Financial Crisis Survey conducted by the Enterprise Surveys unit of the World Bank, revisited firms participating in the 2008 BEEPS in six countries and asked about the effects of the crisis and their responses to it. The results show approximately 60 percent of firms that participated in the 2008 BEEPS had reduced their workforce by 2009.

Of firms participating in both surveys, many reported that they are planning to reduce their full-time permanent workforce (see Figure B4.6.1). The highest value is seen in Lithuania, where 42 percent of firms speculated they will reduce their workforce in response to the crisis.

Figure B4.6.1. Firms Planning to Downsize

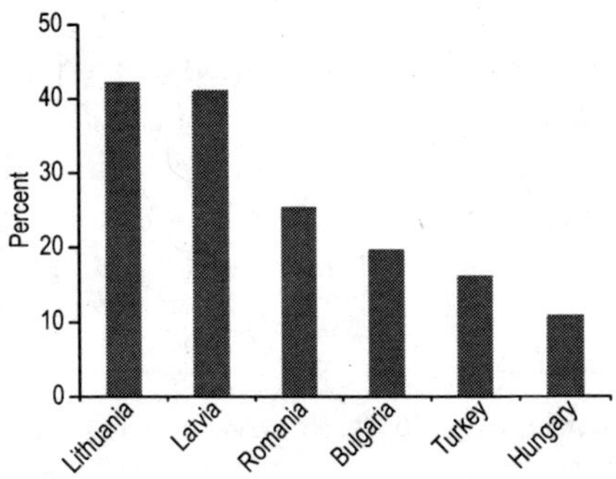

Source: Financial Crisis Survey, 2009.

Figure B4.6.2. Skills and Education of Labor as No Obstacle and Plans to Downsize

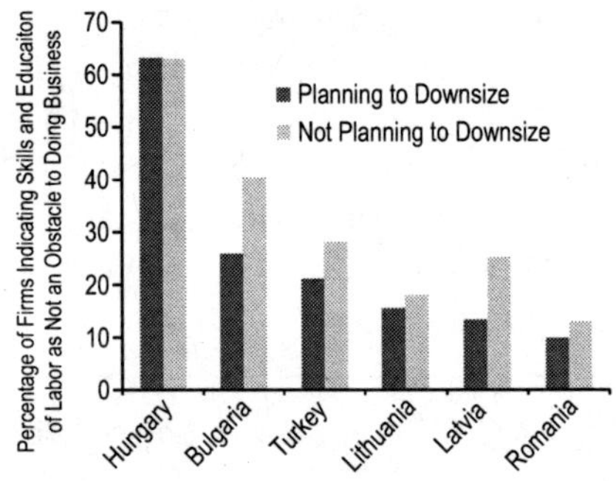

Source: BEEPS 2008, Financial Crisis Survey, 2009.

Firms that planned to downsize in 2009 were more dissatisfied with their quality of labor in 2008.[38] Across all firms participating in the survey, only 22 percent of firms planning to downsize stated skills and education of labor was not an obstacle in 2008, compared to 33 percent of firms that were not planning to downsize.[39] However, the differences across countries are dramatic. See Figure B4.6.2. The difference in perceptions of labor quality between firms that are planning to downsize versus those that are not planning to downsize does not vary for Hungary, and although there are visible differences across the other 5 countries, the difference is only statistically significant in Latvia. Latvian firms that are not planning to downsize are significantly more satisfied with the quality of their labor. For those firms planning to downsize, the crisis may provide an opportunity to shed ineffective workers and capitalize on the increased pool of available workers resulting from the rise in unemployment due to the crisis.

Source: Financial Crisis Survey, 2009.

Effects of the Crisis on Labor

The data for the 2008 BEEPS describes the period before the financial crisis, and the effects of the crisis will undoubtedly have implications for labor in ECA. Firms may shed workers and cut capacity and/or production, which may reverse the positive trend seen in perceptions of labor regulations as redundancy and termination costs rise. The financial crisis may also affect the perceptions of skills and education of labor. As the pool of candidates grows, due to some firms contracting, other firms may be able to capitalize on the crisis by hiring better-skilled workers. However, even if there is more skilled labor on the market, dissatisfaction may persist either because firms become more selective or because in the post-crisis environment, less skilled labor is produced by the education system due to mismatches between the skills needs of firms and the existing curricula in the educational systems.[40] The early effects of the crisis on BEEPS firms in selected countries are discussed in Box 4.6.

Though the crisis may provide temporary relief to firms hampered by the skills constraint, the shortage of relevant skills may eventually prove to be a drag on growth and economic recovery if left unaddressed. Other regional reports[41] have recommended a greater role for lifelong learning through various training schemes. At the same time, where reforms to labor market institutions remain incomplete, labor rigidity may constrain job creation.

Conclusion

In the three years since the previous BEEPS was conducted in 2005, two distinct trends have emerged. First, skills and education of labor has become a top-five obstacle to firms across the ECA region, while at the same time, firms' relative perceptions of labor regulations have improved. The trend in labor regulations suggests greater flexibility in the employment decisions of the private sector made possible by recent reforms to labor market institutions and employment regulation.[42] Despite this flexibility, firms report greater dissatisfaction with the educational and skills qualifications of their workforce. This increase in the skills constraint is a more recent phenomenon, but one that is widespread and significant and is consistent with other data sources and what is known more broadly of labor markets in the ECA region. Although satisfaction with labor quality has been on the decline for the last decade, the skills constraint is becoming an urgent issue for firms in ECA.

There is evidence of a skills shortage driven in part by features of the transition process, including the structural transformation that shifted the demand for labor from low-skilled to high-skilled, international emigration, and the inability of educational systems in the region to respond adequately to the changing needs of enterprises. These drivers predate the recent rise in skills constraints, but there is evidence that they have become more important drivers of skills shortages in recent years.

The rising skills constraint has a measurable impact on labor productivity. While some firms are able to provide training in response to the skills constraint, others cannot. In addition, firms that do provide training are also more likely to report that skills and education of labor is a major obstacle, which may suggest that the added burden of cultivating an effective workforce using their own resources is hindering enterprise performance. Further, firms in high-income countries provide more training to their workers. If firms in poorer countries cannot provide adequate training to complement the skills acquired by their workers through formal education, the gaps in enterprise performance and productivity between rich and poor countries may widen further.

One important finding is that the solution to the problem of the rising skills constraint does not appear to reside in formal education, but in developing relevant skills. Although BEEPS does not capture perceptions of a range of employer-desired skills, such as the ability of individuals to solve problems, work independently, and use IT-based applications, it is clear that there is a lack of fundamental skills in these countries. Other recent regional reports identify early education as an area for countries to aim policies and resources, as well as enhancing job-relevant skills of the current and future workforce. However, this approach is a long-term solution, and does not address the immediate problem of the long-term unemployed.

In the aftermath of the financial crisis, reducing long-term unemployment is a rising concern. In the short term, enhancing the skills of existing workers and unemployed workers can be achieved through policy measures such as re-training programs. While some argue that these government programs may be unnecessary, they may provide relief for stressed state budgets and employers in the long-term by reducing the amount spent on social welfare programs and by reducing labor costs to firms. In addition, retraining these workers could be an important step toward replenishing the stock of qualified workers, which in turn will enhance competitiveness. However, longer-term sustainable measures that bring together the private sector and educational institutions should be considered to achieve better congruence between firms' needs in the changing economy and fundamental skills taught in secondary and post-secondary institutions.

Notes

1. See Alam et al. (2005).
2. See, for example, Rutkowski (2007). Rutkowski rules out other explanations such as emigration from the new EU member states to the older member states, arguing that although such an outflow may explain the fall in unemployment rate, it does not explain rising job creation.
3. See, for example, Schreiner (2008). This refers to year-on-year, four-quarter moving average, for the new EU member states as a group.
4. The regional averages are calculated so that each country has an equal weight.
5. O'Higgins (2010) traces a longer history, spanning the last 15 years or so, behind the effort to deregulate EPL.
6. Stricter EPL theoretically can benefit the firm (Cazes and Mesporova 2003), as it can lead to enhanced productivity though results of prior studies on the relationship between EPL and productivity are mixed (e.g. Scarpetta and Tressel 2004). What is clear is that stricter EPL can also increase the cost of labor for individual firms and may reduce a firm's propensity to hire, particularly for full-time positions, favoring short term or temporary arrangements which may be less costly, unless EPL also has strict regulations governing contractual employment.
7. Scarpetta and Tressel (2004) found that stringent EPL has a significant negative impact on firm productivity, particularly for innovative firms.
8. This finding is based on a generalized ordered logit model that uses perceptions of labor regulations as the dependent variable as informed by Pierre and Scarpetta (2006). Results are significant at p= 0.10 or better. See Table A1.15 in Appendix 1 for results.
9. See Table A1.15 in Appendix 1 for results.
10. See Table A1.17 in Appendix 1 for results.
11. See Table A1.19 in Appendix 1 for results.
12. See Table A1.17 in Appendix 1 for results.
13. This is somewhat surprising. Smaller firms are expected to face higher barriers in the business environment, due to resource and access constraints and their limited ability to provide employ-

ment benefits that larger firms do, but instead larger firms appear to be more constrained. See Table A1.16 in Appendix 1.
14. See Table A1.16 in Appendix 1 for results.
15. Results of the multivariate regression analysis show the skills constraint to have a negative relationship with labor productivity, significant at the 0.08 level. See Table A1.19 in Appendix 1.
16. See Table A1.16 in Appendix 1 for results.
17. See Table A1.19 in Appendix 1 for results.
18. There is a large literature documenting the rising demand for skilled labor as a result of the structural transformation and the transition process, more generally. The relevant studies include Brixiova et al (2009), Tan et al (2007) and Commander and Kollo (2003). In the Western Balkans, the relevant literature is a comprehensive review by Fetsi et al (2007). Further, preliminary evidence on Poland also shows enterprise restructuring has been associated with a pronounced shift of labor demand away from less skilled blue collar labor toward highly skilled white collar labor. Respectively, newly created jobs tend to differ in skill content from the old jobs they replace. Consequently, workers who lose their jobs due to enterprise restructuring often lack skills that are required in the newly created jobs. This gives rise to an excess supply of some skills, which often coexists with the shortage of other skills—those needed in new and expanding activities. Educational systems and labor markets in general have not been able to catch up with this phenomenon. This is reflected in employers' perceptions on skills.
19. Rutkowski (2007).
20. One exception is Belarus, where the employment rate is 51 percent for those with a tertiary education. A similar picture is seen in Georgia and Ukraine, which had tertiary unemployment rates of 42 percent and 39 percent respectively. In all three countries, the unemployment rate of workers with tertiary education rose between 2004 and 2007.
21. See World Bank (2009) for details.
22. See World Bank (2009).
23. See Rutkowski, Scarpetta, et al (2005: 239).
24. See, for example, Alam, Asad et al (2005) on wage increases from 1997 to 2003.
25. See Table A1.16 in the Appendix for results.
26. Research has shown that workers who possess a higher level of education than what the job requires may be more prone to report job dissatisfaction and reduce their work effort, resulting in lower productivity of the firm overall. See Buchel (2000) and Tsang and Levin (1985).
27. See O'Higgins (2010).
28. See Table A1.20 in Appendix 1 for results.
29. See Table A1.17 in Appendix 1 for results.
30. See Table A1.18 in Appendix 1 for results.
31. See Table A1.19 in Appendix 1 for results.
32. See Table A1.19 in Appendix 1 for results.
33. The question on provision of formal training was included only on the Manufacturing Module of the BEEPS survey.
34. See Table A1.18 in Appendix 1 for results.
35. However, these firms in higher income countries may require more skilled labor as they produce higher value-added goods. This hypothesis cannot be tested with available data.
36. See Storey (2004).
37. See Table A1.18 in Appendix 1 for regression results on firm characteristics and provision of training.
38. T-test significant at p=0.000.
39. Based on the full weighted sample of the Enterprise Surveys Financial Crisis Survey 2009.
40. See for example, World Bank (2010); Mitra, Selowsky and Zalduendo (2010).
41. World Bank (2010); Mitra, Selowsky and Zalduendo (2010).
42. Nonetheless, some caution is warranted in interpreting these developments. Although it is possible to demonstrate the links between reforms to labor market institutions and the changing perception of labor regulation, it is extremely difficult to isolate reforms to employment protection legislation from other reforms. In particular, because labor and product markets are interrelated, the impact of reforms in one market is likely to be affected by how heavily other markets continue to be regulated.

References

Ahn, S. 2002. "Competition, Innovation and Productivity Growth: A Review of Theory and Evidence." OECD Economics Department Working Papers, No. 317. OECD Publishing.

Alam, Asad, Mamta Murphy, Ruslan Yemtsov, Edmundo Murrugarra, Nora Dudwick, Ellen Hamilton, and Erwin Tiongson. 2005. *Growth, Poverty, and Inequality: Eastern Europe and the Former Soviet Union.* Washington, DC: World Bank.

Alam, Asad, Paloma Anós Casero, Faruk Khan, and Charles Udomsaph. 2008. *Unleashing Prosperity: Productivity Growth in Eastern Europe and the Former Soviet Union.* Washington, DC: World Bank.

Agenor, P., and B. Moreno-Dodson. 2006. "Public Infrastructure and Growth: New Channels and Policy Implications." Policy Research Working Paper Series 4064. Washington, DC: World Bank.

Arbore and Ordanini. 2006. "Broadband divide Among SME's The role of Size, Location and Outsourcing Strategies." *International Small Business Journal* 24(1): 83–99.

Aslund, Anders. 2009. "Implications of the Crisis for Eastern Europe." *Development and Transition* 13: 2–4.

Aterido, Reyes, Mary Hallward-Driemeier, and Carmen Pagés. 2007. "Investment Climate and Employment Growth: The Impact of Access to Finance, Corruption and Regulations Across Firms." IZA Discussion Paper No. 3138 (Bonn: IZA).

Basu, S., and J. Fernald. 2007. "Information and Communication Technology as a General-Purpose Technology: Evidence from U.S. Industry Data." *German Economic Review* 8: 146–173.

Beck, Thorsten, Aslı Demirgüç-Kunt, and Vojislav Maksimovic. 2005. "Financial and Legal Constraints to Firm Growth: Does Firm Size Matter?" *Journal of Finance* 60(1, February): 137–177.

Beck, Thorsten, Aslı Demirgüç-Kunt, and Vojislav Maksimovic. 2008. "Financing Patterns around the World: Are Small Firms Different?" *Journal of Financial Economics* 89(3).

Belaid, H. 2004. "Telecommunication, infrastructure and economic development." mimeo.

Bonin, John P., Iftekhar Hasan, and Paul Wachtel. 2005. "Privatization Matters: Bank Efficiency in Transition Countries." *Journal of Banking and Finance* 28(8–9): 2155–2178.

Brown, D., M. Fay, J. Felkner, S. Lall, and H. Wang. 2009. "Profiting from Proximity: Rising Economic Densities in the Russian Federation." Mimeo. Washington, DC: World Bank.

Boswell, C., S. Stiller, and T. Straubhaar. 2004. "Forecasting Labor and Skills Shortages: How Can Projections Better Inform Labor Migration Policies?" HWWA Hamburg Migration Research Group.

Bresnahan, T., E. Brynjolfsson, and L. Hitt. 2002. "Information Technology, Workplace Organization, and the Demand for Skilled Labor: Firm Level Evidence." *The Quarterly Journal of Economics* 117(1): 339–376.

Brixiova, Zuzana. 2009. "Labor Market Flexibility in Estonia: What More Can Be Done?" OECD Working Paper (Paris: OECD).

Brixiova, Zuzana, Wenli Li, and Tarik Yousef. 2009. "Skill Shortages and Labor Market Outcomes in Central Europe." *Economic Systems* 33: 45–59.

Byrd, W., and M. Raiser. 2006. "Economic Cooperation in the Wider Central Asia Region." World Bank Working Paper No. 75. Washington, DC: World Bank.

Cadot, O., L.H. Roller, and A. Stephan. 2006. "Contribution to Productivity or Pork Barrel? The Two Faces of Infrastructure Investment." *Journal of Public Economics* 90: 1133–1153.

Calderon, C. 2007. "Infrastructure and Productivity Growth in the ECA Region—A Macroeconomic Approach." Mimeo. Washington, DC: World Bank.

Calderon, C., W. Easterly, and L. Serven. 2003. "Latin America's Infrastructure in the Era of Macroeconomic Crises." Mimeo. Washington, DC: World Bank.

Calderon, C., and L. Serven. 2005. "The Effects of Infrastructure Development on Growth and Income Distribution." World Bank Working Paper WPS3400. Washington, DC: World Bank.

Caprio Jr., G., and D. Klingebiel. 2003. "Episodes of Systemic and Borderline Financial Crises." Mimeo. Washington, DC: World Bank.

Claessens, S., T. Gurcanlar, J. Mercado Sapiani, and N. Van Horen. 2008, "Foreign Bank Presence in Developing Countries 1995–2006: Data and Trends." Mimeo. http://papers.ssrn.com/sol3/papers.cfm?abstract_id=1107295.

Claessens, S., and N. Van Horen. 2008. "Location Decisions of Foreign Banks and Institutional Competitive Advantage." De Nederlandsche Bank Working Paper, n. 172, April.

Clarke, George R.G. 2010. "Are Managers' Perceptions of Constraints to Growth Reliable? Evidence from a Natural Experiment in South Africa." Texas A&M International University, Sanchez School of Business. Mimeo.

Commission on Growth and Development. 2008. "The Path to Prosperity: Productivity Growth in Eastern Europe and the Former Soviet Union." Washington, DC: World Bank.

Correa, Paulo, and Mariana Iootty. 2009. "The Impact of the Global Economic Crisis on the Corporate Sector in Europe and Central Asia: Evidence from a Firm-Level Survey." Enterprise Note 9. Washington, DC: World Bank.

———. 2010. "Will the Crisis Affect the Economic Recovery in Eastern European Countries? Evidence from Firm Level Data." World Bank Policy Research Working Paper number 5278. Washington, DC: World Bank.

Corsetti, Giancarlo, Paolo Pesenti, and Nouriel Roubini. 1999. "What Caused the Asian Currency and Financial Crisis?" *Japan and the World Economy* 11(3): 305–373.

Crystal, Jennifer, B. Gerard Dages, and Linda S. Goldberg. 2001. "Does Foreign Ownership Contribute to Sounder Banks in Emerging Markets? The Latin American Experience." Open Doors: Foreign Participation in Financial Systems in Developing Countries, April 19–21.

Crystal, Jennifer, B. Gerard Dages, and Linda S. Goldberg. 2002. "Has Foreign Bank Entry Led to Sounder Banks in Latin America?" *Federal Reserve Bank of New York, Current Issues in Economic and Finance* 8(1), January.

Cull, Robert, and Maria Soledad Martinez Peria. 2008. "Crises as Catalysts for Foreign Bank Activity in Emerging Markets." In Justin Robertson, ed., *Power and Politics After Financial Crisis: Rethinking Foreign Opportunism in Emerging Markets.* New York: Palgrave Macmillan.

———. 2010. "Foreign Bank Participation in Developing Countries: What Do We Know About the Drivers and Consequences of this Phenomenon?" World Bank Policy Research Working Paper 5398. Washington, DC: World Bank.

Cull, Robert, María Soledad Martínez Pería, and Natalia Teplitz. 2011. "Foreign Bank Claims to Developing Countries Before, During, and After the 2007–2008 Crisis." Mimeo. Washington, DC: World Bank.

Dages, B. Gerard, Linda S. Goldberg, and Daniel Kinney. 2000. "Foreign and Domestic Bank Participation in Emerging Markets: Lessons from Mexico and Argentina." NBER Working Paper No. W7714. New York: Federal Reserve Bank of New York.

Das, Rohit, and Esha Mendiratta. 2007. "CEE's Dwindling Skilled Labor Supply: The Vagaries of Unfavorable Demographics." Technical Paper December 2007. London: Watson Wyatt Worldwide.

De Haas, R., and I. Naaborg. 2006, "Foreign Banks in Transition Countries: To Whom Do They Lend and How Are They Financed?" *Financial Markets, Institutions & Instruments* 15(4): 159–99.

De Haas, Ralph, and Iman van Lelyveld. 2006. "Foreign Banks and Credit stability in central and Eastern Europe. A Panel Data Analysis." *Journal of Banking and Finance* 30(7): 1927–1952.

———. 2010. "Internal Capital Markets and Lending by Multinational Bank Subsidiaries." *Journal of Financial Intermediation* 19(1): 1–25.

Desai, Raj, and Itzhak Goldberg, eds. 2007. "Enhancing Russia's Competitiveness and Innovative Capacity." Report No. XX. Washington, DC: World Bank.

Duffy-Deno. 2003. "Business Demand for Broadband Access Capacity." *Journal of Regulatory Economics* 24:3 359–372.

Ebinger, J. 2006. "Measuring Financial Performance in Infrastructure: An Application to Europe and Central Asia." World Bank Working Paper Series No. 3992. Washington, DC: World Bank.

Esfahania, H.S., and M.T. Ramirez. 2003. "Institutions, Infrastructure, and Economic Growth." *Journal of Development Economics* 70: 443–477.

European Bank for Reconstruction and Development (EBRD). 2010. *Transition Report 2010: Recovery and Reform.* London: European Bank for Reconstruction and Development.

———. 2005. *Transition Report 2005: Business in Transition.* London: European Bank for Reconstruction and Development.

———. 2002. *Transition Report 2002: Agricultural and Rural Transition.* London: European Bank for Reconstruction and Development.

Fay, M., and A. Estache. 2009. "Current Debates on Infrastructure Policy." Washington, DC: World Bank.

Fernald, J. 1999. "Roads to Prosperity—Assessing the Link between Public Capital and Productivity." *American Economic Review* 89(3): 619–638.

Fetsi, Anastasia, and Manuela Prina. 2009. "The Role of Vocational Education and Training in Transition Economies: Lessons Learned for Asian Countries." Paper prepared for 3rd China-ASEAN Forum on Social Development and Poverty Reduction, 4th ASEAN+3 High-Level Seminar on Poverty Reduction, and Asia-wide Regional High-level Meeting on The Impact of the Global Economic Slowdown on Poverty and Sustainable Development in Asia and the Pacific. Manila: Asian Development Bank.

Fetsi, Anastasia, ed. 2007. "Labor Markets in the Western Balkans: Challenges for the Future." Turin: European Training Foundation.

Freel, M. 1999. "Where Are the Skills Gaps in Innovative Small Firms?" *International Journal of Entrepreneurial Behavior & Research* 5(3): 144+.

Gamberoni, Elisa, Erik Von Uexkull, and Sebastian Weber. 2010. "The Roles of Openness and Labor Market Institutions for Employment Dynamics during Economic Crises." *Economic Premise* 29. Washington, DC: World Bank.

Gashi, Ardiana N., and Nick Adnett. 2009. "Technology, Training and Transition: Evidence from the Western Balkans." Working Paper.

Giannetti, M., and S. Ongena. 2009a. "Financial Integration and Firm Performance: Evidence from Foreign Bank Entry in Emerging Markets." *Review of Finance, Oxford University Press for European Finance Association* 13: 181–223.

———. 2009b. "'Lending by Example: Direct and Indirect Effects of Foreign Banks in Emerging Markets."Second Singapore International Conference on Finance 2008, AFA 2009 San Francisco Meetings Paper and ECGI—Finance Working Paper No. 221/2008.

Gimpelson, Vladimir, Rostislav Kapeliushnikov, and Anna Lukiyanova. 2009. "Stuck Between Surplus and Shortage: Demand for Skills in the Russian Industry." IZA Discussion Paper No. 3934. Bonn: IZA.

Goldberg, Itzhak, Branko Radulovic, and Mark Schaffer. 2005. "Productivity, Ownership and the Investment Climate: International Lessons for Priorities in Serbia." World Bank Policy Research Working Paper No. 3681. Washington, DC: World Bank.

Grabowska-Lusinska, Izabela. 2007. "Skill Shortages, Emigration and Unemployment in Poland—Causes and Implications." Focus on Central and Eastern Europe May 2007. Prague: Multicultural Center.

Griffith, Rachel, Elena Huergo, Jacques Mairesse, and Bettina Peters. 2006. "Innovation and Productivity Across Four European Countries." *Oxford Rev Econ Policy* 22(4): 483–498.

Grigoriou, C. 2007. "Landlockedness, Infrastructure and Trade: New Estimates for Central Asian Countries." World Bank Policy Research Working Paper 4335. Washington, DC: World Bank.

Grigorian, D. and V. Manole. 2006. "Determinants of Commercial Bank Performance in Transition: An Application of Data Envelopment Analysis." *Comparative Economic Studies* 48(3): 497–522.

Hallward-Dreimer, M., G. Khun-Jush, and L. Pritchett. 2009. "Deals versus Rules: Uncertainty in Policy Implementation in Africa." World Bank Policy Research Working Paper 5321. Washington, DC: World Bank.

Hulten, C., E. Bennathan, and S. Srinivasan. 2003. "Infrastructure, Externalities, and Economic Development—A Study of Indian Manufacturing Industry." World Bank working paper. Washington, DC: World Bank.

Iimi, A. 2008. "Effects of Improving Infrastructure Quality on Business Costs: Evidence from Firm-Level Data." World Bank Policy Research Working Paper 4581. Washington, DC: World Bank.

International Labour Organization (ILO). 2008. "Young People and Their Transition to Decent Work in the Western Balkans." A background paper for the Informal Meeting of Ministers of Labour and Social Affairs during the International Labour Conference.

International Monetary Fund (IMF). 2010a. *Regional Economic Outlook: Europe: Building Confidence.* Washington, DC: The International Monetary Fund.

———. 2010b. *World Economic Outlook: October 2010.* Washington, DC: The International Monetary Fund.

Janz, N., H. Lööf, and B. Peters. 2004. "Innovation and Productivity in German and Swedish Manufacturing Firms: Is there a Common Story?" *Problems & Perspectives in Management* 2: 184–204.

Kaczmarczyk, P. and M. Okólski. 2008. "Economic Impacts of Migration on Poland and the Baltic States." Fafo-Paper 2008: 1, Oslo.

Kahanec, Martin, Anzelika Zaiceva, and Klaus F. Zimmermann. 2009. "Lessons from Migration after EU Enlargement." Discussion Paper No. 4230. IZA, DIW Berlin, Bonn University and Free University of Berlin.

Kamil, Herman, and Kulwant Rai. 2010. "The Global Credit Crunch and Foreign Banks' Lending to Emerging Markets: Why Did Latin America Fare Better?" IMF Working Paper WP/10/102. Washington, DC: International Monetary Fund.

Kaufmann, D., A. Kraay, and M. Mastruzzi. 2009. "Governance Matters VIII: Governance Indicators for 1996–2008." World Bank Policy Research Working Paper 4978. Washington, DC: World Bank.

Kessides, C., and S. Khan. 2009. "Infrastructure." In *Fiscal Policy and Economic Growth: Lessons for ECA.* Washington, DC: World Bank.

Kiraly, J., B. Majer, L. Matyas, B. Ocsi, A. Sugar, and E. Varhegyi. 2000. "Experience with Internationalization of Financial Service Providers—Case Study: Hungary." In Claessens, S. and Marion Jansen, eds., *The Internationalization of Financial Services: Issues and Lessons for Developing Countries.* Boston, MA.: Kluwer Academic Press.

Kolding, Marianne, and Vladimír Kroa. 2005. "Networking Skills in Europe: Will an Increasing Shortage Hamper Competitiveness in the Global Market?" IDC White Paper. London: IDC.

La Porta R., F. López-de-Silanes, A. Shleifer, and R. Vishny. 1999. "The Quality of Government." *Journal of Laws, Economics, and Organization* 15(1): 222–279.

Lehmann, Hartmut, and Alexander Muravyev. 2009. "How Important Are Labor Market Institutions for Labor Market Performance in Transition Countries?" IZA Discussion Paper No. 4673. Bonn: IZA.

Marton, K., and C. H. McCarthy. 2008. "From State to Foreign Ownership: The Banking Sector in Eastern and Central Europe." *2008 Global Economy Journal* 8(3), Article 8.

Lopez-Garcia, Paloma. 2005. "Business Environment and Labor Market Outcomes in Europe and Central Asia Countries." World Bank Policy Research Working Paper No. 3885. Washington, DC: World Bank.

Lynch, L., and S. Black. 1998. "Beyond the Incidence of Employer-Provided Training." *Industrial and Labor Relations Review* 52(1): 64–81.

Marin, Dalia. 2005. "A New International Division of Labor in Europe: Outsourcing and Offshoring to Eastern Europe." Paper prepared for the Papers and Proceedings of the European Economic Association Congress, Amsterdam.

Miluka, Juna, and Andrew Dabalen. 2009. "Exploring the Role of Albanian International Migration on Education." Mimeo. Washington, DC: World Bank.

Mitra, Pradeep, Marcelo Selowsky, and Juan Zalduendo. 2010. *Turmoil at Twenty: Recession, Recovery, and Reform in Central and Eastern Europe and the Former Soviet Union.* Washington, DC: World Bank.

Molnar, E., and L. Ojala. 2003. "Transport and Trade Facilitation Issues in the CIS 7, Kazakhstan and Turkmenistan." Mimeo. Washington, DC: World Bank.

Mussio, Irene. 2008. "Who Has What It Takes? Determining the Main Constraints of Labor Markets in BRIC and Eastern Europe." *Insight,* February 2009. London: Watson Wyatt Worldwide.

Nikiel, E. M., and T. P. Opiela. 2002. "Customer Type and Bank Efficiency in Poland: Implications for Emerging Market Banking." *Contemporary Economic Policy* 20(3): 255–71.

O'Higgins, Niall. 2010. "Youth Labour Markets in Europe and Central Asia." IZA Discussion Paper No. 5094. Bonn: IZA.

Paci, Pierella, Erwin Tiongson, Mateusz Walewsi, Jacek Liwinski, and Maria Stoilkova. 2007. "Internal Labor Mobility in Central Europe and the Baltic Region." Working Paper No. 105. Washington, DC: World Bank.

Pavlova, Olga, and Oleksandr Rohozynsky. 2005. "Labor Markets in CIS Countries." Center for Social and Economic Research (CASE) Studies and Analysis No. 311. Warsaw: CASE.

Pierre, Gaelle, and Stefano Scarpetta. 2006. "Employment Protection: Do Firms' Perceptions Match with Legislation?" *Economics Letters* 90: 328–334.

———. 2004. "Employment Regulations through the Eyes of Employers: Do They Matter and How Do Firms Respond to Them?" IZA Discussion Paper No. 1424. Bonn: IZA.

Röeller, L., and L. Waverman. 2001. "Telecommunications Infrastructure and Economic Development—A Simultaneous Approach." *American Economic Review* 91(4): 909–923.

Rutkowski, Jan. 2007. "From the Shortage of Jobs to the Shortage of Skilled Workers: Labor Markets in the EU New Member States." IZA Discussion Paper 3202. Bonn: Institute for the Study of Labor.

———. 2006. "Labor Market Development during Economic Transition." World Bank Policy Research Working Paper No. 3894. Washington, DC: World Bank.

Rutkowski, Jan, and Stefano Scarpetta with Arup Banerji, Philip O'Keefe, Gaëlle Pierre, and Milan Vodopivec. 2005. *Enhancing Job Opportunities: Eastern Europe and the Former Soviet Union.* Washington, DC: World Bank.

Salt, Bernard. 2008. "The Global Skills Convergence." Melbourne: KPMG.

Scarpetta, Stefano, and Thierry Tressel. 2004. "Boosting Productivity Via Innovation and Adoption of New Technologies: Any Role for Labor Market Institutions?" The World Bank Social Protection Discussion Paper Series No. 0406. Washington, DC: World Bank.

Schreiner, Josef. 2008. "Labor Markets in Central, Eastern and Southeastern European EU Member States: General Trends and Migration Effects." Focus on European Economic Integration No. 01/08.

Semih Yildirim, H. and G. C. Philippatos. 2007. "Efficiency of Banks: Recent Evidence from the Transition Economies of Europe, 1993–2000." *The European Journal of Finance* 13(2): 123–43.

Shepherd, B. and J. Wilson. 2006. "Road Infrastructure in Europe and Central Asia: Does Network Quality Affect Trade?" World Bank mimeo. Washington, DC: World Bank.

Shima, Isilda. 2010. "Return Migration and Labour Market Outcomes of the Returnees: Does the Return Really Pay Off? The Case Study of Romania and Bulgaria." FIW Research Reports 2009/10, No. 07. Vienna: FIW.

Storey, D. 2004. "Exploring the Link among Small Firms between Management Training and Firm Performance: A Comparison between the UK and Other OECD Countries." *International Journal of Human Resource Management* 15: 112–130.

Straub, S. 2008. "Infrastructure and Growth In Developing Countries: Recent Advances and Research Challenges." World Bank Policy Research Working Paper 4460. Washington, DC: World Bank.

Tan, Hong, Vladimir Gimpelson, and Yevgeniya Savchenko. 2007. "Upgrading Skills." In Raj M. Desai and Itzhak Goldberg, eds., *Enhancing Russia's Competitiveness and Innovative Capacity*. Washington, DC: World Bank.

Tan, Hong, Yevgeniya Savchenko, Vladimir Gimpelson, Rostislav Kapelyushnikov, and Anna Lukyanova. 2007. "Skills Shortages and Training in Russian Enterprises." IZA Discussion Paper No. 2751. Bonn: Institute for the Study of Labor.

Tsang, M., and Levin. 1985. "The Economics of Overeducation." *Economics of Education Review* 4(2): 93–104.

Verme, Paolo. 2006. "Constraints to Growth and Job Creation in Low-Income Commonwealth of Independent States Countries." World Bank Policy Research Working Paper No. 3893. Washington, DC: World Bank.

Wagstyl, Stefan, Jan Cionski, Kester Eddy, and Thomas Escritt. 2008. "Gone West: Why Eastern Europe is Laboring under an Abundance of Jobs." *Financial Times*, Comments & Analysis, January 17

World Bank. 2010. "Stepping Up Skills for More Jobs and Higher Productivity." Washington, DC: World Bank.

———. 2010a. *Global Economic Prospects, Summer 2010*. Washington, DC: World Bank.

———. 2010b. *EU10 Regular Economic Report: November 2010*. Washington, DC: World Bank.

———. 2010c. *Russian Economic Report No. 23: November 2010*. Washington, DC: World Bank.

———. 2009. "Are Skills Constraining Growth in Bosnia and Herzegovina?" Report No. 54901-BA. Washington, DC: World Bank.

———. 2008. *Innovation, Inclusion, and Integration: From Transition to Convergence in Eastern Europe and the Former Soviet Union.* Washington, DC: World Bank.

———. 2008. *Migration and Remittances: Eastern Europe and the Former Soviet Union, World Bank.* Washington, DC: World Bank.

———. 2008. "Unleashing Prosperity: Productivity Growth in Eastern Europe and the Former Soviet Union." World Bank mimeo. Washington, DC: World Bank.

———. 2007. "The Cost of State Regulation of Enterprise Activity." Chisinau. Washington, DC: World Bank.

———. 2006. Infrastructure in Europe and Central Asia Region: Approaches to Sustainable Services. Washington, DC: World Bank.

———. 2005. "FYR of Macedonia Poverty Assessment for 2003-2003." Report No. 34324-MK. Washington, DC: World Bank.

Appendixes

Appendix 1. Technical Notes and Data Tables

BEEPS 2008 Survey Questions

Problems Doing Business: Access to Finance, Electricity, Telecommunications, Transport, Labor Regulations and Skills and Education of Labor

Access to Finance
Q.K30: Is **access to finance**, which includes availability and cost, interest rates, fees and collateral requirements, No Obstacle, a Minor Obstacle, a Moderate Obstacle, a Major Obstacle, or a Very Severe Obstacle to the current operations of this establishment? (No obstacle=0 Minor obstacle=1 Moderate obstacle=2 Major obstacle=3 Very severe obstacle=4)

Electricity
Q.C30a: Is **electricity** No Obstacle, a Minor Obstacle, a Moderate Obstacle, a Major Obstacle, or a Very Severe Obstacle to the current operations of this establishment? (No obstacle=0 Minor obstacle=1 Moderate obstacle=2 Major obstacle=3 Very severe obstacle=4)

Telecommunications
Q.C30b: Is **telecommunications** No Obstacle, a Minor Obstacle, a Moderate Obstacle, a Major Obstacle, or a Very Severe Obstacle to the current operations of this establishment? (No obstacle=0 Minor obstacle=1 Moderate obstacle=2 Major obstacle=3 Very severe obstacle=4)

Transport
Q.D30a: Is **transport** No Obstacle, a Minor Obstacle, a Moderate Obstacle, a Major Obstacle, or a Very Severe Obstacle to the current operations of this establishment? (No obstacle=0 Minor obstacle=1 Moderate obstacle=2 Major obstacle=3 Very severe obstacle=4)

Labor Regulations
Q.L30a: Are **labor regulations** No Obstacle, a Minor Obstacle, a Moderate Obstacle, a Major Obstacle, or a Very Severe Obstacle to the current operations of this establishment? (No obstacle=0 Minor obstacle=1 Moderate obstacle=2 Major obstacle=3 Very severe obstacle=4)

Inadequately Educated Workforce
Q.L30b: Is an **inadequately educated workforce** No Obstacle, a Minor Obstacle, a Moderate Obstacle, a Major Obstacle, or a Very Severe Obstacle to the current operations of this establishment? (No obstacle=0 Minor obstacle=1 Moderate obstacle=2 Major obstacle=3 Very severe obstacle=4)

Overdraft Facility
Q.K7: At this time, does this establishment have an overdraft facility? (Yes=1 No=2)

Credit Line
Q.K8: At this time, does this establishment have a line of credit or a loan from a financial institution? (Yes=1 No=2)

Innovation
Q.O.1: In the last three years, has this establishment introduced new products or services? (Yes=1 No=2)

Power Outages
Q.C7: In a typical month, over fiscal year **2007**, how many power outages did this establishment experience? Average number of power outages per month:

Duration of Power Outages
Q.C8: How long did these power outages last on average? Average duration of power outages (hours)___. Less than 1 hour=1.

Losses due to Power Outages
Q.C9: Please estimate the losses that resulted from power outages either as a percentage of total annual sales or as total annual losses.
- Loss as percent of total annual sales due to power outages ___% (Q.C9a)
- Annual losses due to power outages ___ (LCU) (Q.C9b)

Email Use
Q.C22a: At the present time, does this establishment use any of the following: Email to communicate with clients or suppliers? (Yes=1 No=2)

High-speed Internet
Q.C23: Does this establishment have a high-speed Internet connection on its premises? (Yes=1 No=2)

Training
Q.L10: Over fiscal year **2007**, did this establishment have formal training programs for its permanent, full-time employees? (Yes=1 No=2)

Professionalism of Labor
Q.69: What percent of this establishment's labor force employed at the end of fiscal year **2007** had a university degree? ___%

Foreign and Domestic Competition
Q.63: How important are each of the following factors in affecting decisions to develop new products or services and markets? (Not at all important=1 Slightly important=2 Fairly important=3 Very important=4)
- Pressure from domestic competitors (Q.63a)
- Pressure from foreign competitors (Q.63b)

Notes on Regional and Subregional Averages

For many graphs and tables, the regional and subregional averages are presented. The following notes describe the composition of the ECA region and subregional averages (unless otherwise stated in individual table and figure notes).

- The ECA average for BEEPS 2008 indicators includes 29 countries: Albania, Armenia, Azerbaijan, Belarus, Bosnia and Herzegovina, Bulgaria, Croatia, Czech Republic, Estonia, Georgia, Hungary, Kazakhstan, Kosovo, Kyrgyz Republic, Latvia, Lithuania, FYR Macedonia, Moldova, Montenegro, Poland, Romania, Russian Federation, Serbia, Slovak Republic, Slovenia, Tajikistan, Turkey, Ukraine and Uzbekistan.

- Northern FSU (FSU-N) averages include Belarus, Kazakhstan, Russia, and Ukraine.
- Southern FSU (FSU-S) averages include Armenia, Azerbaijan, Georgia, Kyrgyz Republic, Moldova, Tajikistan, and Uzbekistan.
- South Eastern Europe (SEE) averages include Albania, Bosnia and Herzegovina, Croatia, FYR Macedonia, Kosovo, Montenegro, and Serbia.
- European Union-10 (EU-10) averages include Bulgaria, Czech Republic, Estonia, Hungary, Latvia, Lithuania, Poland, Romania, Slovak Republic, and Slovenia.
- Turkey is included in the ECA average, but is not included in any subregional category.

Enterprise Surveys Data-Based Regional Averages

For many graphs and tables, data from Enterprise Surveys is used to show the regional comparison between the ECA region and other regions covered by Enterprise Surveys. The following notes describe the composition of the individual regions (unless otherwise stated in individual table and figure notes).

- East Asia & Pacific: Fiji, Indonesia, Lao PDR, Micronesia, Mongolia, Philippines, Samoa, Timor Leste, Tonga, Vanuatu, Vietnam.
- South Asia: Afghanistan, Bangladesh, Bhutan, India, Nepal, Pakistan.
- Latin America & Caribbean: Argentina, Bolivia, Brazil, Chile, Colombia, Ecuador, El Salvador, Guatemala, Honduras, Mexico, Nicaragua, Panama, Paraguay, Peru, Uruguay, República Bolivariana de Venezuela.
- Africa: Angola, Benin, Botswana, Burkina Faso, Burundi, Cameroon, Cape Verde, Chad, Republic of Congo, Democratic Republic of the Congo, Eritrea, Ethiopia, Gabon, The Gambia, Ghana, Guinea, Guinea Bissau, Côte d'Ivoire, Kenya, Lesotho, Liberia, Madagascar, Malawi, Mali, Mauritania, Mauritius, Mozambique, Namibia, Niger, Nigeria, Rwanda, Senegal, Sierra Leone, South Africa, Swaziland, Tanzania, Togo, Uganda, Zambia.
- Eastern Europe and Central Asia: Albania, Armenia, Azerbaijan, Belarus, Bosnia and Herzegovina, Bulgaria, Croatia, Czech Republic, Estonia, FYR Macedonia, Georgia, Hungary, Kazakhstan, Kosovo, Kyrgyz Republic, Latvia, Lithuania, Moldova, Montenegro, Poland, Romania, Russia, Serbia, Slovak Republic, Slovenia, Tajikistan, Turkey, Ukraine, Uzbekistan.
- Middle East and North Africa: Algeria, the Arab Republic of Egypt, Jordan, the Syrian Arab Republic, West Bank and Gaza, the Republic of Yemen.

And the years that the surveys for each country were conducted in are as follows.

- 2006: Angola, Argentina, Bolivia, Botswana, Burundi, Chile, Colombia, Democratic Republic of the Congo, Ecuador, El Salvador, Ethiopia, The Gambia, Guatemala, Guinea, Guinea Bissau, Honduras, India, Jordan, Mauritania, Mexico, Namibia, Nicaragua, Panama, Paraguay, Peru, Rwanda, Swaziland, Tanzania,

Uganda, Uruguay, República Bolivariana de Venezuela, and the West Bank and Gaza.

- 2007: Albania, Algeria, Bangladesh, Croatia, Ghana, Kenya, Mali, Mozambique, Nigeria, Pakistan, Senegal, South Africa, and Zambia.
- 2008: Afghanistan, Belarus, Egypt, Georgia, Tajikistan, Turkey, Ukraine, and Uzbekistan.
- 2009: Armenia, Azerbaijan, Benin, Bhutan, Bosnia and Herzegovina, Brazil, Bulgaria, Burkina Faso, Cameroon, Cape Verde, Chad, Congo, Cote d'Ivoire, Czech Republic, Eritrea, Estonia, Fiji, FYR Macedonia, Gabon, Hungary, Indonesia, Kazakhstan, Kosovo, Kyrgyz Republic, Lao PDR, Latvia, Lesotho, Liberia, Lithuania, Madagascar, Malawi, Mauritius, Micronesia, Moldova, Mongolia, Montenegro, Nepal, Niger, Philippines, Poland, Romania, Russian Federation, Samoa, Serbia, Sierra Leone, Slovak Republic, Slovenia, the Syrian Arab Republic, Timor Leste, Togo, Tonga, Vanuatu, and Vietnam.
- 2010: the Republic of Yemen.

Table A1.1. Regression Controls: Summary of BEEPS-Based Control Variables

Firm Size: Small dummy	Assigned a value of 1 if the firm is a small firm (between 5 and 19 employees, inclusive), zero otherwise.
Firm Size: Medium dummy	Assigned a value of 1 if the firm is a medium firm (between 20 and 99 employees, inclusive), zero otherwise.
Firm Size: Large dummy	Assigned a value of 1 if the firm is a large firm (100 or more employees), zero otherwise.
Manufacturing sector dummy	A dummy variable indicating the firm operates in the manufacturing sector. The variable is assigned a value of 1 for yes, zero otherwise.
Service sector dummy	A dummy variable indicating the firm operates in the service sector. The variable is assigned a value of 1 for yes, zero otherwise.
Foreign-Owned dummy	Assigned a value of 1 if the firm is 10% foreign-owned or higher, zero otherwise.
Government-Owned dummy	Assigned a value of 1 if the firm is 10% state-owned or higher, zero otherwise.
Exporting Firm dummy	Assigned a value of 1 if the firm has any direct exports, zero otherwise.
Domestic competition	Importance of pressure from domestic competition in developing new products or services, based on BEEPS Q.63a.
Foreign competition	Importance of pressure from foreign competition in developing new products or services, based on BEEPS Q.63b.
Innovation dummy	Assigned a value of 1 if the responding firm answered yes to the question of "In the last three years, has this establishment introduced new products or services?" zero otherwise.
IT Use/Email	Assigned a value of 1 if the responding firm indicated that it uses email to communicate with customers or suppliers, zero otherwise.
Labor Growth dummy	A dummy variable indicating the firm expanded the number of full-time permanent employees from 2004 to 2007. The variable is assigned a value of 1 for yes, zero otherwise.
Education constraint	Firm perception of an inadequately educated labor force as a problem.
Training	Assigned a value of 1 if the responding firm provided training to its permanent full-time employees, zero otherwise.
Professionalism of Labor	The percentage of workers with a university degree (see Q.69).
Percentage of Skilled Labor	The percentage of skilled workers within a firm.
Percentage of Unskilled Labor	The percentage of unskilled workers within a firm
LN(GDP)	The natural log of GDP per capita at PPP in 2007 (in constant 2005 international dollars).
LN(age)	Natural log of the firm's age.

EU-10 dummy	Assigned a value of 1 if the firm is located in an EU-10 country, zero otherwise.
FSU-N dummy	Assigned a value of 1 if the firm is located in an FSU-N country, zero otherwise.
FSU-S dummy	Assigned a value of 1 if the firm is located in an FSU-S country, zero otherwise.
SEE dummy	Assigned a value of 1 if the firm is located in an SEE country, zero otherwise.
Country-specific dummies	A dummy for each country in the BEEPS 2008, based on the country in which the firm is located.
City-size dummies	A set of dummies for the locality size the firm is in, based on question a3 in the BEEPS 2008.

Chapter 2: Access to Finance

Figure Notes

Figure 2.1 presents the change in liquid liabilities as a share of GDP for various regions from 1996 to 2008. Source: World Bank Database of Financial Development and Structure. http://go.worldbank.org/X23UD9QUX0. Regions include the following countries:

- Europe and Central Asia: Albania, Armenia, Bulgaria, Croatia, Czech Republic, Estonia, Georgia, Hungary, Kazakhstan, Kyrgyz Republic, Latvia, Lithuania, Moldova, FYR Macedonia, Poland, Romania, Russian Federation, Serbia, Slovak Republic, Slovenia, and Turkey.
- East Asia and the Pacific: Cambodia, Fiji, Indonesia, Lao PDR, Malaysia, Mongolia, Myanmar, Papua New Guinea, Philippines, Samoa, Solomon Islands, Thailand, Timor-Leste, Tonga, Vanuatu, and Vietnam.
- Latin America and the Caribbean: Argentina, Belize, Bolivia, Brazil, Chile, Colombia, Costa Rica, Dominica, Dominican Republic, Ecuador, El Salvador, Grenada, Guatemala, Guyana, Haiti, Honduras, Jamaica, Mexico, Panama, Paraguay, Peru, St. Kitts and Nevis, St. Lucia, St. Vincent and Grenadines, Suriname, and Uruguay.
- Middle East and North Africa: Algeria, the Arab Republic of Egypt, the Islamic Republic of Iran, Jordan, Libya, Morocco, the Syrian Arab Republic, Tunisia, and the Republic of Yemen.
- South Asia: Bangladesh, Bhutan, India, Nepal, Pakistan, and Sri Lanka.
- Sub-Saharan Africa: Angola, Benin, Botswana, Burkina Faso, Burundi, Cameroon, Cape Verde, the Central African Republic, Chad, the Democratic Republic of Congo, the Republic of Congo, Côte d'Ivoire, Ethiopia, Gabon, the The Gambia, Ghana, Guinea-Bissau, Kenya, Lesotho, Madagascar, Malawi, Mali, Mauritania, Mauritius, Mozambique, Niger, Nigeria, Rwanda, Senegal, Seychelles, Sierra Leone, South Africa, Sudan, Swaziland, Tanzania, Togo, Uganda, and Zambia.

Figure 2.2 displays the percent of total banking sector assets that were held by foreign banks from 1996 to 2005 for various regions. Source: Claessens, Van Horen, Gurcanlar and Mercado, 2008. "Foreign Bank Presence in Developing Countries. 1995–2006: Data and Trends," mimeo, Washington, DC: The World Bank.

Regions include the following countries:

- Europe and Central Asia: Albania, Armenia, Azerbaijan, Belarus, Bosnia and Herzegovina, Bulgaria, Croatia, Czech Republic, Estonia, Georgia, Hungary, Kazakhstan, Kyrgyz Republic, Latvia, Lithuania, FYR Macedonia, Moldova, Poland, Romania, Russian Federation, Serbia, Slovak Republic, Slovenia, Turkey, Ukraine, and Uzbekistan.
- East Asia and the Pacific: Cambodia, China, Indonesia, Republic of Korea, Malaysia, Mongolia, Philippines, Thailand, and Vietnam.
- Latin America and the Caribbean: Argentina, Bolivia, Brazil, Chile, Colombia, Costa Rica, Cuba, Dominican Republic, Ecuador, El Salvador, Guatemala, Haiti, Honduras, Jamaica, Mexico, Nicaragua, Panama, Paraguay, Peru, Trinidad and Tobago, Uruguay, and República Bolivariana de Venezuela.
- Middle East and North Africa: Algeria, the Arab Republic of Egypt, the Islamic Republic of Iran, Jordan, Lebanon, Libya, Morocco, Oman, Tunisia, and the Republic of Yemen.
- South Asia: Bangladesh, India, Nepal, Pakistan, and Sri Lanka.
- Sub-Saharan Africa: Angola, Benin, Botswana, Burkina Faso, Burundi, Cameroon, the Democratic Republic of Congo, Côte d'Ivoire, Ethiopia, Ghana, Kenya, Madagascar, Malawi, Mali, Mauritania, Mauritius, Mozambique, Namibia, Niger, Nigeria, Rwanda, Senegal, Seychelles, South Africa, Sudan, Swaziland, Tanzania, Togo, Uganda, Zambia, and Zimbabwe.

Figure 2.3 presents regional averages from 1996 to 2008 of total credit provided to the private sector by banks and other financial institutions divided by GDP. Source: World Bank Database of Financial Development and Structure. http://go.worldbank.org/X23UD9QUX0. The country groupings match those of Figure 2.1.

Figure 2.4 presents regional averages from 1996 to 2008 of total foreign claims as a share of GDP on an immediate risk basis. The data was obtained from the Bank of International Settlements. Regional groupings are set up as follows:

- Europe and Central Asia: Albania, Armenia, Azerbaijan, Belarus, Bosnia and Herzegovina, Bulgaria, Croatia, Czech Republic, Estonia, Georgia, Hungary, Kazakhstan, Kyrgyz Republic, Latvia, Lithuania, FYR Macedonia, Moldova, Montenegro, Poland, Romania, Russian Federation, Serbia, Slovak Republic, Slovenia, Tajikistan, Turkey, Turkmenistan, Ukraine, and Uzbekistan.
- East Asia and the Pacific: Cambodia, China, Fiji, Indonesia, Kiribati, Lao PDR, Malaysia, Micronesia, Mongolia, Palau, Papua New Guinea, Philippines, Samoa, Solomon Islands, Thailand, Timor Leste, Tonga, Vanuatu, and Vietnam.
- Latin America and the Caribbean: Argentina, Belize, Bolivia, Brazil, Chile, Colombia, Costa Rica, Dominica, Dominican Republic, Ecuador, El Salvador, Grenada, Guatemala, Guyana, Haiti, Honduras, Jamaica, Mexico, Nicaragua, Panama, Paraguay, Peru, St. Lucia, St. Vincent, Surinam, Uruguay, and República Bolivariana de Venezuela.
- Middle East and North Africa: Algeria, Djibouti, the Arab Republic of Egypt, the Islamic Republic of Iran, Iraq, Jordan, Lebanon, Libya, Morocco, the Syrian Arab Republic, Tunisia, and the Republic of Yemen.
- South Asia: Afghanistan, Bangladesh, Bhutan, India, Maldives, Nepal, Pakistan, and Sri Lanka.

- Sub-Saharan Africa: Angola, Benin, Botswana, Burkina Faso, Burundi, Cameroon, Cape Verde, Central African Republic, Chad, Comoros Islands, Congo, the Democratic Republic of Congo, Côte d'Ivoire, Eritrea, Ethiopia, Gabon, The Gambia, Ghana, Guinea, Guinea Bissau, Kenya, Lesotho, Madagascar, Malawi, Mali, Mauritania, Mauritius, Mozambique, Namibia, Niger, Nigeria, Rwanda, São Tomé and Príncipe, Senegal, Seychelles, Sierra Leone, South Africa, Sudan, Swaziland, Tanzania, Togo, Uganda, Zambia, and Zimbabwe.

Figure B2.1.1 displays the correlation between the percentage change in credit to the private sector from 2004 to 2007, obtained from the World Bank Database of Financial Development and Structure. http://go.worldbank.org/X23UD9QUX0, and the GDP growth for each corresponding country in 2009 from the World Development Indicators data set. The correlation coefficient is −0.4831 and is significant at 0.027.

Figure B2.1.2 plots the relationship between the percentage change in foreign bank claims as a percent of GDP from 2004 to 2007, obtained from the Bank of International Settlements and the GDP growth for each corresponding country in 2009 from the World Development Indicators data set. The correlation coefficient is −0.43 and is significant at 0.025.

Figure 2.5 presents the percentage of firms indicating that access to finance was not an obstacle to doing business, by firm size. The figure is based on the panel data set covering the BEEPS 2002, 2005, and 2008.[1] The firm sizes are determined by the number of employees the firm has in the survey year, with small firms having 5–19 employees, medium firms having 20–99 employees, and large firms having 100 or more employees. The percentages are calculated as a simple division of the number of firms (of specific size) answering "no obstacle" to the access to finance as a problem question by the total number of firms of the same size answering that question (for each survey year).

Figure 2.6 presents the percentage of firms indicating that they applied for a loan or line of credit in the previous fiscal year, by firm size. The figure is based on the panel data set covering the BEEPS 2002, 2005, and 2008. The firm sizes are determined by the number of employees the firm has in the survey year, with small firms having 5–19 employees, medium firms having 20–99 employees, and large firms having 100 or more employees. The percentages are calculated as a simple division of the number of firms (of specific size) stating that they applied for a loan or line of credit in the last fiscal year by the total number of firms of the same size answering that question (for each survey year).

Figure 2.7 compares the predicted probabilities that a firm would indicate that access to finance was not an obstacle to doing business, by level of foreign ownership of banking sector assets across the BEEPS survey years. The figure is based on the panel data set covering the BEEPS 2002, 2005 and 2008. The level of foreign ownership categories are defined as low if the level of foreign ownership in 1999 was less than 20 percent, medium

1. The question wording for access to finance as an obstacle in 2002 and 2005 is as follows: Can you tell me how problematic are these different factors for the operation and growth of your business? Access to financing (e.g., collateral required or financing not available from banks) (No obstacle=1 Minor obstacle=2 Moderate obstacle=3 Major obstacle=4).

if the level was greater than or equal to 20 percent and less than 60 percent, and large if the level was 60 percent or higher. The probabilities are calculated based on Table A1.3, model 2, with all variables assigned their mean values except for the level of foreign ownership.

Figure 2.8 compares the predicted probabilities that a firm will apply for a loan, by level of foreign ownership of banking sector assets across the BEEPS survey years. The figure is based on the panel data set covering the BEEPS 2002, 2005, and 2008. The level of foreign ownership categories are defined in the same way as in Figure 2.7. The probabilities are calculated based on Table A1.3, model 3.

Figure 2.9 presents the predicted probability that a firm will indicate access to finance is not an obstacle to doing business, by the level of the current account deficit of the country that the firm is located in for countries with a fixed exchange rate regime, across BEEPS survey years. The figure is based on the panel data set covering the BEEPS 2002, 2005 and 2008. The probability calculations are based on Table A1.3, model 2 and current account deficit levels are assigned such that low current account deficits correspond to 0–4 percent of GDP, medium to 4–8 percent, and high to above 8 percent. All other variables are assigned their mean values.

Figure 2.10 presents the same relationship as Figure 2.9, but for countries that use a crawling exchange rate regime. The figure is based on the panel data set covering the BEEPS 2002, 2005, and 2008. The probability calculations are based on Table A1.3, model 2 and current account deficit levels are assigned as in Figure 2.9. All other variables are assigned their mean values.

Figure 2.11 presents the predicted probability that a firm will apply for a loan, by the level of the current account deficit of the country that the firm is located, across BEEPS survey years. The figure is based on the panel data set covering the BEEPS 2002, 2005, and 2008. The probability calculations are based on Table A1.3, model 3 and current account deficit levels are assigned as in Figure 2.9.

Figure 2.12 shows the relationship between firm size and the predicted probability of firm survival. Shorter bars correspond to a lower likelihood that a firm will cease operations. Data is based on the regression model discussed in the firm survival regression results section.

Figure 2.13 shows the relation between firm age and the predicted probability of firm survival. Shorter bars correspond to a lower likelihood that a firm will cease operations. Data is based on the regression model discussed in the firm survival regression results section.

Table 2.1 data comes from the following: Percentage of assets held by foreign banks comes from Claessens et al. (2008). WGI indicators are from the World Bank Governance Indicators database. GDP per capita is from the World Development Indicators (World Bank). Banking and crisis data were taken from Caprio and Klingebiel (2003), "Database on Episodes of Systemic and Broderline Financial Crises" at http://go.worldbank.org/5DYGICS7B0. Legal origin variables are taken from La Porta et al. (1999).

Empirical Analysis

Two types of empirical analyses were conducted to explain the relative severity of the recent global economic crisis across firms in the ECA region. As described above, the first exploits data on whether firms survived from the follow-ups to the 2008 BEEPS surveys conducted in June and July 2009 in six countries. The second exploits variation over time in firms' reported financial constraints for a balanced panel of respondents to the 2002, 2005, and 2008 BEEPS surveys. For both types of analysis, the basic regression is:

$$Y_{it} = \alpha + \beta X_{it} + \gamma F_{it} + \delta C_{it} + \lambda S_{it} + \mu T_i + \varepsilon_{it}$$

Where Y is a dummy variable = 1 if a firm died for the survival analysis,[2] or a dummy variable = 1 if the firm owner reported that access to finance was not an obstacle to its operations for the financial constraints analysis. Note that the survival analysis is cross-sectional because information on whether a firm survived was available at only one point in time (mid-2009). The subscript "t" therefore is relevant only for the analysis of perceived financial constraints.

X represents a matrix of firm characteristics that includes the number of employees, the age of the firm, exports as a percent of sales, the shares of foreign and private ownership, and a dummy variable indicating whether the firm was privatized. In some specifications, a control variable capturing ISO certification was added as an additional measure of firm quality. It was expected that all of these variables would help to relax firms' financial constraints and improve their prospects for surviving the crisis.

In the financial constraints regressions, firm size, as measured by the number of employees, was interacted with the year of the survey to test whether large firms were differentially affected by the crisis relative to small and medium-sized firms. For the reasons described above, it was expected that larger firms would have better access to external finance in non-crisis periods (2002 and 2005) and thus report less severe constraints, and become more constrained in the crisis (2008) due to their reliance on dwindling sources of external funding.

The X matrix also includes measures of firm performance including employment growth and a dummy variable indicating whether the firm made investments in the prior year. Unfortunately, only the employment growth variable is available in a consistent format across the three rounds of the BEEPS. It is therefore the only firm performance variable that enters the financial constraints regressions. The full set of performance variables enters the survival regressions.

2. The 2,501 firms from the third round of the BEEPS survey can be divided into four groups: (i) those that were still operating and were interviewed in the follow-up survey; (ii) those that were still operating but were not interviewed during the follow-up survey because enough firms had been interviewed, an interview could not be scheduled, or the firm manager refused to participate in the survey; (iii) firms that could not be located; and (iv) firms that had closed. The approach of Ramalho et al. (2010) is employed it is assumed that firms were no longer operating if they fell into categories (iii) or (iv), or if they were in category (i) but reported that they had filed for insolvency or bankruptcy. Firms that could not be located because they had temporarily shut down, rather than closed permanently, are implicitly included in the category of firms that are no longer operating. This classification carries some limitations—some firms that could not be located might have had contact information recorded incorrectly during the BEEPS survey and some firms that were still operating but were not interviewed might have filed for insolvency or bankruptcy. However, it is probably the most reasonable breakdown possible given the available information.

To ensure that firms that were no longer operating at the time of the second survey can be included in the survival regressions, the firm characteristics are all taken from the original BEEPS survey (2008). An additional advantage of this approach is that it reduces the likelihood of reverse causality. One particular concern is that firm performance is likely to have been affected by the crisis and those affected most seriously are also most likely to be forced to close during the crisis. To reduce these concerns, where possible, variables such as firm size and growth are measured in fiscal year 2007 or earlier.

F represents of matrix of variables that summarize firms' use of financial services. These are particularly relevant for the firm survival regressions. All else equal, firms that had readier access to finance are expected to be more likely to survive. Although having access to finance would not affect firms that were basically insolvent, it might allow firms that have temporary liquidity problems due to the drop in demand to survive the crisis. To reduce concerns about reverse causation, measures of access to finance prior to the crisis would be ideal. Unfortunately, the two best measures in the survey—whether the firm has a loan and whether the firm has a line of credit or overdraft—were asked 'at the current time' (i.e., at the time of the survey). Since the surveys were mostly conducted between September and December of 2008, these questions were asked after the onset of the crisis. To the extent that banks either extended loans or overdrafts to firms that they believed had long-term potential if they could survive temporary liquidity problems or ended lines of credit or loans for firms that they believed were the most likely to fail during the crisis, this could affect estimates. Still, it is likely that a large share of the repercussions of the crisis in terms of access to credit for firms in ECA were yet to be felt at the time of the last round of the BEEPS survey.

Because the financial constraints regressions are designed to summarize firms' access to financial services, this set of variables represented by F is obviously less relevant, though in some specifications a dummy variable for whether the firm applied for a loan in the past year was included to control for its demand for finance.

C represents a matrix of country characteristics. Because the survival analysis is based on a cross-section and because the FCS was done in only six countries, it is not possible to include a full set of country-level controls in those regressions, and so country dummy variables were included instead. Because the BEEPS data offer time series variation and cover a much broader set of countries, a rich set of country-level variables in the financial constraints regressions are able to be included. These include GDP per capita, the WGI index of institutional development,[3] inflation, and GDP growth. All except inflation are likely to be associated with less severe financial constraints. Population and population-density were included in the constraints regressions, though it is less clear how those variables are expected to affect financial constraints. The GDP growth variable was interacted with dummy variables for the year of the survey to test whether that variable had differential effects on financial constraints in crisis and non-crisis years, in line with some predictions from the literature.

3. This is the measure of broad institutional development created by Kaufmann, Kraay, and Maztruzzi (2007).

The country variables also include the share of banking sector assets in state-owned and foreign owned banks. For the reasons described above, and elaborated on in Chapter 2, the foreign bank participation variable is measured in 1999. That variable was then interacted with year dummies to test whether well-established foreign banks helped firms to weather the crisis as reflected in less severe financial constraints compared with those of firms in countries that did not have well-established foreign presence in banking.

Finally, controls were introduced for each country's exchange rate regime with dummy variables for pegged and crawling exchange rates. The coefficients on those variables reflect differences in constraints relative to the omitted category, firms in countries with floating exchange rates. For the reasons described above, the combination of large current account deficits and exchange rates based on fixed or crawling pegs coincided with explosive credit growth in the run-up to the crisis. Therefore, interaction of the exchange rate regime dummy variables with the current account deficit were introduced to test whether the coefficients on those variables indicate looser financial constraints prior to the crisis (2002 and 2005) and steep increases in constraints in 2008.

S is a matrix of sector dummy variables because financial constraints and the probability of survival could vary across industries. T represents variables that control for the timing of surveys. In the case of the financial constraints, these are simple dummy variables corresponding to the round of the survey. For the survival analysis, time dummies indicating the month that the firm was surveyed in the 2008 BEEPS survey were also used. Although the FCS were conducted within a tight two-month window (June and July 2009), most of the 2008 BEEPS were conducted over a three to six month period in individual countries. The dummies indicating the month of the 2008 BEEPS are included to partially control for differences in survival possibilities for firms interviewed before the global crisis and those interviewed in the early part of the crisis.

The timing of the 2008 BEEPS survey was introduced in a simple cross-sectional regression of the 2008 financial constraints, though it was not significant. This could be because perceptions of financial constraints are forward looking and thus all respondents had a good sense of the coming crisis, regardless of the month in which they were interviewed. In any event, the month of 2008 survey was not controlled for in the financial constraints regressions presented below. Both types of regressions are estimated via a standard Probit model.

Regression Results

Firm Survival

Base Results. Table A1.2 shows the results from the base regressions. The results in column 1 omit the financial sector variables. The coefficients on the variables indicating firm size at the end of 2007 and the age of the firm are both statistically significant and negative. This suggests that larger firms and older firms were more likely to be operating at the time of the second survey than other firms. Based upon the coefficient estimates and estimating the effects at sample means of all variables, increasing the number of workers by 10 reduces the likelihood that the firm is no longer operating by about

0.1 percentage points. Similarly, increasing age by 1 year reduces the likelihood by 0.4 percentage points. Firms that had ISO or other international certifications were about 4 percentage points less likely to be no longer operating—suggesting that firms attuned to international standards might have been more likely to survive.

Inclusion of financial variables. Including a dummy variable (model 2, Table A1.2) indicating that the firm had either a loan or an overdraft at the time of the first interview (i.e., in 2008 or early 2009) does not have a notable effect on most of the other variables. In particular, the coefficients on the variables representing the age of the firm and whether the firm has ISO certification remain negative and statistically significant. In contrast, the coefficient on the variable representing the size of the firm becomes smaller and becomes statistically insignificant. This suggests that one reason why large firms might have fared better in terms of surviving is that they had better access to finance than smaller firms did, in line with the literature described above.

The coefficient on the dummy variable representing whether the firm has a loan, line of credit or overdraft is negative and statistically significant. The coefficient suggests that firms with loans or overdrafts were about 4 percentage points more likely to still be operating in mid-2009 than firms without. This suggests that retaining access to financing was important for survival. Given that the most common concern about the impact of the crisis on firm performance was the effect of a drop in demand, one explanation is that firms with access to finance were better able to maintain access to external sources for replenishment of working capital and to manage the drop in demand than firms that were not.

Given that overdrafts and lines of credit might be better for financing working capital and other expenses during a temporary drop in demand, it is worthwhile to separate the variable into two components: whether the firm has a loan and whether it has an overdraft or line of credit. Although there is considerable overlap between these categories—about 73 percent of firms in the sample with overdrafts had loans compared to 40 percent of firms without overdrafts—potentially leading to multicollinearity, the differences in the estimated coefficients could be instructive.

The coefficients in model 3 (Table A1.2) confirm the intuition in that the marginal effect of the dummy variable indicating that the firm has an overdraft is larger and more highly statistically significant than on the dummy variable indicating that the firm has a loan. However, the coefficient is smaller and less statistically significant than that on the joint variable. Results for the overdraft variable by itself, moreover, tend to be less robust than for the combined variable.

Performance Variables. One concern is that better performing firms might be more likely to survive the crisis and to have bank credit. Because of this, included is a set of variables intended to measure firm performance: a dummy variable indicating that the firm invested in fixed assets in 2007, and employment growth between 2005 and 2007. As noted above, these performance metrics are measured before the start of the crisis. The coefficients on these variables are mostly statistically insignificant (model 4, Table A1.2) and do not appear to have a significant impact on the other results. The main exception is that the coefficient on firm size becomes smaller and even less statistically significant. In contrast, the coefficient on the dummy variable indicating that the firm had access to credit becomes slightly larger (in absolute value) and remains statistically significant.

Financial Constraints

Firm Characteristics. In an unreported regression that does not include interactions (for firm size, GDP growth, foreign bank participation in 1999, and exchange rate regimes), the likelihood of reporting finance is no obstacle is highest in 2005 (i.e., there are negative coefficients for 2002 and 2008). This is encouraging in that the dependent variable is picking up both the easing of financial constraints from 2002 to 2005 and the effects of the crisis from 2005 to 2008. When the interaction terms are included, the coefficients for the simple year dummies (2002, 2008) are no longer significant (model 1, Table A1.3). In that sense, the interaction terms are isolating the types of firms responsible for the negative coefficients on the year dummies in the simpler unreported models.

The key firm characteristic in the financial constraints analysis is size. As suggested by Figure 2.1 and for the reasons described above, it is expected that the effect of firm size will be discontinuous—since large firms had much better access to external sources of funding, they were more vulnerable to a credit crunch. Rather than use the continuous size variable based on number of workers (as was done in the analysis of firm survival), dummy variables corresponding the BEEPS definitions of small, medium, and large firms: <=19 workers, 20–99 workers, and >=100 workers are used, respectively. The omitted category in the regressions is small firms, and thus the insignificant coefficient for medium-sized firms indicates no significant difference in financial constraints across those two groups (Table A1.3, model 1). The model interacts the dummy variable for large firms with dummies for the 2005 and 2008 BEEPS. Thus the positive significant coefficient for the large firms dummy indicates that they were much more likely than smaller firms to report finance as being no obstacle in 2002. Large firms were still more likely to report finance as no obstacle in 2005 as reflected in the insignificant coefficient on Large*2005. However, the coefficient for large firms in 2008 is negative and of a magnitude similar to that for the large firm dummy. To calculate the effects of large size on "finance as an obstacle" in 2008 the 'Large size' and 'Large*2008' coefficients must be summed. Doing so wipes out the advantage of being a large firm that was evident for 2002 and 2005, that is, the hypothesis that sum of the two coefficients is zero for large firms in 2009 cannot be rejected. This confirms Figure 2.1, where large firms come to look a lot more like the others in terms of reported financial constraints in 2008. The external financing patterns of large firms, therefore, could be seen as being more affected by the crisis.

This pattern only becomes stronger when a dummy indicating that the firm had applied for a loan in the past year to control for its demand for credit is included (Table A1.3, model 2). In fact, the coefficient for Large*2008 is negative and significant. The applied for a loan variable is itself negative and highly significant and improves the overall fit of the regression (pseudo r-squared improves from 0.07 to 0.10). In model 3 (in Table A1.3), the dependent variable is the 'applied for a loan' dummy, to get a sense of which firms came to demand more credit during the crisis. The results indicate that large firms were much more likely to apply for credit in 2002 than others, a gap that was maintained in 2005. That gap grew significantly larger in 2008 as reflected in the positive significant coefficient on Large*2008, indicating that large firms were much more apt than others to apply for external sources of funding in response to the dramatic drop in demand documented in Correa and Iootty (2009, 2010). Taken together, the steep decline in the share of large firms that reported finance was not an obstacle to their firms' operations in 2008 and the steep increase in the share of large firms applying for loans shows that they were the firms most affected by crisis. None of the other firm characteristics is significant in the financial constraints regressions (though some of them are in the loan application regression).

Country Characteristics. Based on the literature on multinational banking, it is conjectured that the crisis might have compelled foreign banks to pull back from countries where growth prospects were weak if the substitution motive dominated (Morgan et al., 2004). To test this hypothesis GDP growth is interacted with the dummy variables for the BEEPS rounds. If this conjecture were true, it is expected that the coefficient for GDP growth*2008 will be positive and significant, but it is not. Insignificance could arise for a number of different reasons. As described above, multinational banks have both substitution and support motives in assigning funds across affiliates in developing countries. Insignificance could arise because those motives cancel each other out, which could also account for the insignificant coefficients in the non-crisis years (2002, 2005). Another possible explanation may be that information about future growth prospects at a country level is already subsumed within the foreign bank participation variable or that current growth is not a strong predictor of future growth, especially during crisis (although other papers have found links between host country growth and foreign bank participation). If anything, the negative, nearly significant (p-value, 0.188) coefficient for GDP growth in 1999 provides some weak evidence for the support motive, in line with other findings on the stabilizing effects of foreign bank participation during crises (de Haas and Van Lelyveld, 2006, 2010).

Population density is the only other variable among the country characteristics that is significant in the financial constraints regressions (though again, there are some significant country variables in the loan application regression). The negative, significant coefficient for population density in model 1 (Table A1.3) goes away when the loan application dummy is included in the regression in model 2 (Table A1.3), suggesting that greater reported financial obstacles in densely populated countries are due to greater demand for external sources of funds. The general insignificance of the country level variables in the financial constraints regressions might also arise because correlation between errors at the country level is allowed (i.e., clustered standard errors are used).

Banking Sector Variables. State ownership of banking sector assets is not significantly associated with either reported financial constraints or loan applications in Table A1.3. However, the key banking sector variable is the share of banking sector assets held by foreign-owned banks in 1999, which we interact with the dummy variables for the latter two survey rounds of the BEEPS (2005, 2008). The negative, significant coefficient for foreign participation level in 1999 therefore represents the effects of that variable on the 2002 responses, indicating that financial constraints were more severe, at that time, in countries with greater foreign participation. The positive, significant coefficient for 1999 foreign bank participation share multiplied by the BEEPS 2005 dummy is of similar magnitude to the negative association for 2002, indicating that by 2005 constraints were similar across countries regardless of their level of foreign bank participation in 1999. However, the interaction term for the 2008 BEEPS is positive, significant, and twice as large (in absolute value) as the negative association for 2005, which indicates that financial constraints were substantially less severe during the crisis in countries with a high-level foreign bank participation in 1999. The pattern of results is robust to using different measures of foreign bank participation and different years between 1999 and 2002.[44]

For the reasons described above, and analyzed in greater detail in the next section, foreign bank participation level in 1999 is viewed as an indicator of well-established presence and commitment to a local market. The pattern of results is therefore supportive of the hypothesis that reported obstacles were much less severe during the early stages of the economic crisis in countries with high foreign bank participation levels. The results also do not support the hypothesis that the increase in reported financial constraints would be less severe in countries with well-established foreign bank participation. But this is because reported constraints are less severe in 2008 than they were in 2005 and, especially, 2002 in countries with such participation. This suggests that foreign banks had entered relatively credit-starved countries seeking profit opportunities and were trying to meet that demand in 2002. Demand was being better met by 2005 in that constraints were on par with other countries in the region, and by 2008, constraints were less severe than ever despite the crisis. The loan application regression (model 3 in Table A1.3) also indicates that demand was highest in countries with a high level of foreign participation in 2002, and then dropped to levels prevalent in the region in 2005 and 2008, consistent with demand for credit being better met over time in countries with a well-established foreign bank presence.

It must be acknowledged that, although the signs of the coefficients for the foreign participation variables are identical when these regressions are run on the full BEEPS sample, magnitudes and significance levels are smaller than for the balanced panel of BEEPS respondents. It should therefore be kept in mind that these results hold for a sample that differs slightly from the full one in that the firms come from smaller countries on average with a greater tendency toward fixed rather than floating exchange rate regimes, and have a slightly higher degree of foreign ownership and greater likelihood of being in the trade industry.

4. We use the 1999 share of total banking assets held by foreign-owned banks from Claessens and Van Horen (2008). We derive similar results when we use the foreign claims on the countries in the ECA region (as a share of GDP) as reported by the Bank for International Settlements.

Table A1.2. Results from Probit Regression of Firm Exit on Enterprise Characteristics

	Firm no longer operating at time of the FCS survey			
Model number	**(1)**	**(2)**	**(3)**	**(4)**
Observations	**2203**	**2174**	**2138**	**1699**
Country Dummies	Yes	Yes	Yes	Yes
Sector Dummies	Yes	Yes	Yes	Yes
Month of Interview Dummies	Yes	Yes	Yes	Yes
Bank Credit				
Firm has loan, line of credit or overdraft		−0.038**		−0.048***
(dummy)		(−2.49)		(−2.66)
Firm has line of credit or overdraft			−0.030**	
(dummy)			(−2.01)	
Firm has loan			−0.004	
(dummy)			(−0.30)	
Firm Characteristics				
Number of workers	−0.011**	−0.009	−0.009*	−0.007
(natural log)	(−2.05)	(−1.57)	(−1.71)	(−1.03)
Age of firm	−0.041***	−0.041***	−0.040***	−0.028*
(natural log)	(−4.35)	(−4.26)	(−4.13)	(−1.85)
Exports	0	0	0	0
(% of sales)	(−0.52)	(−0.68)	(−0.85)	(−0.27)
Foreign-owned	0.009	0.005	0.012	−0.034
(dummy)	−0.34	−0.2	−0.46	(−1.23)
Firm has ISO certification	−0.039***	−0.037**	−0.037**	−0.043**
(dummy)	(−2.58)	(−2.48)	(−2.47)	(−2.52)
Firm Performance				
Firm Growth 2005-2007				0
(employment growth, %)				(−0.8)
Firm invested in 2007				−0.004
(dummy)				(−0.22)
Joint test for significance of overdraft and loan variables			5	
P-value			0.08	
Pseudo R-Squared	0.07	0.07	0.07	0.06

Source: Authors' calculations based upon World Bank Enterprise Surveys
Note: ***,**,* Significant at 1, 5, and 10 percent level. t-statistics in parentheses. All regressions include dummy variables indicating sector, country, and month of first interview (i.e., in 2008 or early 2009). Marginal effects calculated at sample means for each variable are shown in place of coefficients. The dependent variable is dummy variable indicating a firm in existence in late 2008/early 2009 was no longer operating at the time of the FCS second survey.

Table A1.3. Probit Models, Financial Constraints Analysis

	Dependent Var =1 if finance is no obstacle		Dep. Var = 1 if applied for loan
Model number	**(1)**	**(2)**	**(3)**
Applied for Loan		-0.384***	
		(0.066)	
2002	0.117	-0.096	-0.088
	(0.199)	(0.306)	(0.441)
2008	-0.142	-0.066	0.165
	(0.320)	(0.271)	(0.288)
Firm Characteristics			
Medium size	0.071	0.172	0.655***
	(0.110)	(0.156)	(0.119)
Large size	0.390*	0.628**	0.801***
	(0.233)	(0.251)	(0.260)
Large*2005	0.047	0.002	-0.032
	(0.244)	(0.307)	(0.289)
Large*2008	-0.421	-0.484*	0.617*
	(0.258)	(0.247)	(0.342)
Firm Age	-0.062	0.003	-0.054
(natural log)	(0.092)	(0.126)	(0.085)
% Employment Growth	-0.008	-0.001	0.114*
	(0.049)	(0.047)	(0.069)
% Private Owned	-0.001	-0.001	0.010***
	(0.002)	(0.003)	(0.002)
% Foreign Owned	0.001	0.0004	0.004
	(0.002)	(0.003)	(0.004)
Privatized	0.063	0.086	-0.206**
	(0.157)	(0.179)	(0.097)
Export Share	-0.001	0.0001	0.003
	(0.003)	(0.003)	(0.003)
Country Characteristics			
GDP Growth*2002	-0.035	0.004	-0.053
	(0.036)	(0.055)	(0.054)
GDP Growth*2005	0.023	-0.017	-0.045
	(0.016)	(0.020)	(0.034)
GDP Growth*2008	-0.030	-0.030	0.008
	(0.024)	(0.023)	(0.023)

(Table continues on next page)

Table A1.3 (continued)

	Dependent Var =1 if finance is no obstacle		Dep. Var = 1 if applied for loan
Model number	**(1)**	**(2)**	**(3)**
GDP Per Capita	0.007	0.026	0.145***
(1000s)	(0.032)	(0.026)	(0.036)
WGI Instit. Develop.	0.207	0.152	-0.686***
	(0.217)	(0.189)	(0.216)
Population Density	-0.005***	-0.003	0.004**
	(0.002)	(0.002)	(0.002)
Population (millions)	-0.0003	-0.0003	0.002
	(0.014)	(0.017)	(0.002)
Inflation	0.001	-0.004	-0.021**
	(0.005)	(0.006)	(0.009)
Banking Sector			
% State Bank Assets	0.001	0.001	0.0001
	(0.003)	(0.004)	(0.003)
% Foreign in 1999	-0.006*	-0.007**	0.013***
	(0.003)	(0.003)	(0.004)
% Foreign1999*2005	0.007**	0.006	-0.014**
	(0.003)	(0.004)	(0.006)
% Foreign1999*2008	0.013***	0.012***	-0.016***
	(0.003)	(0.003)	(0.005)
Exchange Rate Regime			
Fixed Peg*current account	0.023	0.023	-0.003
deficit*2002	(0.017)	(0.027)	(0.036)
Fixed Peg*current account	0.068***	0.082***	0.087***
deficit*2005	(0.014)	(0.020)	(0.029)
Fixed Peg*current account	0.006	0.010*	0.026***
deficit*2008	(0.005)	(0.005)	(0.008)
Crawling*current account	0.062**	0.053*	-0.066
deficit*2002	(0.029)	(0.029)	(0.047)
Crawling*current account	0.044**	0.064**	0.093**
deficit*2005	(0.018)	(0.031)	(0.038)
Crawling*current account	0.003	0.006	0.024**
deficit*2008	(0.011)	(0.010)	(0.010)
Sector Dummies	Yes	Yes	Yes
Observations	920	731	748
Pseudo R-squared	0.07	0.10	0.16

Note: Robust standard errors in parentheses. Errors clustered at country level.
Note: ***,**, * Significant at 1, 5, and 10 percent level.

Table A1.4. Comparison of Balanced BEEPS Panel and Full Sample, BEEPS 2002, 2005, and 2008

	Balanced Panel					Full BEEPS Sample		
Variable	**Obs.**	**Mean**	**St. Dev.**	**Min**	**Max**	**Obs.**	**Mean**	**St. Dev.**
Finance No Obstacle (dummy)	920	0.35	0.48	0	1	22340	0.34	0.47
Small Firms (<=19 workers)	920	0.50	0.50	0	1	22340	0.47	0.50
Medium Firms (20-99 workers)	920	0.32	0.47	0	1	22340	0.32	0.46
Large Firms (>=100 workers)	920	0.18	0.38	0	1	22340	0.22	0.41
Firm Age (Years)	920	16.6	16.8	1	141	22340	15.6	16.4
Employment Growth (%)	920	24.0	96.7	-96.7	1400	22340	33.9	220.8
Private ownership share (%)	920	79.0	38.1	0	100	22340	82.5	35.7
Foreign ownership share (%)	920	12.8	30.9	0	100	22340	9.2	26.6
Privatized (dummy)	920	0.23	0.42	0	1	22340	0.14	0.35
Exports as a % of sales	920	10.1	24.1	0	100	22340	10.5	24.8
GDP Growth %	920	5.8	4.6	-4.6	26.4	22340	5.8	4.0
GDP per capita (1000s $US 2002)	920	3.2	3.1	0.3	13.7	22340	3.4	2.5
% of banking assets in state banks	920	14.7	20.6	0.0	75.2	22340	18.6	20.4
% of banking assets, foreign banks 1999	920	31.6	30.1	0.0	92.3	22340	31.4	28.5
WGI, Institutional development	920	-0.02	0.66	-1.06	1.04	22340	-0.001	0.61
Population density, residents per sq .mile	920	76.3	32.2	5.5	135.0	22340	77.1	38.3
Population (millions)	920	12.4	21.5	1.3	145.0	22340	28.4	40.0
Inflation (%)	920	9.1	9.6	0.2	53.4	22340	9.4	8.5
Hotel, Services Industry (dummy)	920	0.13	0.34	0	1	22340	0.14	0.35
Construction Industry (dummy)	920	0.13	0.33	0	1	22340	0.09	0.29
Trade Industry (dummy)	920	0.37	0.48	0	1	22340	0.26	0.44
Transport Industry (dummy)	920	0.06	0.24	0	1	22340	0.06	0.23
Manufacturing Industry (dummy)	920	0.30	0.46	0	1	22340	0.40	0.50
Pegged Exchanged Rate (dummy)	920	0.36	0.48	0	1	22340	0.22	0.42
Crawling Peg Exch. Rate (dummy)	920	0.53	0.50	0	1	22340	0.54	0.50
Band, Managed floating Ex. Rate (dummy)	920	0.09	0.29	0	1	22340	0.16	0.37
Current Account Deficit as % GDP	920	7.0	6.2	0.0	25.2	22340	6.6	6.5

Chapter 3: Infrastructure Bottlenecks

Data Notes

Calculated Variables

Power outage costs. There are two methods to calculate the costs incurred from power outages, which are presented throughout the paper and used in the regression analyses. Both methods rely on answers to the questions c9a (losses from power outages as a percentage of annual sales) and c9b (annual losses from power outages in terms of local currency units (LCU)), but they differ in which firms are included. The first method, which is used to calculate regional averages, considers only firms that experienced a power outage in the previous year. The value for the costs of power outages is set to c9a, if this is unavailable then the cost is set to c9b as a share of the firm's sales (in LCU) for the previous year. The second method, whose resulting values are used in regressions, is nearly identical except that it considers all firms. It uses the same methodology to calculate outage costs from firm responses to c9a and c9b, but it assigns zero as the outage cost to those firms that did not experience a power outage in the previous year (in contrast to being left a missing value as in the first method).

Labor Productivity is the ratio of a firm's total annual sales (as given by question d2 and converted to U.S. dollars) to its number of employees. The number of employees is determined as a sum of the answers to questions l1 (the number of permanent full-time employees) and l6 (the number of temporary full-time employees).

Figure Notes

For figures using Enterprise Surveys data, refer to the Note on Regional and Subregional Averages at the beginning of Appendix 1.

Figure 3.1 presents the differences in electricity as not an obstacle to doing business between 2005 and 2008. Upward arrows reflect positive change as they indicate an increase in the percentage of firms stating electricity is not a problem. The downward arrows indicate negative change. The base of the arrow indicates the value in 2005, while the black lines indicate the 2008 value. Both values are based on the truncated samples.

Figure 3.2 compares electricity not an obstacle across the World Bank regions and ECA subregions. The figure uses BEEPS 2008 data for ECA countries and data from Enterprise Surveys covering 2006–2010 for non-ECA countries to present the average number of firms, by region, that indicate electricity is not an obstacle to doing business. Within each region, country-level averages are calculated and then the regional average is calculated as the simple mean of these country-level values. Higher values indicate that electricity is less of an obstacle within the region.

Figure 3.3 presents the correlation between power outages and the natural log of GDP per capita (2007). The vertical axis is the percentage of firms that experienced a power outage in 2007 based on the BEEPS 2008. The underlying GDP per capita values are on a purchasing power parity basis (in constant 2005 international dollars), from the World Bank's World Development Indicators data set. The coefficient of correlation is -0.397 and is significant at 0.033.

Figure 3.4 compares the percentage of firms that experienced electrical outages in the previous year across regions. The regional means are based on data from the BEEPS 2008 for ECA regions and subregions, and Enterprise Surveys data for non-ECA countries that covers the period 2006–2010. Within each region, country-level averages are calculated and then the regional average is calculated as the simple mean of these country-level values.

Figure 3.5 displays the average percentage of sales lost due to power outages by country for ECA, based on the BEEPS 2008 data.

Figure 3.6 shows country-level averages for power outage losses within ECA by income classification. Countries are assigned to an income classification based on the 2009 World Bank Income Classifications.

Figure 3.7 presents the percentage of firms owning or sharing a generator by various firm characteristics for manufacturing firms. Using the non-weighted BEEPS 2008 data for each of the categories (R&D, Exports, Ownership, and Innovation), a simple mean is taken of the generator ownership dummy.

Figure 3.8 presents the differences in telecommunications as not an obstacle to doing business between 2005 and 2008. Upward arrows reflect positive change as they indicate an increase in the percentage of firms stating telecommunications is not a problem. The downward arrows indicate negative change. The base of the arrow indicates the value in 2005, while the black lines indicate the 2008 value. Both values are based on the truncated samples.

Figure 3.9 presents the correlation between email use and GDP. The vertical axis is the percentage of firms that use email as calculated from the BEEPS 2008. The horizontal axis shows the natural log of 2007 GDP per capita values on a purchasing power parity basis (in 2005 constant international dollars), as taken from the World Bank's World Development Indicators data set. The coefficient of correlation is 0.8469 and is significant at 0.000.

Figure 3.10 presents the correlation between email use and labor productivity. The vertical axis is the percentage of firms that use email and the horizontal axis is the natural log of labor productivity (see above note on labor productivity). Each is based on the BEEPS 2008. The coefficient of correlation is 0.8489 and is significant at 0.000.

Figure 3.11 depicts the relation between power outage costs from the BEEPS 2008 and the government effectiveness indicator as determined by WGI (2000–2008). The levels for these values were calculated such that a "medium" level is any score within one standard deviation of the mean score. Scores below this range were classified as "low" and scores above this range were classified as "high." Higher values represent larger costs to firms due to power outages.

Figure 3.12 depicts the relation between power outage costs from the BEEPS 2008 and the government corruption indicator as determined by WGI (2000–2008). The levels for these values were calculated such that a "medium" level is any score within one standard deviation of the mean score. Scores below this range were classified as "low" and scores above this range were classified as "high." Higher values represent larger costs to firms due to power outages.

Figure 3.13 depicts the relation between access to high-speed Internet from the BEEPS 2008 and the government effectiveness indicator as determined by WGI (2000–2008). The levels for these values were calculated such that a "medium" level is any score within one standard deviation of the mean score. Scores below this range were classified as "low" and scores above this range were classified as "high." Higher values (longer bars) represent a higher percentage of firms with access to high-speed Internet.

Figure 3.14 depicts the relation between access to high-speed Internet from the BEEPS 2008 and the government corruption indicator as determined by WGI. The levels for these values were calculated such that a "medium" level is any score within one standard deviation of the mean score. Scores below this range were classified as "low" and scores above this range were classified as "high." Higher values (longer bars) represent a higher percentage of firms with access to high-speed Internet.

Figure B3.3.1 presents the differences in transport as not an obstacle to doing business between 2005 and 2008. Upward arrows reflect positive change as they indicate an increase in the percentage of firms stating transport is not a problem. The downward arrows indicate negative change. The base of the arrow indicates the value in 2005, while the black lines indicate the 2008 value. Both values are based on the truncated samples.

Regression Results

Complementary Regressions

Tables A1.5, A1.7, A1.10, and A1.11 are based on results from complementary regressions on labor productivity. Complementary regressions are set up such that the costs of electrical outages (or other variable of interest, such as government effectiveness) are segregated into mutually exclusive groups, which are based on the firm-level characteristic of interest (e.g. foreign owned, firm size, etc.). For example, the regression to determine the effect of foreign ownership on power-outage costs is set up as follows:

$$Y_i = \beta_1 D_i C_i + \beta_2 F_i C_i + \beta_3 F_i + \ldots$$

Whereby Y_i is labor productivity of firm i, F a dummy which is equal to 1 for domestic firms and equal to zero for foreign firms, $D = (1 - F)$ a dummy for domestic firms, and β_1, β_2 parameters to be estimated.

β_1 measures the impact of the *costs of power outages* on *labor productivity* among *domestic firms*. β_2 measures the impact of the *costs of power outages* on *labor productivity* among *foreign firms*. The estimates of specification show directly if the impact of *costs of power outages* on *labor productivity* are significantly different from zero between the two firm groups.

Regression Controls

All complementary regressions included a base set of controls including firm size, ownership, export activity, innovation activity and others. See Table A1.1. For complementary regressions, the segregating dummy variable (e.g. foreign ownership in the above example) was added as a control if it was not already included in the standard control set. For example, in the regression that determined the difference in the productivity impact between low-growth and high-growth countries, the high-growth dummy was included as a control since it was not in the standard control set.

For the marginal effects regressions, the same set of controls was used with the exception of country-specific dummies, which were not included.

WGI-indicators were converted to dummy variables that represented low government effectiveness, low control of corruption, etc. (0) and high government effectiveness, high control of corruption, etc. (1), and used as regressors. The median value of each indicator was used to determine the low and high classifications.

Table A1.5. Regressions on the Effects of Power Outage Costs on Labor Productivity Based on Varying Firm Characteristics

Firm Characteristics	LN(Labor Productivity)								
Small size	–1.735***								
	(–4.272)								
Medium size	–1.791***								
	(–3.515)								
Large size	–0.0324								
	(–0.0574)								
Panel size firms	–3.991								
	(–1.337)								
Domestically owned		–1.267***							
		(–4.302)							
Foreign Owned[1]		–2.766**							
		(–2.411)							
Non-innovating			–0.859**						
			(–2.118)						
Innovating			–1.772***						
			(–4.658)						
Non–exporting				–1.336***					
				(–4.253)					
Exporting				–1.396**					
				(–2.146)					
Low Access to Credit					–1.469***				
					(–3.866)				
Good Access to Credit					–1.709***				
					(–3.078)				
Low Country Growth[2]						–0.786*			
						(–1.932)			
High Country Growth[2]						–2.008***			
						(–4.535)			
Subsidiary							–1.154		
							(–1.339)		
Independent Firm							–1.365***		
							(–4.537)		
Low-Income Country[3]								–1.576***	
								(–4.337)	
Medium-Income Country[3]								–3.736**	
								(–1.965)	
High-Income Country[3]								–0.781	
								(–1.607)	
Ownership of a Generator									0.218***
									(3.633)
Constant	–3.139***	–3.168***	–3.168***	–3.173***	–4.571***	–3.242***	–3.168***	–1.899***	7.825***
	(–5.570)	(–5.626)	(–5.626)	(–5.632)	(–9.076)	(–5.748)	(–5.627)	(–3.220)	(6.214)
Observations	7,160	7,160	7,160	7,160	6,836	7,072	7,160	7,160	3,593
R–squared	0.417	0.417	0.417	0.417	0.426	0.420	0.417	0.417	0.425

Notes: t-statistics in parentheses.
*** p<0.01, ** p<0.05, * p<0.1
1. Firms are considered foreign owned if they are at least 10% foreign owned.
2. Fast growing countries are those that grew with an average growth rate of more than 6% from 2000 to 2008.
3. Income thresholds are 8,000 and 13,000 GDP per capita at PPP in 2007.

Table A1.6. Regressions on the Effects of Power Outage Costs on Productivity by Firm Productivity Quintile

	Quintiles of Labor Productivity				
	10%	25%	50%	75%	90%
Power Outage Costs	-1.834***	-1.868***	-1.196***	-1.210***	-0.964**
	(-4.583)	(-6.130)	(-3.791)	(-2.729)	(-1.969)
Constant	-6.586***	-5.632***	-3.954***	-1.402*	0.130
	(-7.087)	(-8.528)	(-6.181)	(-1.772)	(0.140)
Observations	7,160	7,160	7,160	7,160	7,160
Pseudo R-squared	0.2951	0.2987	0.2704	0.2243	0.1793

Notes: t-statistics in parentheses
*** p<0.01, ** p<0.05, * p<0.1

Table A1.7. Regressions on the Effects of High-Speed Internet Access on Firm Productivity Based on Varying Firm Characteristics

Firm Characteristics	LN(Labor Productivity)		
Low-Income Country	0.783***		
	(8.750)		
Medium-Income Country	0.239**		
	(2.023)		
High-Income Country	0.524***		
	(5.282)		
Small size		0.559***	
		(7.022)	
Medium size		0.492***	
		(5.081)	
Large size		0.703***	
		(4.211)	
Panel size		0.781***	
		(3.713)	
Fast-Growth Country			0.628***
			(8.351)
Low-Growth Country			0.440***
			(4.506)
Constant	-4.106***	-2.678***	2.071*
	(-4.035)	(-2.619)	(1.856)
Observations	2,637	2,637	2,586
R-squared	0.418	0.421	0.421

Notes: t-statistics in parentheses
*** p<0.01, ** p<0.05, * p<0.1

Table A1.8. Regressions on the Effects of Email Use on Productivity by Firm Productivity Quintile

	Quintiles of Labor Productivity				
Variables	**10%**	**25%**	**50%**	**75%**	**90%**
Email	0.610***	0.557***	0.475***	0.458***	0.584***
	(10.72)	(13.37)	(14.12)	(8.925)	(9.442)
Constant	-4.936***	-4.694***	-3.381***	-1.588**	0.592
	(-6.314)	(-8.301)	(-7.483)	(-2.297)	(0.718)
Observations	8,437	8,437	8,437	8,437	8,437
Pseudo R-squared	0.3003	0.3017	0.2751	0.2275	0.1796

Notes: t-statistics in parentheses
*** p<0.01, ** p<0.05, * p<0.1

Table A1.9. Regressions on the Effects of High-Speed Internet Access on Productivity by Firm Productivity Quintile

	Quintiles of Labor Productivity				
Variables	**10%**	**25%**	**50%**	**75%**	**90%**
Internet access	0.574***	0.518***	0.441***	0.502***	0.526***
	(5.637)	(7.551)	(5.590)	(6.922)	(5.988)
Constant	-5.237***	-6.222***	-4.955***	-2.580**	-1.303
	(-3.043)	(-5.277)	(-3.756)	(-2.207)	(-0.954)
Observations	2,637	2,637	2,637	2,637	2,637
Pseudo R-squared	0.3077	0.2963	0.2715	0.2314	0.1999

Notes: t-statistics in parentheses
*** p<0.01, ** p<0.05, * p<0.1

Table A1.10. Regressions on the Effects of Power Outage Costs in Countries with Good Governance, Good Control of Corruption, and Good Government Regulation on Labor Productivity

Government Characteristics	**LN(Labor Productivity)**		
Effective Governance	-0.945		
	(-1.550)		
Non-effective Governance	-1.462***		
	(-4.479)		
Good Control of Corruption		-0.977	
		(-1.603)	
Bad Control of Corruption		-1.453***	
		(-4.451)	
Good Government Regulation			-0.973*
			(-1.847)
Bad Government Regulation			-1.505***
			(-4.383)
Constant	4.232***	-2.023**	0.0223
	(4.971)	(-2.421)	(0.0342)
Observations	7,160	7,160	7,160
R-squared	0.417	0.417	0.417

Notes: t-statistics in parentheses
*** p<0.01, ** p<0.05, * p<0.1

Table A1.11. Regressions on the Effects of High-Speed Internet Access in Countries with Good Governance, Good Control of Corruption, and Good Government Regulation on Labor Productivity

Government Characteristics	LN(Labor Productivity)		
Effective Governance	0.353***		
	(3.714)		
Non-effective Governance	0.691***		
	(9.309)		
Good Control of Corruption		0.250***	
		(2.597)	
Bad Control of Corruption		0.744***	
		(10.10)	
Good Government Regulation			0.413***
			(4.407)
Bad Government Regulation			0.661***
			(8.812)
Constant	3.344	-2.531*	-2.238**
	(1.292)	(-1.726)	(-2.161)
Observations	2,637	2,637	2,637
R-squared	0.420	0.422	0.419

Notes: t-statistics in parentheses
*** p<0.01, ** p<0.05, * p<0.1

Table A1.12. Marginal Effects of Generalized Ordered Logit Models of the Effects of Various Firm Characteristics on Electricity Perceptions

	Electricity Perception				
	Major or Very Severe Obstacle				Not an Obstacle
Number of power outages	0.007***				
	(8.14)				
Losses from outages as a percent of sales		1.884***			
		(12.34)			
Generator ownership			0.130***		
			(5.70)		
Access to high-speed Internet				0.069***	
				(3.58)	
Labor growth					-0.024**
					(-2.13)
Observations	3,916	8,385	4,258	3,191	8,942
Pseudo R-squared	0.077	0.078	0.056	0.070	0.053

Notes: t-statistics in parentheses
*** p<0.01, ** p<0.05, * p<0.1

Table A1.13. Regression Results for World Governance Indicators on Power Outage Costs and Access to High-Speed Internet

	Power Outage Costs		High-Speed Internet Access	
	Government Effectiveness	Control of Government Corruption	Government Effectiveness	Control of Government Corruption
Power Outage Costs	−0.0898***	−0.1108***		
	(−11.37)	(−19.23)		
High-Speed Internet Access			0.2817***	0.1611
			(6.40)	(1.44)
Constant	0.3418***	−.2733***	−1.442**	−0.5033
	(10.36)	(−8.77)	(−2.04)	(−0.90)
Observations	8470	8470	3220	3220
R-squared	0.172	0.172	0.308	0.308

Notes: t-statistics in parentheses
*** p<0.01, ** p<0.05, * p<0.1

Table A1.14. Estimated Power Outage Costs and Access to High-Speed Internet

	Estimated Power Outage Costs (Percent of Sales)	Estimated Percent of Firms with Access to High-Speed Internet
Low Government Effectiveness	12.29%	33.82%
High Government Effectiveness	0.52%	70.74%
Low Control of Corruption	16.50%	43.44%
High Control of Corruption	3.01%	63.04%

Estimates are based on regression results from Table A1.13, the survey-population means for the controls, and assumed low and high levels of the WGI indicator (defined as the mean indicator-value across ECA countries plus or minus one standard deviation).

Chapter 4: Labor: Challenges Ahead of the Crisis

Data Notes

BEEPS-BASED VARIABLES OF INTEREST:

Skills as No Obstacle comes from the 2005 and 2008 BEEPS datasets, using the question, "Is an inadequately educated workforce no obstacle, a minor obstacle, a moderate obstacle, a major obstacle or a very severe obstacle to the current operations of this establishment?" The variable is assigned a value of 1 if the firm reported "no obstacle," zero otherwise.

Skills as a Major Obstacle comes from the 2008 BEEPS dataset, using the question, "Is an inadequately educated workforce no obstacle, a minor obstacle, a moderate obstacle, a major obstacle or a very severe obstacle to the current operations of this establishment?" The variable is assigned a value of 1 if the firm reported "major obstacle" or "very severe obstacle," zero otherwise.

Labor Regulations as No Obstacle comes from the 2005 and 2008 BEEPS datasets, using the question, "Are labor regulations no obstacle, a minor obstacle, a moderate obstacle, a major obstacle or a very severe obstacle to the current operations of this establishment?" The variable is assigned a value of 1 if the firm reported "no obstacle," zero otherwise.

Labor Regulations as a Major Obstacle comes from the 2008 BEEPS dataset, using the question, "Are labor regulations no obstacle, a minor obstacle, a moderate obstacle, a major obstacle or a very severe obstacle to the current operations of this establishment?" The variable is assigned a value of 1 if the firm reported "major obstacle" or "very severe obstacle," zero otherwise.

Labor Productivity is the ratio of a firm's total annual sales (as given by question d2 and converted to U.S. dollars) to its' number of employees. The number of employees is determined as a sum of the answers to questions l1 (the number of permanent full-time employees) and l6 (the number of temporary full-time employees).

Other Variables:

EPL Rigidity is defined as the value of the Rigidity of Employment Index for 2008 from Doing Business. Values range from 0–100. Higher values reflect more stringent employment regulations.

Unemployment 2007 data comes from the World Bank, and is the percentage of total unemployment for 2007.

Figures and Tables

When using Enterprise Surveys data, regions are comprised as shown in the Note on Regional and Sub-regional Averages at the beginning of Appendix 1.

Table 4.1 data comes from the KILM (6th Edition) and authors' calculations. The groupings show unweighted averages.

Table 4.2 shows the percentage of firms stating that labor regulations and skills and education of labor respectively are major or very severe obstacles to doing business. Each subregion is calculated so that each country has an equal weight.

Figure B4.1.1 is based on a simple correlation between labor regulations as no obstacle and the log of GDP 2007 on a purchasing power parity basis (in constant 2005 international dollars). The correlation between the two variables graphed is -0.65, significant at the 0.001 level. This relationship is significant at the firm level when controlling for other factors in generalized logit models. See Table A1.15 in the Regression Results section below.

Figure B4.1.2 is based on a simple correlation between EPL Rigidity defined as the Rigidity of Employment Index from Doing Business 2008 and the percentage of firms innovating (introducing a new product or service in the last three years) from BEEPS 2008. The correlation between the two variables graphed is 0.36, significant at the 0.06 level.

Figure 4.1 presents the differences in skills and education of labor as not an obstacle to doing business between 2005 and 2008. Upward arrows reflect positive change as they indicate an increase in the percentage of firms stating skills and education of labor are not a problem. The downward arrows indicate negative change. The base of the arrow indicates the value in 2005, while the black lines indicate the 2008 value. Both values are based on the truncated samples.

Figure 4.2 shows the averages for skills and education of labor as no obstacle by income classification including both ECA and countries in other regions using BEEPS 2008 and Enterprise Surveys 2006–2010. Countries are assigned to an income classification based on the 2009 World Bank Income Classifications. Averages are calculated so that each country has an equal weight.

Figure 4.3 is based on a simple correlation between the country-level mean value of skills and education of labor as an obstacle from the 2008 BEEPS and the log of labor productivity. The correlation between the two variables graphed is -0.24, but is not significant at the country level (significant at the 0.20 level).

Figure B4.3.1 and *Figure B4.3.2* data comes from KILM 6th Edition, 2009

Figure B4.4.1 data comes from the IMF Balance of Payments 2008.

Figure B4.4.2 is based on a simple correlation between skills and education of labor as no obstacle from BEEPS 2008 and migrants remittances as a percent of GDP from the IMF Balance of Payments, 2008. The correlation between the two variables graphed is -0.05, and is not significant (significant at the 0.81 level).

Figure B4.4.3 is based on a simple correlation between skills and education of labor as no obstacle from BEEPS 2008 and the emigration rate of the tertiary educated from the World Bank Migration and Remittances Factbook, 2008. The correlation between the two variables graphed is 0.29, and is not significant (significant at the 0.15 level).

Figure 4.4 is based on a simple correlation between the country-level mean value of skills and education of labor as an obstacle from BEEPS 2008 and the unemployment rate for 2007. The correlation between the two variables graphed is -0.43, and is significant at the 0.06 level. This relationship is significant at the firm level when controlling for other factors in generalized logit models.

Figure 4.5 is based on a simple correlation between the country-level mean value of skills and education of labor as an obstacle from BEEPS 2008 and the percentage rate of unemployment of those with a tertiary education. The correlation between the two variables graphed is 0.45, and is significant at the 0.05 level.

Figure 4.6 is based on a simple correlation between the country-level mean value of skills and education of labor as an obstacle from BEEPS 2008 and the percentage rate of unemployment of those with a secondary education. The correlation between the two variables graphed is -0.22, but is not significant (significant at the 0.36 level).

Figure 4.7 shows the regional and subregional averages for the percentage of firms providing formal training to permanent full-time employees for ECA and countries in other regions using BEEPS 2008 and Enterprise Surveys 2006–2010. Averages are calculated so that each country has an equal weight.

Figure 4.8 shows the averages for the percentage of firms providing formal training to permanent full-time employees including both ECA and countries in other regions using BEEPS 2008 and Enterprise Surveys 2006–2010 by Income Classification. Countries are assigned to an income classification based on the 2009 World Bank Income Classifications. Averages are calculated so that each country has an equal weight.

Figure 4.9 is based on a simple correlation between the country-level mean value of skills and education of labor as an obstacle and the percentage of firms providing formal training to permanent full-time employees from BEEPS 2008. The correlation between the two variables graphed is 0.31 and is significant at the 0.10 level.

Figures B4.6.1 and *B4.6.2* data come from the Enterprise Surveys Financial Crisis Survey 2009.

Analytic Results

Analysis of Obstacles to Doing Business

The primary method of analysis used to examine the obstacles doing business is a generalized ordered logit model, based on the model proposed by Pierre and Scarpetta (2004, 2006). The dependent variable can take on values from 0 to 4; 0 if the aspect of the business environment is not an obstacle, and a value of 4 if it is a very severe obstacle. For the purposes of this analysis, the values for major and very severe obstacle were combined to capture differences in perceptions between no obstacle and severe obstacle. This transformation was completed to be consistent with the approach used by Pierre and Scarpetta (2004, 2006).

Pierre and Scarpetta (2004 and 2006) argue the use of ordinal regression models often results in a violation of assumptions, and this method allows flexibility in the proportional odds assumption on the data. The generalized ordered logit models relaxes these assumptions and "allows the effects of explanatory values to vary with the point at which the categories of the dependent variables are dichotomized" (Maddala, 1983 cited in Pierre and Scarpetta, 2006, p. 330).

A totally unconstrained general ordered logit model is notated as:

$$P(Y_i > j) = g(X\beta) = \frac{\exp(\alpha_j + X_i\beta_j)}{1 + [\exp(\alpha_j + X_i\beta_j)]},\ j = 1, 2, \ldots m - 1$$

The generalized ordered logit model estimates a set of coefficients for each of the $m-1$ points at which the dependent variable can be dichotomized. From this set of k coefficients (B_k), using the logistic cumulative distribution, it is possible to derive formulas for the probabilities that y will take on each of the values 0, 1, ..., m:

$P(y = 0) = F(-X\beta_1)$ $P(y = 0) = F(-X\beta_1)$
$P(y = j) = F(-X\beta_{(j+1)}) - F(-X\beta_j)$ $j = 1, \ldots, m-1$
$P(y = m) = 1 - F(-X\beta_m)$

The variables of interest including EPL rigidity, innovation, and a set of control variables (see Table A1.1) are regressed on the perception of labor regulations and skills and education of labor as an obstacle, respectively. Using this method, the coefficients of the explanatory variables can be determined and the marginal effects on the dependent variable can be interpreted. These marginal effects allow for more careful interpretation of the effects of the variables on a discrete change in the dependent variable, for example, the change in value from 0 to 1 or from 2 to 3. Only the results for no obstacle and major or very severe obstacle are presented for consistency with the results discussed in the chapter. See Tables A1.15 and A1.16.

All models include control variables including those for firm size, sector, location, ownership, export activity, firm age, and innovation, subregion (FSU N, FSU S, SEE, EU-10), and others. The set of control variables were informed by previous literature (see for example, Pierre and Scarpetta 2004, 2006). Additional control variables were inserted for consistency with the models employed in Chapter 3.

In addition to the general ordered logit models, standard logit models are used to examine the probability of provision of training and the propensity to innovate. Multivariate regression models are used to examine the effects of variables of interest on labor productivity and the professionalism of labor. These models also included the control variables listed above.

Table A1.15. Marginal Effects of Primary Variables on Labor Regulations as No Obstacle and Major Obstacle (General Ordered Logit Models)

Firm Characteristic	Labor Regulations No Obstacle	Labor Regulations Major Obstacle	Labor Regulations No Obstacle	Labor Regulations Major Obstacle
EPL Rigidity			−0.002*	0.001*
			(0.001)	(0.001)
Unemployment (2007)	0.008***	−0.004***	0.006***	−0.003**
	(0.002)	(0.001)	(0.002)	(0.001)
Log of Firm Age	0.004	0.000	0.004	0.000
	(0.010)	(0.007)	(0.010)	(0.007)
Innovation dummy	−0.028**	0.023***	−0.027**	0.022***
	(0.014)	(0.009)	(0.014)	(0.009)
Small firm dummy	−0.053	−0.005	−0.056	−0.003
	(0.039)	(0.026)	(0.039)	(0.026)
Medium firm dummy	−0.073*	0.018	−0.076*	0.019
	(0.039)	(0.027)	(0.039)	(0.027)
Large firm dummy	−0.110***	0.023	−0.114***	0.024
	(0.039)	(0.028)	(0.039)	(0.029)
Manufacturing firm dummy	−0.023	0.009	−0.024	0.010
	(0.017)	(0.011)	(0.017)	(0.011)
Service firm dummy	−0.027	0.017	−0.027	0.017
	(0.018)	(0.012)	(0.018)	(0.012)
Log of GDP 2007	0.100***	−0.122***	0.021	−0.076**
	(0.033)	(0.019)	(0.053)	(0.031)
Observations	6175	6175	6175	6175
Pseudo R-squared	0.0414	0.0414	0.0417	0.0417

Notes: Values presented are marginal effects with standard errors in parentheses
*** p <0.01, **p<0.05, * p<0.1

Table A1.16. Marginal Effects of Primary Variables on Skills and Education of Labor as No Obstacle and Major Obstacle (General Ordered Logit Models)

Firm Characteristics	Skills Not an Obstacle	Skills Major Obstacle	Skills Not an Obstacle	Skills Major Obstacle	Skills Not an Obstacle	Skills Major Obstacle	Skills Not an Obstacle	Skills Major Obstacle	Skills Not an Obstacle	Skills Major Obstacle
Innovation	−0.075***	0.096***								
	(0.009)	(0.010)								
Training			−0.045***	0.022						
			(0.014)	(0.016)						
Email Use					−0.039***	0.071***				
					(0.013)	(0.013)				
Professionalism of Labor							0.000	0.001***		
							(0.000)	(0.000)		
Log of Labor Productivity									0.007**	−0.006
									(0.004)	(0.004)
Firm Size: Small	−0.111***	0.073*								
	(0.025)	(0.039)								
Firm Size: Medium	−0.160***	0.104***								
	(0.024)	(0.039)								
Firm Size: Large	−0.020***	0.139***								
	(0.021	(0.041)								
Log of GDP	0.111***	−0.093***								
	(0.011)	(0.013)								
Service Sector	−0.017	−0.001								
	(0.012)	(0.013)								
Manufacturing Sector	−0.042***	−0.005								
	(0.011)	(0.012)								
Observations	10,248	10,248	4,330	4,330	10,230	10,230	9,847	9,847	8,445	8,445
Pseudo R-Squared	0.0476	0.0476	0.0495	0.0495	0.0488	0.0488	0.048	0.048	0.0471	0.0471

Notes: Values presented are marginal effects with standard errors in parentheses
*** $p < 0.01$, ** $p < 0.05$, * $p < 0.1$

Table A1.17. Results of the Innovation and ICT Use Logit Models

Firm Characteristics	Innovation Activity		ICT Use (Email)	
EPL Stringency	0.013*** (0.002)			
Log of Labor Productivity		0.160*** (0.018)	0.363*** (0.027)	
Professionalism of labor				0.022*** (0.001)
Skilled Labor				-0.011*** (0.003)
Unskilled Labor				-0.006 (0.004)
Firm Size: Small	0.220 (0.139)	0.214 (0.151)	0.521*** (0.183)	0.621* (0.386)
Firm Size: Medium	0.387*** (0.139)	0.331** (0.152)	1.296*** (0.187)	1.688*** (0.391)
Firm Size: Large	0.449*** (0.142)	0.385** (0.156)	2.381*** (0.206)	3.102*** (0.419)
Exporting Firm	0.696*** (0.058)	0.606*** (0.063)	1.095*** (0.129)	1.366*** (0.155)
Foreign-Owned	0.294*** (0.075)	0.188** (0.082)	0.599*** (0.152)	0.394* (0.205)
Log of GDP	0.549** (0.070)	0.164*** (0.061)	0.594*** (0.077)	0.882*** (0.121)
Constant	-7.650*** (0.719)	-5.178*** (0.596)	-9.193*** (0.787)	-8.593*** (1.311)
Observations	10189	8582	8573	4094
Pseudo R-Squared	0.0560	0.0644	0.3480	0.3332

Notes: Values presented are coefficients with standard errors in parentheses
*** p <0.01, **p<0.05, * p<0.1

Table A1.18. Regression Results of the Training Logit Models

Firm Characteristics	Provision of Training			
Innovation	0.910*** (0.072)			
Labor Growth		0.365*** (0.073)		
Professionalism of Labor			0.005*** (0.002)	
Email Use				0.756*** (0.117)
Firm Size: Small	0.314 (0.401)			
Firm Size: Medium	1.065*** (0.400)			
Firm Size: Large	1.679*** (0.403)			
Exporting Firm	0.257*** (0.079)			
Foreign-Owned	0.282*** (0.110)			
Log of GDP	0.227** (0.010)			
Constant	-3.690*** (1.044)	-3.159*** (1.087)	-3.251*** (1.066)	-3.284*** (1.063)
Observations	4404	3884	4221	4396
Pseudo R-Squared	0.1280	0.1306	0.1272	0.1356

Notes: Values presented are coefficients with standard errors in parentheses.
*** p <0.01, **p<0.05, * p<0.1

Table A1.19. Regression Results of Labor Productivity Models

Firm Characteristics	Ln(Labor Productivity)		
Skills Constraint	-0.020* (0.012)		
Labor Growth	0.203*** (0.030)		
Innovation	0.252*** (0.030)		
Provision of Training		0.301*** (0.045)	
Email Use			0.756*** (0.117)
Firm Size: Small	0.175* (0.092)		
Firm Size: Medium	0.273** (0.093)		
Firm Size: Large	0.263*** (0.095)		
Log of GDP	0.885*** (0.036)		
Constant	3.062*** (0.359)	3.160*** (0.590)	-3.284*** (1.063)
Observations	8445	3612	4396
R-Squared	0.3778	0.3862	0.1356

Notes: Values presented are coefficients with standard errors in parentheses
*** p <0.01, **p<0.05, * p<0.1

Table A1.20. Regression Results of the Professionalism of Labor Model

Firm Characteristics	Professionalism of Labor
Email use	10.897*** (0.632)
Constant	2.383 (5.937)
Observations	10000
R-Squared	0.2488

Notes: Values presented are coefficients with standard errors in parentheses
*** p <0.01, **p<0.05, * p<0.1

Appendix 2. Notes on Sampling and the Survey Methodology

Over 11,000 firms were interviewed for the 2008 round of BEEPS in 29 ECA countries. The number of firms surveyed varied from a low of 116 in Montenegro to more than 1,000 in Russia and Turkey. Most surveys were conducted between April 2008 and March 2009, and most quantitative questions (e.g. sales, employment, etc.) refer to the firm's operations in the calendar year 2007.

The firms vary by size, sector of operation, and ownership, and were selected to be representative of the non-agricultural private sector in each nation. The firms were chosen using stratified random sampling (firms were stratified by size, sector of operations, and geographical location). Datasets include weights in order to extrapolate to the overall population of firms in each country.

The sampling methodology used in 2008 differs from that of prior rounds in several ways:

- The 2008 round of BEEPS utilized stratified random sampling, moving away from the use of simple random sampling supplemented by elements of quota sampling used in 2005 and earlier rounds of BEEPS.
- In order to extrapolate the stratified sample to the targeted population of firms, the BEEPS 2008 utilized weights, while the BEEPS 2005 sample was designed to be self-weighted.
- The self-weighted sample for BEEPS 2005 was designed to be "as representative as possible" to the population of firms within the industry and service sectors subject to the various minimum quotas for the total sample (e.g. x% of state-owned enterprises, y% of large enterprise, z% from the capital city, etc.).
- The sectoral composition of the sample changed from 2005 to 2008. For example, a number of sectors were excluded from the 2008 sampling frame: mining and quarrying, advertising and other business services, welfare services, and others.
- While the 2005 sampling frame included firms with two or more employees (including the owner), in 2008 the firm size strata changed to include only firms with five or more employees (including the owner), although in both cycles, a panel component included firms with less than five employees.
- The 2005 sampling frame included firms that were 100 percent state owned, while in 2008, 100 percent state owned firms were excluded.
- The 2005 sampling frame was restricted to include only firms that had been operating for three years or more, while the 2008 frame included firms of all ages.

For analyses that focus on 2008, i.e. do not require a cross-period comparison, all firms from the 2008 BEEPS are included in the weighted averages. In comparisons of 2005 and 2008 results—such as changes in perceptions of obstacles over time—an intersection of two sample populations was sought, i.e. the firm samples were modified as follows to maximize comparability:

- *Sector*: Restricted to sectors present in both 2005 and 2008 samples. Firms operating in a number of manufacturing and service sectors were dropped from the 2008 database, while firms in certain other sectors (e.g. mining and quarrying, business services and welfare services among others) were dropped from the 2005 data.

- *Size*: Firms in the 2005 data with fewer than five employees were dropped to match the 2008 approach.
- *Ownership*: Firms that were 100 percent state owned were dropped from the 2005 sample to match the 2008 approach.
- *Age*: Firms that were established after 2006 were dropped from the 2008 sample to match the 2005 approach.

These modifications result in dropping approximately 35 percent of firms surveyed in 2005 and approximately 6 percent of those surveyed in 2008. In analyses comparing 2005 to 2008, therefore, the 2008 estimates exclude data from 6 percent of firms region-wide, varying from less than 1 percent for several countries to as high as 14 percent in Armenia. In contrast, analyses based purely on 2008 data do not require comparability with the 2005 sample, so no firms are excluded. This means that readers will sometimes encounter two different country-level figures for the same indicator for 2008. Both are correct, but for differing purposes.

Results for two countries in the BEEPS 2008—Albania and Croatia—are based on two different surveys: (i) from BEEPS 2008 for ECA-specific questions not included in the Enterprise Surveys, and (ii) from the 2007 Enterprise Surveys for all other questions. Due to the small universe of firms coupled with "survey fatigue"[1] in Albania and Croatia, it was not possible to conduct the full BEEPS survey on a large sample of firms in 2008.

1. Survey fatigue results from over-surveying. When someone who recently completed a survey from a particular organization is inundated with invitations to complete other surveys, they feel tired or "fatigued" when it comes to taking surveys. Once a respondent forms an opinion that a survey organization doesn't respect him/her because of over-surveying, it is very difficult to restore the organization's image. Other effects of survey fatigue can include lower response rates and lower-quality data.

Table A2.1. Sample Summary 2005 and 2008

Country	2005 Sample for All Countries: Total Firms Surveyed in 2005	Total Firms Excluded (Size, Sector, and Ownership)	Percent of Firms Excluded	Reduced Sample Size	2008 Sample for All Countries: Total Firms Surveyed in 2008	Total Firms Excluded (Size and Age)	Percent of Firms Excluded	Reduced Sample Size	Dates of Data Collection 2008/2009
ALB[1]	204	50	24.5	154	304	1	0.3	303	12/2007–3/2008
ARM	351	79	22.5	272	374	52	13.9	322	10/2008–2/2009
AZE	350	63	18.0	287	380	25	6.6	355	9/2008–2/2009
BLR	325	116	35.7	209	273	9	3.3	264	5/2008–8/2008
BIH	200	56	28.0	144	361	26	7.2	335	9/2008–3/2009
BGR	300	138	46.0	162	288	37	12.9	251	9/2008–12/2008
HRV[1]	236	88	37.3	148	633	3	0.5	630	1/2007–12/2007
CZE	343	176	51.3	167	250	20	8.0	230	9/2008–3/2009
EST	219	91	41.6	128	273	7	2.6	266	4/2008–10/2008
MKD	200	88	44.0	112	366	40	10.9	326	9/2008–1/2009
GEO	200	90	45.0	110	373	19	5.1	354	4/2008–8/2008
HUN	610	170	27.9	440	291	22	7.6	269	8/2008–2/2009
KAZ	585	150	25.6	435	544	44	8.1	500	9/2008–1/2009
KGZ	202	60	29.7	142	235	16	6.8	219	9/2008–3/2009
LVA	205	100	48.8	105	271	19	7.0	252	9/2008–10/2008
LTU	205	76	37.1	129	276	23	8.3	253	9/2008–3/2009
MDA	350	71	20.3	279	363	39	10.7	324	9/2008–2/2009
POL	975	447	45.9	528	455	36	7.9	419	8/2008–3/2009
ROM	600	145	24.2	455	541	38	7.0	503	9/2008–12/2008
RUS	601	209	34.8	392	1004	35	3.5	969	9/2008–3/2009
SRB	282	139	49.3	148	388	35	9.0	353	9/2008–12/2008
SVK	220	110	50.0	110	275	27	9.8	248	9/2008–3/2009
SVN	223	110	49.3	113	276	17	6.2	259	9/2008–3/2009
TJK	200	66	33.0	134	360	38	10.6	322	5/2008–8/2008
TUR	557	183	32.9	374	1152	27	2.3	1125	4/2008–1/2009
UKR	594	238	40.1	356	851	46	5.4	805	6/2008–8–2008
UZB	300	98	32.7	202	366	3	0.8	363	4/2008–8/2008
KSV*					270	12	4.4	258	10/2008–2/2009
MNE*					116	5	4.3	111	9/2008–2/2009
Total	**9,637**	**3,407**	**35.4**	**6,235**	**11,909**	**721**	**6.1**	**11,188**	

Notes: *Kosovo and Montenegro were included in the 2008 cycle.

1. Results for two countries in the BEEPS 2008—Albania and Croatia—are based on two different surveys: (i) from the 2007 Enterprise Surveys and (ii) from BEEPS 2008 for ECA-specific questions not included in the Enterprise Surveys. Due to a small universe of firms coupled with survey fatigue in Albania and Croatia, it was not possible to conduct the full BEEPS survey on a large sample of firms in 2008.

The numbers in the table above correspond to the Enterprise Surveys 2007 data sets. The 2008 BEEPS dataset for Albania consisted of a total of 175 firms. In order to best match the 2008 sample to that of 2005, the sample was adjusted. Seven firms (4.0 percent of the sample) were excluded on the basis of size and age. The reduced sample size was 168 firms for 2008. The dates of data collection for the 2008 BEEPS in Albania were from 10/2008 to 2/2009.

For Croatia, the BEEPS 2008 dataset consisted of a total of 159 firms. To adjust the 2008 sample to that of 2005, 17 firms (10.7 percent of the sample) were excluded on the basis of size and age. The reduced sample size was 142 firms for 2008. The dates of data collection for the 2008 BEEPS in Croatia were from 9/2008 to 3/2009.

Appendix 3. Summary of Obstacles Doing Business

Table A3.1. Problems Doing Business: Ranking of Problems 2008

	Tax Rates	Corruption	Electricity	Skills and Education of Workers	Access to Financing	Crime, Theft, and Disorder	Tax Administration	Telecom	Courts	Access to Land	Business Licensing and Permits	Transport	Labor Regulations	Customs and Trade Regulations
ALB	4	2	1	3	9	8	5	10	14	7	12	11	13	6
ARM	1	3	9	10	2	4	7	5	12	11	14	6	13	8
AZE	3	1	9	6	4	7	5	13	11	2	8	12	14	10
BLR	1	10	5	2	8	3	9	6	13	7	4	11	14	12
BIH	1	2	9	7	3	8	4	13	5	14	6	12	10	11
BGR	2	1	9	6	8	3	5	4	7	13	12	11	10	14
HRV	1	5	7	4	6	11	3	9	2	12	10	13	8	14
CZE	3	9	1	4	8	10	7	2	6	12	13	5	11	14
EST	2	10	5	1	8	6	11	4	13	9	12	7	3	14
MKD	3	4	7	10	1	5	6	12	2	9	8	13	14	11
GEO	3	9	1	5	2	4	10	7	11	6	13	8	14	12
HUN	1	3	6	11	7	12	2	8	9	14	4	10	5	13
KAZ	2	3	4	1	6	5	8	9	12	11	10	7	14	13
KSV	11	2	1	5	4	3	12	6	7	8	13	10	14	9
KGZ	3	2	1	8	7	5	6	4	10	11	12	9	14	13
LVA	1	3	10	2	5	6	4	13	8	9	11	7	12	14
LTU	1	5	4	2	7	3	6	9	12	13	10	11	8	14
MDA	3	5	8	2	4	6	10	7	9	1	13	12	14	11
MNE	2	6	1	5	3	11	4	14	10	13	8	7	9	11
POL	1	8	3	2	7	6	5	9	11	12	10	13	4	14
ROM	1	3	10	4	5	9	2	14	7	11	6	12	8	13
RUS	2	3	4	1	8	6	10	7	12	5	11	9	14	13
SRB	3	1	6	5	2	10	9	14	4	13	12	11	8	7
SVK	2	3	1	5	8	4	9	7	6	13	10	11	12	14
SVN	1	13	4	7	2	9	11	5	10	8	12	6	3	14
TJK	1	3	2	4	5	6	9	12	13	7	10	11	14	8
TUR	1	2	7	3	9	13	5	6	8	14	4	11	10	12
UKR	1	2	10	6	8	7	4	9	5	3	11	12	14	13
UZB	4	7	3	2	5	1	6	8	11	9	10	13	12	14
Total Countries Where the Rank <=3	26	17	1C	11	7	5	3	1	2	3	0	0	2	0
Total Countries Where the Rank <=7	28	23	21	25	21	19	18	12	10	7	5	7	4	2

Source: BEEPS 2008.

Table A3.2. Problems Doing Business: Ranking of Problems 2005

	Tax Rates	Corruption	Electricity	Skills and Education of Workers	Access to Financing	Crime, Theft, and Disorder	Tax Administration	Telecom	Courts	Access to Land	Business Licensing and Permits	Transport	Labor Regulations	Customs and Trade Regulations
ALB	1	2	4	9	7	13	3	14	5	12	8	10	11	6
ARM	2	5	13	12	3	14	1	10	8	7	6	9	11	4
AZE	2	3	7	13	4	8	1	14	11	10	6	12	9	5
BLR	2	9	14	5	1	11	4	13	10	7	3	12	8	6
BIH	3	4	11	12	1	7	6	13	2	14	8	9	10	5
BGR	1	3	11	5	6	8	4	12	2	14	7	13	9	10
HRV	2	3	13	6	4	9	10	12	1	14	5	11	7	8
CZE	1	3	14	9	4	8	2	13	5	11	10	12	6	7
EST	7	3	13	2	4	12	8	14	9	11	5	10	1	6
MKD	3	1	10	12	4	8	5	11	2	14	6	13	9	7
GEO	1	4	2	8	3	5	10	14	7	13	11	9	12	6
HUN	1	8	14	4	2	11	3	12	9	13	7	10	5	6
KAZ	2	5	13	6	4	10	1	14	8	9	3	12	11	7
KSV														
KGZ	1	3	12	5	7	4	2	14	6	10	8	13	11	9
LVA	1	4	14	3	10	8	2	12	9	13	6	11	5	7
LTU	1	4	12	2	11	8	6	14	7	3	9	13	5	10
MDA	1	7	13	9	5	10	2	14	4	11	6	12	8	3
MNE														
POL	1	6	14	8	3	9	2	13	4	11	10	12	5	7
ROM	2	3	13	8	6	10	1	14	4	11	5	12	7	9
RUS	2	3	13	4	6	8	1	14	7	10	5	12	11	9
SRB	1	4	14	9	2	10	5	12	3	11	8	13	7	6
SVK	2	3	12	4	9	5	6	14	1	13	8	11	7	10
SVN	2	9	13	5	6	11	1	14	3	7	8	12	4	10
TJK	1	4	5	9	6	11	2	14	8	10	3	12	13	7
TUR	1	4	10	8	3	6	2	13	7	14	9	12	5	11
UKR	1	3	12	2	5	10	4	14	6	8	7	13	11	9
UZB	1	9	6	8	3	7	2	14	10	13	4	11	12	5
Total Countries Where the Rank <=3	26	13	1	4	9	0	16	0	8	1	2	0	1	0
Total Countries Where the Rank <=7	27	24	4	13	25	7	24	0	18	4	16	0	11	17

The problems are presented in the table in the order that they rank in severity ECA-wide for 2008. The most severe problem, Tax Rates, is presented first in the table. The least severe problem, Customs and Trade Regulations, is presented last. No data is presented for Kosovo or Montenegro.

Source: BEEPS 2005.

Table A3.3. Factors that are Not a Problem Doing Business, Percentage Point Changes and Statistical Significance

	Tax Rates	Corruption	Electricity	Skills and Education of Workers	Access to Financing	Crime, Theft, and Disorder	Tax Administration	Telecom	Courts	Access to Land	Business Licensing and Permits	Transport	Labor Regulations	Customs and Trade Regulations	Sig. Positive Changes	Sig. Negative Changes
ALB	17.5	7.9	-12.5	-13.0	6.1	-4.6	19.5	-2.1	32.7	-11.5	22.7	-5.8	4.7	13.8	6	3
ARM	4.3	6.8	-15.6	-3.2	10.2	-10.4	28.1	-11.5	24.4	25.9	31.1	-4.2	11.4	11.3	9	3
AZE	5.7	-11.6	-4.8	-36.0	5.0	-26.6	21.0	-10.8	-21.9	-42.6	7.9	-15.9	4.3	26.1	5	7
BLR	-28.2	-30.4	-55.2	-31.8	-1.9	-59.8	-23.0	-50.6	-32.1	-26.3	-15.4	-45.9	-9.3	-17.6	0	13
BIH	-4.7	1.0	-8.5	-13.2	8.1	-0.7	-7.5	-2.0	7.8	3.3	-3.7	9.9	8.5	28.8	5	3
BGR	-8.0	-5.7	-38.1	-3.6	-13.0	-16.9	-6.0	-38.9	5.4	-14.8	-4.5	-25.3	-9.2	6.7	1	9
HRV	-6.4	4.0	-20.6	-10.5	-3.9	-4.5	-32.7	-19.6	0.8	-11.9	16.5	-9.6	-11.9	10.8	2	8
CZE	6.0	15.2	-38.3	-5.6	2.9	-0.4	14.5	-40.4	7.1	5.1	6.2	-24.4	3.2	29.5	5	4
EST	-24.6	10.0	-11.4	-14.2	8.5	-21.8	6.3	-19.9	18.9	1.7	16.5	-9.5	26.9	21.1	6	6
MKD	-0.2	3.5	-9.6	-7.6	-4.5	2.0	-2.9	0.4	7.1	-4.5	1.5	-4.2	9.4	11.6	2	1
GEO	21.2	27.4	-1.8	-5.1	-1.6	15.0	5.7	-15.5	12.3	-12.7	18.0	4.6	13.1	28.4	7	2
HUN	-7.2	-33.3	-20.3	36.3	32.0	3.1	-17.8	-8.8	6.1	11.3	-20.5	3.2	2.8	24.4	5	6
KAZ	-4.0	-22.8	-46.3	-26.4	-19.4	-26.7	8.2	-39.0	-9.6	-16.6	-12.3	-37.8	3.8	-0.6	1	11
KGZ	-8.1	-6.2	-60.9	-19.0	-23.4	-11.5	4.6	-52.4	-8.7	-18.2	8.5	-39.4	-5.0	3.1	1	10
LVA	-5.7	-23.3	-19.1	15.0	-28.8	-18.3	12.7	-16.1	-22.8	-19.9	-1.7	-24.3	2.0	3.8	2	9
LTU	-3.1	-3.2	-38.5	-4.8	-35.4	-8.8	-6.3	-36.3	20.2	30.5	-9.8	-25.8	4.0	25.8	3	7
MDA	15.7	7.0	-21.1	-5.1	4.0	-1.9	18.5	-27.8	20.0	-24.1	20.3	-15.5	35.7	23.1	7	5
POL	-3.2	0.3	-33.9	-15.5	4.2	-10.9	9.5	-23.9	13.0	-19.4	-9.7	-14.8	-1.9	22.0	4	8
ROM	-9.1	-2.1	-19.6	-8.8	-3.4	-3.6	-5.4	-10.6	6.2	-14.7	-3.2	-15.6	0.9	9.1	2	9
RUS	-9.0	-16.4	-45.6	-27.9	-19.0	-21.4	5.7	-62.9	-8.6	-27.1	-9.1	-35.5	-0.1	8.1	2	11
SRB	10.6	4.0	-16.2	-12.9	9.1	-2.4	13.6	8.8	18.9	-0.4	7.7	-7.9	8.2	9.6	8	3
SVK	-32.5	-31.4	-45.2	-19.2	-41.5	-36.4	-38.3	-48.2	-32.5	-31.5	-33.3	-30.5	-22.0	-4.6	0	13
SVN	-5.4	6.2	-32.2	5.5	-9.7	-30.9	30.2	-26.7	19.1	-8.3	2.7	-35.3	-4.5	13.3	3	6
TJK	-2.2	-6.2	-10.1	-19.5	-10.4	-7.0	25.7	-0.6	18.0	-4.0	14.4	-5.4	13.2	4.0	4	3
TUR	-4.6	-20.1	-4.0	-19.7	11.2	16.9	11.1	-11.8	0.8	-0.5	-15.3	-1.2	0.1	1.5	3	5
UKR	-2.6	-18.5	-42.7	-7.9	-12.4	-18.9	-15.2	-50.6	-16.7	-18.6	-8.8	-37.6	-5.1	0.8	0	12
UZB	1.3	-19.4	-35.5	-32.3	-8.4	-46.9	12.4	-34.2	-5.8	-22.0	3.4	-7.4	-11.7	20.0	2	9
ANALYSIS OF CHANGES																
Positive Change	8	12	0	3	11	4	17	2	18	6	14	3	17	24		
Sig. Pos. Change	7	6	0	2	8	2	14	1	14	3	10	1	8	19		
Negative Change	19	15	27	24	16	23	10	25	9	21	13	24	10	3		
Sig. Neg. Change	13	11	24	19	12	15	9	22	8	17	10	19	6	1		

[1] Shaded cells indicate changes that are statistically significant at p=0.10 or above.

Source: BEEPS 2005, BEEPS 2008.

Note: The table above shows the changes in the percentage of firms indicating a certain factor is not an obstacle to doing business from 2005 to 2008.

ECO-AUDIT

Environmental Benefits Statement

The World Bank is committed to preserving endangered forests and natural resources. The Office of the Publisher has chosen to print World Bank Studies and Working Papers on recycled paper with 30 percent postconsumer fiber in accordance with the recommended standards for paper usage set by the Green Press Initiative, a nonprofit program supporting publishers in using fiber that is not sourced from endangered forests. For more information, visit www.greenpressinitiative.org.

In 2009, the printing of these books on recycled paper saved the following:

- 289 trees*
- 92 million Btu of total energy
- 27,396 lb. of net greenhouse gases
- 131,944 gal. of waste water
- 8,011 lb. of solid waste

*40 feet in height and 6–8 inches in diameter

BEEPS Data Portal: Information at Your Fingertips

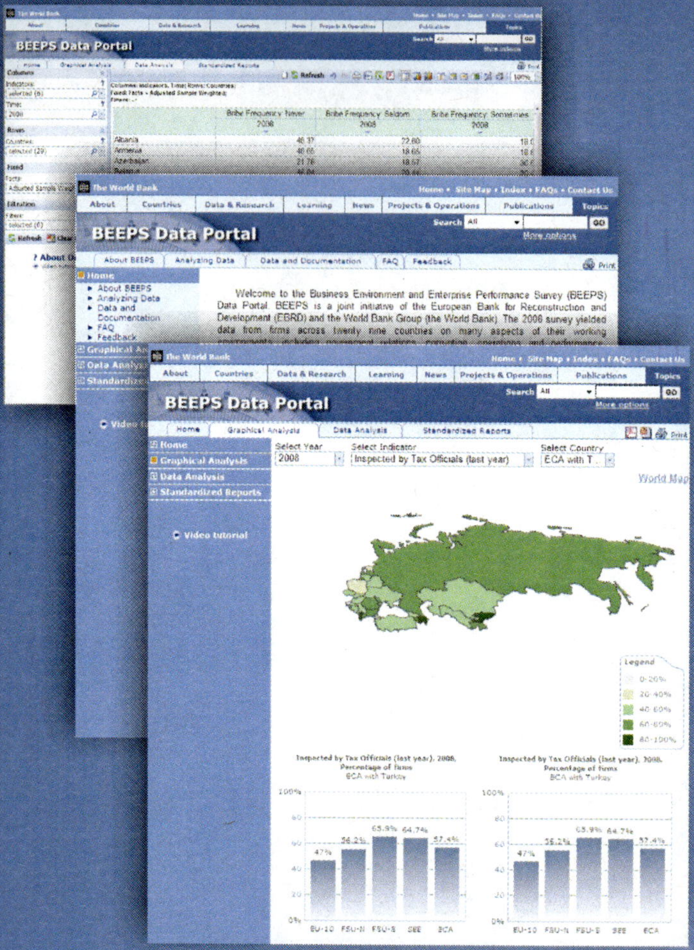

The BEEPS Data Portal is a new interactive tool that allows users to analyze and display data, design custom charts and create dynamic reports using standard templates.

The Portal allows users to manipulate data from the 2005 and 2008 BEEPS surveys and other supplementary sources. Users can view results by country and year and calculate custom indicators in seconds. All reports, charts, and tables can be downloaded into multiple formats for ease of use.

The BEEPS Data Portal is publicly available. For more information on the BEEPS Data Portal and the BEEPS Project, enter the link below in your browser.

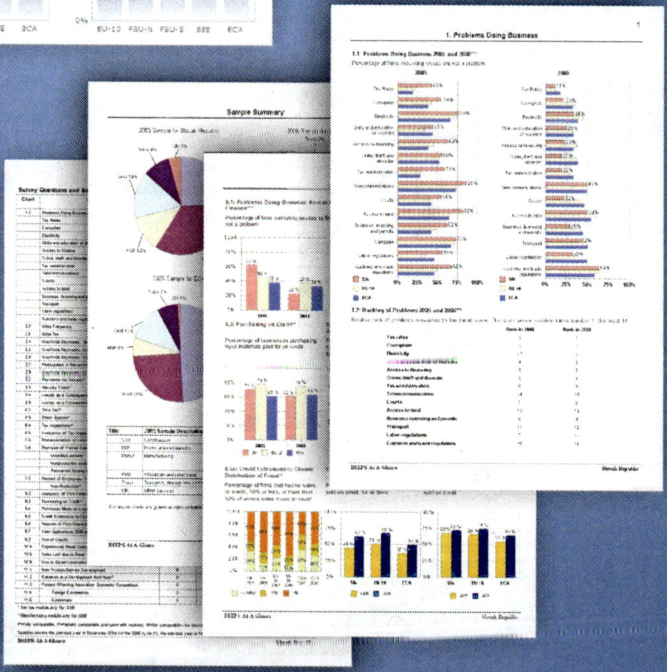

Access the BEEPS Data Portal at: http://beeps.prognoz.com